COMMUNICATION
GAPS
and How to
Close Them

Also Available from Dorset House Publishing

COMMUNICATION GAPS

and How to Close Them

Naomi Karten

DORSET HOUSE PUBLISHING
353 WEST 12TH STREET
NEW YORK, NEW YORK 10014

Library of Congress Cataloging-in-Publication Data

Karten, Naomi.
    Communication gaps and how to close them / Naomi Karten.
        p. cm.
    Includes bibliographical references and index.
    ISBN 0-932633-53-6 (soft cover)
        1. Miscommunication. 2. Communication in organizations. 3. Interpersonal
    communication. I. Title.

    P96.M56 K37 2002
    302.2--dc21

2002067228

Trademark credits: All trade and product names are either trademarks, registered trademarks, or service marks of their respective companies, and are the property of their respective holders and should be treated as such. Perspectoscope™ is a trademark of Karten Associates.

Cover and Interior Illustrations: Mark Tatro, Rotate Graphics
Cover Design: David W. McClintock

Executive Editor: Wendy Eakin
Senior Editor: David W. McClintock
Editor: Nuno Andrade
Assistant Editors: Vincent Au, Benjamin A. Deutsch, Jessica N. Stein

Distributed in the English language in Singapore, the Philippines, and Southeast Asia by Alkem Company (S) Pte., Ltd., Singapore; in the English language in India, Bangladesh, Sri Lanka, Nepal, and Mauritius by Prism Books Pvt., Ltd., Bangalore, India; and in the English language in Japan by Toppan Co., Ltd., Tokyo, Japan.

Printed in the United States of America

Library of Congress Catalog Number: 2002067228

ISBN: 0-932633-53-6   12   11   10   9   8   7   6   5   4   3   2   1

Dedication

To my husband, Howard,
my adventure-mate.

Acknowledgments

Big hugs of appreciation to the following
for your ideas, input, inspiration, feedback, and encouragement:

Marie Benesh
Esther Derby
Valla Dana Fotiades
Ellen Gottesdiener
Paul Jacobson
Jean McLendon
Helen Osborne
Johanna Rothman
David Schmaltz
Patricia Snipp
Robert Snipp
Eileen Strider
Wayne Strider
Jerry Weinberg
Doug Whittle

and of course,
Howard Karten

Thank you to my many clients for inviting me to consult with you and to provide seminars and presentations for your organization. In the stories and examples I've presented in this book, I've changed all names and revealing circumstances to protect . . . well, you know. If you think you recognize yourself in a particular story, read on—it might actually be another story that's about you.

Wendy Eakin, David McClintock, Jessica Stein, Ben Deutsch, Vincent Au, and Nuno Andrade at Dorset House Publishing, my heartfelt appreciation for your diligent and caring attention to both my concepts and my commas.

Mark Tatro, special thanks for cartoons that are so clever and laugh-out-loud funny that you inspire me to keep on writing so that you can continue to provide the artwork.

April 2002   N.K.
Randolph, Massachusetts

Contents

COMMUNICATION

GAPS

and How to Close Them

1

Mind the Gap

Have you ever been in the London subway—or the Underground, as it's called? If you have, you may have noticed that in some stations of the Underground, the tracks and platform curve slightly between the points where the train enters and leaves the station. Because of the curve, there are gaps at several places between the edge of the platform and a stopped train. A voice on a loudspeaker repeatedly warns passengers, "Mind the gap. . . . Mind the gap."

Although you'd be unlikely to fall through this platform gap unless you're thinner than a London telephone book, you could catch your foot or the wheel of a stroller in it, or your keys or wallet could slip through to the track below. Hence, the continuous warnings.

Unlike platform gaps, which result from the configuration of the station and don't vary from one day to another, communication gaps appear unpredictably and in any number of contexts. You can neither create nor eliminate platform gaps, but you can create communication gaps or fall victim to those created by other people. And you *can* eliminate them—or at least reduce the likelihood of their occurring.

Consider the following examples, which I address in this book and which are evidence of communication gaps:

- An organization embarked on a company-wide desktop upgrade. When technical staff arrived to install the new technology, employees asked, "Why are you shoving this down our throats?" The upgrade was a painful experience for both provider and customer personnel.
- At the start of a software development project, the client asked the project manager for a weekly, written status report. The project manager willingly accommodated. After the project's completion—on time, within budget, and to specification—the client filled out a satisfaction survey, in which he reported his dissatisfaction with the project.
- A vendor organization had a four-hour standard for responding to reported malfunctions in its critical hardware components. Unfortunately, vendor and client personnel defined "response" differently, as clients discovered, to their dismay, the first time they called about a malfunction.
- A network-management group undertook the upgrade of networking technology used by its internal customers, many of whom were highly dissatisfied with the group's service delivery. Customers asked to be involved in the effort, so the network group complied. Nevertheless, customers remained unhappy.
- A well-liked manager stopped by the cubicles of several employees on a high-pressure project to see how they were doing and to offer encouragement. She asked one top-notch employee, "How are you feeling?" She was surprised by the employee's negative reaction.
- IT personnel, eager to restore their once-positive reputation, implemented numerous service improvements. They were justifiably proud and expected a gigantic leap in customer satisfaction. However, judging from survey results, customers hardly noticed or cared.

- After a team had wrestled with alternative approaches to solving a thorny problem, the project manager announced the strategy the team would follow. Team members responded quickly and angrily.

Clearly, situations like these can have a damaging or counter-productive impact on projects and relationships. I use the term "communication gap" to refer broadly to a situation in which miscommunication, or the complete lack of communication, adversely affects the work as well as the relationships among the people carrying out the work.

Communication gaps can occur between individuals and groups at all organizational levels, regardless of whether the message is communicated face-to-face, by phone, fax, letter, e-mail, or carrier pigeon. Gaps can occur whenever people offer ideas, present information, introduce change, propose policies, gain input, make recommendations, implement standards, give or receive feedback, or simply converse—whether with customers, suppliers, friends, relatives, coworkers, or team-mates.

Communication gaps *are* pervasive. The vast majority of customer complaints revolve around communication glitches, omissions, and snafus. And few complaints detailed in employee-satisfaction surveys are as prominent as those that involve communication, particularly as it concerns information withheld and distorted. In one large company reeling both from financial difficulties and from the reorganization wrought by a new CEO, e-mail messages to the CEO were top-heavy with complaints, and a survey of more than 7,500 employees revealed widespread anger over poor communication. Such dissatisfaction is not limited to large companies; in fact, the business press regularly reports similar examples from compa-nies of all sizes.

A common misconception is that communication gaps are caused by too little communication. Some are, certainly. Often, however, the problem is the reverse: too much commu-nication. Often, too, the problem isn't simply the quantity of communication but the kind: Gaps are frequently caused by misdirected, one-way, poorly timed, or badly worded communications. In addition, some gaps result from misunderstandings, misinterpretations, and miscommunications. And sometimes, even if you feel you've done everything just right, people will respond in unexpected or puzzling ways.

THE ABILITY TO COMMUNICATE

In information-technology circles, people are becoming increasingly aware of the importance of being communication-savvy. Many years ago, when I was an IT manager, job postings for technical positions in my company included a list of the technical prerequisites for each job. At the end of each list, the final item read, "An ability to communicate, verbally and in writing." The ability to communicate was not at the top of the list, nor was it even in the middle; it was tacked on at the very bottom. Inclusion of this crucial skill on the list seemed almost an afterthought, as if serious contenders need meet only the other requirements. If they could also communicate, jolly good.

It has occurred to me in the years since leaving that company that the placement of this prerequisite at the end of the list was no accident; the company was anything but a role model for effective communication (although whether this was the cause or the effect of its limited emphasis on communication skills is hard to say). Memos and reports written by employees were full of run-on sentences, typos, and grammatical errors. Managers, too, often were punctuational illiterates.

But misspelled words and dangling participles were a minor matter compared to some of the issues this company faced. Communication between departments was strained, at best. People in positions of power routinely gave subordinates a hard time. Faultfinding was common when things went wrong—and much went wrong. Customers also suffered from the company's blaming culture, feeling the impact in the form of service that was, at times, dismal.

It was true that people in the company communicated "verbally and in writing" if you take that phrase to mean hurling words to and fro. E-mail hadn't yet emerged as a means of communication but that wasn't a deterrent: Memos abounded, everyone carbon-copied everyone else, and meetings were finger-pointing events. But congruent communication, with all parties seeking to understand and to be understood, was in short supply. Awareness of how to create strong relationships, build trust, manage expectations, and take responsibility for one's contribution to problems—all of which entail communication—was, at best, limited.

Although I understood that much was wrong in the company, I lacked the vocabulary to describe what I saw, the experience to understand it, and the clout to effect anything more than isolated change. In frustration, I eventually moved on. Since then, as the result of my personal studies, my exposure to wise and caring people, and my business experience as a consultant, speaker, and seminar leader, I'm able to help people—and their organizations—understand their communication difficulties and attain the skills they need to remedy or avoid such problems altogether. This book describes what I have learned about communication gaps.

WHY COMMUNICATION GAPS ARE PREVALENT

Fortunately, most organizations now recognize that the ability to communicate means more than just knowing the difference between nouns and verbs. Indeed, solid communication skills are obligatory for people in positions that entail any type of customer contact as well as for those with managerial responsibilities. So why is it, then, that problems traceable to flawed communication remain prevalent in organizations? Four reasons come immediately to mind.

The first reason is that communication is so fundamental to our very existence that most people don't see the role it has played when matters go awry. For example, as one technical-support specialist put it: "I sent them an e-mail. If they didn't read it, it's not my problem."

Yet a message sent is not necessarily a message received. In fact, the message received may be far removed from the one that was sent. What's sent, how it's sent, whether it's received, how it's received—and for that matter, whether it's actually sent in the first place—all have a bearing on whether communication has taken place. If any of these factors are off, the parties involved will be separated by a communication gap.

The second reason that problems caused by flawed communications are so prevalent is that most people, believing themselves to be capable communicators, deny responsibility for the problems. Therefore, when they create a communication gap or slip into one created by others, they are quick to brush it off as an isolated occurrence: "Just one of those things. Could have happened to anyone." Or they decide that others are at fault: "*They* should have known. . . ." "*They* should have understood. . . ." "*They* should have asked. . . ." It's the They Syndrome in action.

The third reason for the prevalence of problems is the direct opposite of the second: Many people who *aren't* skilled in the art of communication do know they are not, but they have neither the opportunity nor the motivation to improve, most probably because they don't see the connection between their communication weaknesses and their inability to truly succeed in their careers. As they see it, they are managing to make do, and that's good enough.

A fourth explanation for the prevalence of communication gaps is that some human endeavors are so prone to communication glitches that we all fall victim at one time or another. As Donald Norman points out, ". . . if people often seem to be at fault, especially different people over long periods of time, then the first place to look for the explanation is in the situation itself."[1] Take the common act of two people talking to each other, for example. What could be simpler? Yet the opportunities for misinterpretation are endless. The problem is not that people are necessarily poor communicators; rather, we just don't make the effort—or even realize we need to make the effort—to ensure that we understand each other.

---

[1] Donald A. Norman, *Turn Signals Are the Facial Expressions of Automobiles* (Reading, Mass.: Addison-Wesley, 1992), pp. 170–71.

CLOSING THE GAPS

The first step in closing communication gaps is to heed the warning given over the loudspeakers in the London Underground: Mind the gap. Communication gaps and platform gaps are similar in some ways—for example, both can get you into serious trouble if you're unaware of them. However, they differ in how you deal with them once you know they're there. When you're on the train platform and you spot a gap between platform and train, you can avoid the gap simply by stepping over it as you enter the train. Stepping over a gap won't eliminate it, however; the next time you return to that station, the gap between train and platform will still be there.

With communication gaps, by contrast, you can do much more than just bridge them: You can reduce their prevalence, size, and impact. You can accomplish this result by becoming attentive to gaps, appreciating their impact, noticing how they affect you and your organization, taking responsibility for the part you played in creating or maintaining them (or in falling victim to them), and by making changes that will minimize them. Certainly, you won't get rid of every communication gap you encounter; no one can. But you can go a long way toward minimizing the harmful effects. And if we each do what we can, together we can shrink a lot of gaps.

To help you close the gaps, this book

- describes the many ways that communication goes awry and the potentially damaging consequences
- helps you become aware of the communication problems you contribute to or fall victim to
- teaches you ways to become a better observer of the communication problems in your organization
- provides you with models and tools for resolving or preventing communication problems and gives recommendations on how and when to use them
- provides you with terminology, concepts, and information that will help you communicate these ideas to others

Four Contexts

Although gaps come in many sizes, shapes, and forms, there are four contexts in which communication gaps most commonly occur. Each section of this book corresponds to one particular context and recommends methods you can use to minimize or prevent communication gaps. The four sections are outlined below:

Section 1: Gaps in Everyday Interactions. The miracle isn't how poorly we communicate, but how well, given the prevalence of misunderstandings and misinterpretations in our interactions. Still, we could do much better. Chapters 2, 3, and 4 focus on three ways miscommunications occur in everyday interactions. You have experienced all three—I guarantee it!

- As the section's opening chapter, Chapter 2 describes communication flaws that lead the intended recipients of a message to react in ways that the senders then describe as "They didn't listen." This chapter describes senders' responsibilities for ensuring that their messages get through.

- Chapter 3 addresses the way both senders and recipients mislead and are misled by familiar terminology. A comic strip I came across years ago aptly portrays this problem:

John:	Do you have four-volt, two-watt bulbs?
Ron:	For what?
John:	No, two.
Ron:	Two what?
John:	Yes!
Ron:	No.

- Chapter 4 presents a model for analyzing a message recipient's experience upon receiving a message. This chapter explains why a person, on hearing a comment or question, sometimes responds in puzzling ways; the chapter also describes ways to avoid or debug such situations.

Section 2: Gaps in Building Relationships. This section's four chapters discuss the steps individuals and groups can take to work together effectively and to minimize conflict.

- Chapter 5 presents communication strategies for building the foundation for a strong relationship with those with whom you'll be working. The recommendations in this chapter will help you avoid excessive, prolonged, or unresolved conflict.
- Chapter 6 describes differences in communication styles and preferences that can drive you crazy if you don't understand, appreciate, and respect them. The chapter provides practical suggestions on how to accommodate variety—for the good of all concerned.
- Chapter 7 offers ideas for dealing with people whose behavior you find troublesome or stressful. Along with a variety of techniques, this chapter describes the use of a Perspectoscope, a tool I've invented for gaining insight into other people's perspective.

- Chapter 8 focuses on communication techniques to maintain and strengthen relationships throughout a project or work effort. A relationship, like a person, must be cared for if you want it to survive and thrive. This chapter suggests ways of doing that.

Section 3: Service Gaps. Directed at vendors, suppliers, and providers who would rather have deliriously happy customers than ones who are grumpy and irritable, this section contains three highly practical chapters.

- Chapter 9 focuses on the view from the customers' perspective, detailing the role of communication in creating customer satisfaction. When, what, and how you communicate can make all the difference.
- Chapter 10 addresses flaws and failures commonly found when assessing customer satisfaction. The chapter provides essential guidelines for successfully gathering and using customer feedback.
- Chapter 11 describes service level agreements (SLAs), which help providers and customers communicate more effectively. Beginning with a description of the most common flaws in establishing SLAs, the chapter includes guidelines for creating effective SLAs.

Section 4: Change Gaps. This final section is for you if you've faced change in the past and anticipate that you will again in the future—and want to become better at it.

- Chapter 12 describes the experience of change and presents a model for understanding when and how to communicate during times of change.
- Chapter 13 provides recommendations for managers, team leaders, and others who want to excel at introducing and managing change.

The concluding chapter, "On Becoming a Gapologist," offers a special challenge to the readers of this book, by way of a real-life gap that I faced.

Strengthen Your Personal and Organizational Effectiveness

In all four sections, the book focuses on helping you improve your awareness of communication gaps at both the individual and organizational levels so as to enhance your *personal effectiveness* and your *organizational effectiveness.*

Personal effectiveness refers to changes you can make on a personal level, in your own actions, attitude, or behavior, for your own self-improvement, or to help your organization. You can make these changes whether or not your organization backs or supports you. For example, if you were to discover that you sometimes speak in a blaming tone, and you modified that tone, you'd be using your personal effectiveness. You don't need anyone's permission to change your tone of voice; it's your choice. The same is true if you decide to return calls to customers sooner than is customary, or to ask clarifying questions to avoid misinterpreting your teammates' comments. The choice is yours.

To strengthen your personal effectiveness, ask the following questions as you examine the communication gaps discussed in this book:

- What am I currently doing well?
- What communication problems have I noticed?
- How am I part of the problem?
- What can I do better or differently?
- What can I change immediately, and what will take time?
- What commitments am I willing to make?

Notice that these questions focus not just on identifying what you can do differently, but also on recognizing your strengths so that you can use them as tools and catalysts.

Organizational effectiveness refers to changes that require attention and effort at an organizational level, whether that level is your entire organization or a specific subset of it, such as your team or department. These changes to policies and practices may require input, support, or approval by others.

For example, instituting new processes for assessing customer satisfaction would be an example of improved policies and practices. So would building strong relationships with other departments after a reorganization and kicking off a project by establishing group norms.

To strengthen your organizational effectiveness, ask the following variation on the previous set of questions as you examine the communication gaps in this book:

- What are we currently doing well?
- What communication problems have we noticed?
- How are we part of the problem?
- What can we do better or differently?
- What can we start doing immediately, and what will take time?
- What commitments are we willing to make?

These questions, too, focus not just on identifying what your organization can do differently, but also on recognizing your strengths so that you can use them as tools. As you read this book, I encourage you to appreciate what you're already doing well, and to be honest about what you can do to improve your personal and organizational effectiveness.

KEY RECOMMENDATIONS

To give you a head start in strengthening your personal and organizational effectiveness, here are some themes that appear throughout the book:

1. *Communicate early and often.* More precisely, communicate with appropriate parties

   - when a relationship is new—in order to build a strong foundation
   - throughout the relationship to ensure you're in sync and to make adjustments if appropriate

- when you become aware of a communication gap—so that you can take steps to close it before it widens

2. *Communicate in multiple ways.* The workaday world operates at a hectic and often chaotic pace. If you want to ensure that your messages reach your intended destination, convey them in multiple ways, using verbal and written communication, words and images, e-mail and telephone. In addition, alternate between informing and listening, and between providing and requesting clarification.

3. *Communicate about how you're going to communicate.* Let people know how you are going to keep them informed and how you wish to give and receive feedback. Tell them how quickly you expect to respond to their requests, ideas, and suggestions. Discuss how you will respect each other's communication preferences and how you'll handle conflict. The earlier in any undertaking you communicate about how you're going to communicate, the fewer snags you'll run into later.

4. *Give and get clarification.* Don't assume that your message always reaches the other party in the manner you intend or that you always receive the other party's message in the manner it is intended. In both cases, it is important to check and double-check. Ask questions. Verify that you and the other party both understand what is being said. Finally, accept the fact that, despite your best efforts, miscommunication will occur. Try to understand what caused the miscommunication, but be gentle with yourself. Perfection is impossible; just do the best you can.

5. *Apply a generous interpretation.* When someone responds in a puzzling, confusing, or disturbing way to something you say or do, try to refrain from responding in kind, lashing out, finding fault, or jumping to conclusions. Often, the explanation for the person's response is much simpler, and far more positive, than anything

you might imagine. Therefore, start by considering positive interpretations, and ask questions to validate your impressions.

6. *Communicate congruently.* Congruent communication, as described by the late family therapist Virginia Satir, balances self, other, and context—that is, your own needs, desires, and goals (self); those of other parties (other); and the setting or environment in which you're interacting (context).[2] *Incongruent* communication is that which leaves one or more of these out of the mix, resulting in an imbalance.

GAPS GALORE

While studying psychology in graduate school in New York City, I lived not far from the 14th Street IRT Subway station at Union Square. The platform at this station is curved, much like those in some London Underground stations. There's one major difference at this station, though: As the southbound train pulls into the station but before the train doors open, small sections of movable platform emerge at various points along the platform to fill the gap. The announcement over the Union Square loudspeaker repeatedly advises passengers, "Ladies and Gentlemen: Please be careful of the moving platform as trains enter and leave the station. For your safety, please stand away from the platform edge." In other words, mind the gap!

The engineers of the Union Square station found a clever way to close the gap, placing only a small responsibility on the thousands of passengers who pass through this station every day. Perhaps, someday, somehow, we can find as elegant a solution in the realm of communication. In the meantime, I hope you'll find useful ideas in this book to help you improve your skills as a communication "Gapologist."

---

[2] Virginia Satir et al., *The Satir Model: Family Therapy and Beyond* (Palo Alto, Calif.: Science and Behavior Books, 1991).

Section 1
Gaps in Everyday Interactions

Why do people speak so unclearly when they're providing important information? Take phone messages, for example. People sometimes say their names so inaudibly that I can't tell where the first name ends and the last name begins. I once received a message from a fellow whose first and last names together seemed to be a single syllable, and whose phone number sounded like it had only five digits. He probably considered me rude for not returning his call.

Names and numbers aren't the only cryptic parts of phone messages. Sometimes the message itself is befuddling, such as the one I received from a project manager who asked for my help and said I was the only person who understood her something-or-other. I was flattered to be the one who understood, but despite replaying the message a dozen times, I couldn't decipher her words. If you've never heard your own phone messages, tape yourself and have a listen. You might be surprised at how you sound.

Sometimes, muffled messages can be life-threatening. I once took a flight on a plane so tiny that even I, short though I am, risked banging my head on the ceiling. As the plane took off, an announcement came over the loudspeaker. I knew it couldn't be about dining options, beverage choices, or in-flight movies, but what the message was about I couldn't tell because not a word of it was audible over the roar of the plane.

When the 25-minute flight ended and the plane had landed, I waited on board until the eight other passengers had departed. Then, I asked the pilot what the announcement had covered. He replied that it was the safety announcement!

Muffled messages are common on large planes as well, where flight attendants seem unaware that passengers sometimes can't hear what they're saying. When the announcement ends, people turn to their seatmates and ask, "What'd she say?" On one flight I took a few years ago, the pilot made an announcement so softly that he was able to keep it a secret.

These situations illustrate a common trait of communication gaps: a disparity between the message sent and the message received. Most such gaps are merely minor cracks, barely noticeable and of no particular consequence. But some are major chasms, rendering communication impossible.

Why do these gaps occur in the first place, and why are they so common? The chapters of Section 1 tell why, describing several kinds of everyday interactions that lead to miscommunication between sender and recipient:

- Chapter 2 addresses miscommunications that the *sender* of a message creates.
- Chapter 3 focuses on ambiguities to which *both senders and recipients* fall victim.
- Chapter 4 explains why *recipients* of a message sometimes respond in a way that's altogether different from what the sender intended.

Although all three chapters offer ideas on how to avoid, or at least minimize, such gaps, a good place to start being a Gapologist is by noticing phone messages in which you have difficulty deciphering the caller's message. Let these situations alert you to question whether you, too, could be a message muffler. Otherwise, ghp*a)rts st'aa3vz gnt#takv+. Okay?

2

Getting Through

Responsibilities of the Sender

It was a gray and gloomy day when we pulled into the ski-area parking lot, and decided to sit a spell to see whether the sun might break through the clouds. As we waited, a carload of skiers pulled in next to us. Undeterred by the fact that the mountain had now vanished in the fog, they started unloading their gear. Idly watching them, I noticed that they had left their headlights on, and told one of them. The fellow nodded, but he didn't turn out the lights.

Odd, I thought. Why did he ignore what I told him? Why wasn't he paying attention? *Why didn't he listen to me?*

A few minutes later, as group members prepared to set forth, they started speaking to each other—in sign language. Ahhhh! It wasn't that they hadn't listened. It was that they couldn't hear. I pointed to their headlights. They got the message.

Both in our personal lives and in the workplace, most of us have, at times, felt that others weren't listening to us. But by "not listening," we generally don't mean that they were unable to hear. Rather, we mean that we introduced a change, prescribed a standard, offered an idea, proposed a solution, or provided advice—and they didn't do what we wanted them to do, or they did it wrong, or they did something else.

But perhaps it is our way of communicating that leads others to seem not to listen. A manager named Ken showed clear frustration not long ago when he asked me how to get his customers to recognize which products his help desk supports. Ken said his staff had designed a screen of information listing the supported products, yet customers continually asked for help with other tools.

"This product screen is the first thing customers see when they sign onto their PCs. They can't miss it," Ken explained. "They see it every single day, but they still ask for help with products we don't support. How can we get through to them?" In other words, how can we get them to listen?

But was the problem really that customers weren't listening? Certainly, that was a possibility, but other factors also could have contributed. Maybe the customers didn't understand the screen, or maybe they did understand but resented having the standards unilaterally imposed. Or maybe they just didn't see the point of the message since help-desk personnel continued to help them with the very products the screen claimed they didn't support.

Ken's reaction reflects a false assumption to which we all succumb at times: that a message sent is a message received. Ken assumed that because he had put forth some information—in this case, the product screen—his customers must have received, understood, and accepted it. When the customers suggested otherwise, he faulted them for not paying attention.

Everyday experience proves that merely sending a message provides no certainty that it will be received. Letters get misdelivered, voices are drowned out, e-mail messages vaporize in Cyberfluff. But sometimes, the fault does lie with the sender. Therefore, before finding fault elsewhere, it's wise to start by looking within. Ask yourself, "Am I communicating in a way that led the other party to appear not to be listening?"

This chapter describes ten types of messages that don't get through as intended and details the actions you can take to increase the likelihood that they will.

1. Unnoticed messages
2. Misstated messages
3. Missed messages
4. Cluttered messages
5. Hidden messages
6. Off-putting messages
7. One-sided messages
8. Unexplained messages
9. Conflicting messages
10. Befuddling messages

UNNOTICED MESSAGES

Let's say that, like Ken, you want to be sure that your customers read the information you send them. Or maybe you want management to read your proposals in a timely fashion. Or you wish your vendor would respond to your requests.

When people face an information overload, their in-boxes are piled high with number-one priorities, and they need a speed-reading course just to get through their e-mail, conventional methods of getting their attention just won't work. You must *get* their attention before you can *hold* their attention. One way to get *and* hold attention is through "stickiness."

In *The Tipping Point*, Malcolm Gladwell explains the notion of stickiness, the component in a message that makes it so captivating that it "sticks" to the largest possible number of people. Discussing the difficulties of effective communication, Gladwell observes, ". . . the hard part of communication is often figuring out how to make sure a message doesn't go in one ear and out the other. Stickiness means that a message makes an impact."[1] Gladwell concludes that simple changes in the presentation and structuring of information can affect how

---

[1] Malcolm Gladwell, *The Tipping Point: How Little Things Can Make a Big Difference* (Boston: Little, Brown and Company, 2000), pp. 24–25.

memorable a message is and how much impact it has. Taking Gladwell's concept one notch further, I've developed my own set of suggestions for increasing the stickiness of written and spoken messages, as elaborated in the paragraphs below.

Use Creative Titles

Using creative titles is a good place to start the quest for getting and holding attention. The right book title can turn a passerby into a book buyer. Book titles I especially like include *Why We Buy* (by Paco Underhill),[2] and *How We Know What Isn't So* (by Thomas Gilovich).[3]

Notice the titles that intrigue you, and think about how you can create the same kind of intrigue in your material. Aim for titles that will grab people's interest and pique their curiosity. For example, what about a proposal entitled "How to Benefit from Customer Complaints" or a set of guidelines entitled "Seven Surprisingly Simple Steps for Spectacularly Savvy Service"? Or, in Ken's case, how about a product screen labeled "Products You'll Love and the People Who Support Them"?

The same idea applies to e-mail messages. If you want your message to stand out, use a creative subject line: "A defect-tracking idea" is more likely to attract attention than "Hello." Create subject lines that are meaningful; then, more recipients will notice your messages—and actually read them.

Create a Captivating Appearance

A second way to grab people's attention is by making your material appear tantalizing. If your material is yawn-inducing, spruce it up. Use visual images not only in your presentations, but also in your documents, on your envelopes, and in your product screens. Make your material look lively, and people will pay more attention. If Ken's product screen had been

---

[2] Paco Underhill, *Why We Buy: The Science of Shopping* (New York: Simon & Schuster, 1999).

[3] Thomas Gilovich, *How We Know What Isn't So: The Fallibility of Human Reason in Everyday Life* (New York: The Free Press, 1991).

more captivating, customers would have been more likely to notice the standards, particularly if the screen was modified periodically to recapture attention. Of course, getting customers to notice standards doesn't guarantee that they will follow them, but if they *don't* notice the standards, they definitely *won't* follow them.

Use Imaginative Opening Lines

A third way to gain attention is to use opening lines that inspire curiosity. One of my favorite opening lines is this: "On a cold blowy February day a woman is boarding the ten A.M. flight to London, followed by an invisible dog." That's the opening sentence of Alison Lurie's *Foreign Affairs,* which won a Pulitzer Prize for fiction.[4] I don't have patience with novels in which I must wade through 150 pages before the plot begins to thicken. I don't even want to wade through two pages. I want to be hooked by the end of the first sentence, just as I was with Lurie's book.

Consider how you might use provocative opening lines such as the following in your own reports, proposals, memos, and newsletters.

- If you think 2,000 calls per quarter to the Support Center is a lot, wait until you read what customers have accomplished as a result of our help.
- This set of guidelines about security procedures is for people who hate to read guidelines about security procedures.
- For everything you always wanted to know, but didn't know who to ask (about the products we support, that is), call us!

Try New Ways of Communicating Your Message

A fourth way to gain people's attention is to do things differently. If the way you're communicating your message isn't

---

[4] Alison Lurie, *Foreign Affairs* (New York: Avon Books, 1984).

generating the outcome you want, try something different. Otherwise, you'll never know whether what you *could be doing* would work better than what you're *already doing*.

One IT group added whimsical clip art to its new customer procedures. Customers, in contrast to their previous reactions to procedures, actually looked at the new, illustrated documents. And customers who look at new procedures are more likely to follow them than customers who don't. Another group seeking customer approval decided to periodically telephone people in two "test" customer departments just to ask how things were going. Despite no other changes in service, the group found department personnel increasingly pleasant to work with.

To minimize risks, test your new approach before fully implementing it. For example:

- If you'd like to try presenting a two-day course as four half-day sessions, try out the new format with a long-time client who will give you honest feedback and observe how the change affects enrollment, energy levels, retention, and subsequent requests for support.
- If you think customer service could be improved by answering the phone differently, and your usual greeting is "Good morning, service desk," answer every third call with "Service desk, how may I help you?" Observe whether the new wording affects how customers respond.
- Instead of printing all copies of your next survey on white paper, try printing half on bright yellow paper, and see whether people return more yellow copies than white copies.

If the tests have no impact, at least you haven't invested much. And if a test backfires, such as by upsetting or confusing some customers, you can explain that it was only a test of a new method, and then simply return to your previous approach or to something that the customer would view more favorably.

Keep in mind, though, that these attention-getters aren't worth much if the information itself is a snooze-inducer. So, steer away from using the passive voice, and rid yourself of the notion that business writing must be formal. A conversational, down-to-earth style will win you readers, especially if you write as if it's *you* doing the writing, revealing your personality and viewpoint as well as technical content. Remember: Mind-numbingly idiosyncratic multisyllabic circumlocutions will impress people only for as long as it takes them to crumple your document and toss it. Obfuscate at your own risk.

I hasten to add that the satirist and cartoonist Scott Adams offers a somewhat different perspective about obfuscation. In *The Dilbert Principle*, Adams notes that a key to advancing in management is to substitute incomprehensible jargon for common words so as to convince other people of your intelligence. He writes, ". . . a manager would never say, 'I used my fork to eat a potato.' A manager would say, 'I utilized a multi-tined tool to process a starch resource.' The two sentences mean almost the same thing, but the second one is obviously from a smarter person."[5]

MISSTATED MESSAGES

Unfortunately, your message can be noticed but still not get through as you intended because you meant to say one thing and unintentionally said something else instead.

Therefore, if you suspect your message is being ignored, start by questioning whether you yourself might be responsible. I learned this lesson the hard way. During a seminar for an IT group, my client asked that we take an early and short lunch break, so at 11:30, I told the group, "We'll stop for lunch now, and resume in forty-five minutes."

At 12:15, I was ready to continue, but where was everyone else? Ten minutes passed. Three people returned. I started thinking of the rest as The Stragglers. As more minutes passed and The Stragglers still didn't return, I began to think of them very negatively; they were rude, irresponsible, disrespectful.

---

[5] Scott Adams, *The Dilbert Principle: A Cubicle's-Eye View of Bosses, Meetings, Management Fads & Other Workplace Afflictions* (New York: Harper-Business, 1996), p. 41.

Finally at 12:40, my patience exhausted, I announced that we'd get started. "But it's not time yet," one fellow insisted. "You said we'd begin again at twelve forty-five." The other two nodded in agreement.

"What? No way!" I exclaimed. I had said we'd resume in 45 minutes. I know I did. I'm absolutely positive.

At 12:45, the remaining class members filed back into the room. Every one of them. Somehow, they all had heard me say 12:45. I was forced to concede that maybe, just maybe, that's what I *had* said. Despite good intentions, I meant one thing and said another.

Suspect Yourself First

Consider what happened. Being certain (although wrong) about what I had said, I laid the blame for their absence on the class members, never stopping to think of possible alternative reasons for their tardiness. If I hadn't announced at 12:40 that I was going to get started, I would never have discovered that I had misstated myself. Even after the seminar resumed, I would have continued to see the latecomers in a negative light, while they would have been unaware of any problem. After all, I had given them an instruction and they had followed it.

Despite your best efforts, there will be times when you mean to say one thing but say another—and don't realize it. This classroom experience taught me that if something seems at odds with what I intended or anticipated, I have to begin by asking: Could it be me? Could I have said or done something other than what I intended, which somehow accounts for my current situation? These are useful questions to ask before finding fault with others.

MISSED MESSAGES

People are busy. They're not sitting around waiting for your message. Therefore, when it arrives, they can easily miss it, lose it, or forget about it. Intercom announcements that page people at the airport are a great example. They usually take the form:

Person's name—message—person's name

That's the message, from beginning to end. If people aren't anticipating being paged, they might not hear it.

Even if you are certain you said what you meant to say, sending your message just once, or in only one way, may not ensure that it gets through. I remember speaking to a software developer who was angry that a faraway team member had failed to respond to her request for information. She said, "I sent him a message on Monday and he hasn't answered. If I haven't heard from him by Friday, I'll call him."

She was missing the point. If a message you send is truly important, then sending it just once, in only one way, probably is not enough. It's also unwise to wait too long before sending it a second time, especially if you'll spend that time grousing about not having gotten a response. If you want to be sure people get your message, send it again with a note saying "Just in case this didn't reach you the first time . . ." Or follow the first message at intervals with a friendly reminder that you're looking forward to a response.

Sometimes, a person will choose to send a message only once, hoping that it *won't* get through. As Marie Benesh, an IT consultant, astutely observed, sometimes the sender's real message reflects a kind of power trip ("I'm so important and I sent you my important message. Now it's up to you to respond.")[6] But political manipulation is not a true communication issue and is therefore outside the scope of this book. I believe that most people are genuinely interested in having their message get through.

Use Multiple Approaches

If you need to send your message more than once, try using a different format, wording, or communication channel for each subsequent attempt. If your first message was sent as e-mail, telephone the person. If you faxed the previous message, try e-mail or a face-to-face conversation. By trying different approaches, you'll be likely to catch your recipient's attention—at least once.

This multi-message approach worked well when used by a project manager I consulted with some years ago. Engaged in a large software-development project, he had created a team within the larger project's staff to handle a task that was new and unfamiliar. The team leader had written a description of the team's role, and had sent it to the rest of the group, but the group's requests to the newly created team made it clear that many group members did not fully understand the team's role. Team members felt frustrated, but what they experienced was fairly typical. When a new and unfamiliar task is introduced, it's unlikely that everyone will "get it" from a single explanation. The team needed to do more to ensure that its message got through.

---

[6] Marie Benesh, private communication. Benesh (www.mbenesh.com) is coeditor, with James Bullock and Gerald M. Weinberg, of *Roundtable on Project Management: A SHAPE Forum Dialogue* (New York: Dorset House Publishing, 2001).

Once team members were made aware of what the real communication problem was, they clarified their role in different ways, using several formats and channels. First, they issued a written, follow-up explanation to all group members, giving concrete examples of requests that were both within and outside their domain; second, they reiterated the scope of their responsibilities in e-mail to the other project members who sought their services; and, finally, they reinforced the message during face-to-face project meetings.

Similarly, Ken's product screen might have benefited if he had used multiple formats, wordings, or channels to notify customers of product standards. Communication surely will be improved if you find out how your intended recipients prefer to have information sent to them. The better you can accommodate their preferences, the more likely it is that your message will be heard.

Create a Feedback Loop

For important information, it's advisable to create a feedback loop, or "ack" procedure, to acknowledge receipt of an important message. For example, in the rugged sport of mountain climbing, messages between climbing partners require a predefined response. In, say, a two-person climbing team, as one person climbs, the other person secures the rope to which both climbers are attached. Designed to minimize injury if a climber falls, this process is known as belaying. The person belaying says "On belay," which signals that a secured rope has been readied to hold the climber. The climber responds "Climbing." The rope-holder responds "Climb," and only then does the climber climb.

When thousand-foot falls (or the organizational equivalent) are not an imminent risk, such caution may be excessive. However, implementing a simple "ack" procedure is a wise policy. Some e-mail programs allow the sender to ask for a "notification of receipt." Once the e-mail has been opened by the recipient, a message pops up, asking the reader to acknowledge receipt. A message is then automatically sent by the recipient's e-mail client to the sender. Alternatively, if you send important information, and want to make sure it has been received, explicitly ask the recipient to confirm receipt. Or, create a project or team standard stating that people must automatically acknowledge the receipt of certain categories of e-mail. The relief of knowing that your message was received will more than outweigh the nuisance of the extra e-mail.

CLUTTERED MESSAGES

No matter how many times or in how many ways you send a message, if critical parts of it are buried in verbal clutter, recipients might not notice the message you hope to convey. Cluttered messages are especially common in written communication. For example, a consultant I once worked with sent a letter to his colleagues to confirm an upcoming annual meeting and to request their support for an important change in meeting format. Most people who received the letter didn't respond to his request. Why? They hadn't even noticed it.

One reason for the silence was that the format-change request was on the second page of the letter, in a paragraph that included other information. Except for this request, the letter was identical to the ones sent in previous years to confirm the annual meeting. Is it any wonder recipients didn't notice it?

Similarly, a project manager who had created a newsletter was puzzled when customers failed to notice the date of a key meeting described on page one. The problem was that the date was buried deep within the text of an article and printed in the same font as the surrounding text.

When reviewing documents from my clients and others, I frequently find that key information is buried within less essential material. In one noteworthy instance, details pertaining to network security were buried within a section on procedures for registering for training classes.

Simple techniques can help you ensure that critical information stands out, such as by using boldface or italics, an eye-catching font, a contrasting color, a bulleted excerpt, or a border around the key points. In the process of freeing your message from its cluttered surroundings, you might also find you'll need to unclutter people's minds. Consultant and prolific author Jerry Weinberg once told me that a reader suggested that he could communicate more clearly in his writing if he made his examples of inappropriate workplace behavior more distinct from his examples of appropriate behavior, such as by using different fonts. It seems that reader had trouble telling which were which.[7]

Unclutter Your E-mail Messages

E-mail messages that have been designed to communicate essential information often do the opposite, masking the very details they were created to convey. But even if your organization, like most, lacks a standard for formatting e-mail messages, there are ways to make your messages clear. Start, for example, by avoiding one of the most egregious of e-mail errors: the *endless paragraph*, a paragraph that is so long that your brain begs for a time-out.

To improve e-mail readability, keep each line reasonably short; my preference is around seventy-five characters per line. Divide the message into short paragraphs; they're easier on the eye than paragraphs that extend from the top of the screen to the floor. Keep the message brief, focusing on one topic rather than many, if possible.

I confess that I offer this last recommendation strictly as a suggestion, since I'm a frequent offender. Nevertheless, the longer the message and the more topics covered, the less likely it is that anyone, even the most interested reader, will read it all the way through, let alone retain it.

If a long message cannot be avoided, try to place the most important information at the beginning. Newspaper reporters use what they describe as an inverted-pyramid approach to

---

[7] Gerald M. Weinberg, private communication.

writing articles, putting the most important information in the opening paragraph. Each paragraph that follows is successively less important in conveying the essence of the story.[8]

The inverted-pyramid approach accommodates a crucial reality—which is that most people read only the first few paragraphs of a newspaper story. Unfortunately, in composing e-mail messages, most people do not follow the wisdom of newspaper journalists, but instead use a related geometric approach that I whimsically think of as the *inverted rectangle.* No part of a message stands out as more important than any other. Meanwhile, people are lost in an infinity of messages, and I've yet to hear anyone shout "Hooray, another batch of interminable messages!" We could help ourselves and each other by applying the inverted pyramid format to our e-mail messages.

Highlight Important Information

If an e-mail message you send contains crucial information, highlight that information! Let the recipient know what part of your e-mail *you* consider most important. A possible risk of this approach is that your readers may focus only on what's highlighted and ignore the rest. But you, as the sender, can decide which potential pitfall you prefer: the risk of having readers read only the crucial information, or the risk of their not reading the e-mail at all.

Emphasizing what's important is necessary in spoken information as well. I discovered this fact while scuba diving. Since my husband and I were novices, Tom, our instructor, lectured us on what we needed to know. "To check your oxygen level, do this. If you feel pressure in your ears, do that. If your mask fills up with water . . ." *Your mask fills up with water?*

---

[8] The December 11, 2000, issue of *Forbes* quotes Lee Iacocca describing his experience as layout editor of his college newspaper (from his book *Iacocca*), "As the layout editor, I figured out pretty quickly that most people don't read the stories. Instead, they rely on the headlines and subheads. That means that whoever writes those has a helluva lot of influence on people's perception of the news."

As we sped to the dive site in our motorboat, Tom warned us scuba-newbies about staying close to the bottom to avoid the turbulence caused by pockets of fresh water that can propel a diver toward the surface. He didn't stress this point, however, or emphasize its importance, and I barely registered what he had said. When a pocket of turbulence suddenly propelled me to the surface, I got caught in a whirlpool and couldn't catch my breath. Tom emerged quickly from the depths, rescued me, and said, "*Now* do you see what I mean by staying close to the bottom?" Oh!

When speaking, you can use the verbal equivalent of the visual indicators I listed previously, by saying something like, "The following points are particularly important." Or you can use both visual and spoken signals, as e-business guru Paul Jacobson does in his technical training classes. When he presents a particularly important point, he waves a red flag.[9] Is this technique silly? Yes—and it works! Humor can be wonderfully effective in helping people retain key points.

---

[9] Paul Jacobson, private communication. Paul gives wonderful presentations on how to hold an audience's or class's attention. For additional information on his techniques, see the Information Systems Resource Group at www.isrg.com.

Have you ever tried to convey information that's buried in clutter, and then wondered why your audience didn't receive the message you intended? Review the way you communicate in both written and spoken form; you're likely to find examples of cluttered messages.

HIDDEN MESSAGES

A special form of cluttered message is one in which information is right smack in front of the recipient, but it still doesn't get through. At a mom-and-pop grocery store in Vermont, I took my items to the cash register and asked if the store took credit cards. The cashier (I think it was Pop himself) flashed a what-a-dumb-question look and said, "Yes, we do. There are signs all over the store, including right here on the counter."

But locating any particular sign appeared to me to be impossible; this smidgen of a store had posters, cardboard cutouts, grocery displays, lost-and-found notices, and discount offers attached to every shelf, taped to every wall, protruding up from the floor, and even suspended from the ceiling. And the only thing on the counter was my collection of groceries. Unless . . . I moved the groceries aside, and there, taped to the counter, was a sheet of crinkled blue paper on which someone had scribbled a tiny handwritten list of the credit cards accepted by the store.

Pop was correct; there *was* a "sign" on the counter. But it was positioned where few people would have thought to look, and it was in a form they might not have recognized even if they did. Pop assumed that since *he* knew where the information was, then the customers would know, too. If they didn't, it must be their fault—or so his attitude implied. However, information is worthless if the intended recipients can't easily locate it when they need it, or can't see or hear it without strain.

I was a victim of this kind of unintentionally covert communication once at a hotel in which I was a registering guest. At check-in, the clerk told me that I had a message, and he handed me a sheet of paper. Fine, but where was the message?

Then I noticed it in the upper-left corner in a light shade of depleted-cartridge gray:

> Karten, Naomi
>
> 04-10-2002   14:39:31
>
> From: Lee, Stacy
>
> Pls talk to david hall while you're in town about a class he wants

I considered ripping off the top corner of the sheet and returning the rest to the clerk to use in case messages arrived for other guests.

I encountered a similar example of a nearly hidden message when a client asked me to review a draft of his service level agreement. I provide this service for many organizations, but in this instance I had to say no. Why? My client's company must have taken type-size lessons from the aforementioned hotel: I would have needed an industrial-strength magnifying glass to read the agreement. I told my client that if I couldn't read it, it was unlikely that those whose support would be necessary to its success would be able to read it either. Resist the temptation to shrink important information. Unreadable documents don't get read.

If your customers seem to ignore your message, you might want to make sure that they actually have seen it. One way or the other, you do need to get their attention.

Reflection Time

When people read about situations such as the ones I've described in the preceding five sections, they're often quick to respond "Yeah!" and "Right on!" as they think about coworkers, managers, or customers who are prone to these flaws and flubs. Certainly, *they* have room for improvement. Clearly, so do I, and perhaps, so do you as well.

The questions posed in Chapter 1 are good ones to review as we consider how we each can increase our personal effectiveness:

- What are you currently doing well?
- In what ways are you part of the problem?

- What can you do better or differently?
- What can you change immediately, and what will take time?
- What commitments are you willing to make?

OFF-PUTTING MESSAGES

Sometimes, your message is perfectly clear. It hasn't been unnoticed, misstated, missed, cluttered, or hidden. Yet, people don't behave as if they received it. In such situations, the problem may be that you communicated the message with an attitude that recipients found irritating, making them unreceptive to this message, and perhaps to future messages as well.

That's exactly the attitude I heard when I listened to a client's telephone support staff as representatives assisted callers with technical problems. In diagnosing a caller's problem, one support rep asked that oh-so-common question: "Have you changed anything?"

The caller gave that oh-so-common response: "No."

The discussion that followed led the support rep to realize that the caller had, in fact, changed some settings.

The rep's comment? "Oh, so you *did* make a change."

The rep didn't say, "You stupid customer! I suspected it all along! You said you didn't, but actually you did!" Unfortunately, though, her voice communicated this message, nevertheless.

"Attitude" is one of those words whose very use suggests a negative connotation. If we talk about someone's positive attitude, we're likely to describe the way in which it's positive: We say that it's an agreeable attitude, or an enthusiastic attitude, or a service-oriented attitude. When we simply say that someone "has an attitude," however, we usually mean an offensive, arrogant, or displeasing attitude. Do you communicate with an attitude? How you say something is at least as important as what you say if you want others to accept your policies, proposals, and advice.

As Richard Farson points out in *Management of the Absurd*, ". . . it's crucial to listen to the music as well as the lyrics, the feeling behind the words as well as the words themselves."[10] Often, though, the music so overpowers the lyrics that listeners hear only the music. In fact, if there's a certain edge to your voice, the other party may reject your ideas, no matter what they are. Even the best advice is unlikely to get a fair hearing if the recipient is insulted, offended, or put off by the manner in which you communicate it.

Unfortunately, we're not always the best judge of how we come across when we communicate. I once turned on the radio in the midst of an interview program that invites callers' questions, and the first voice I heard was my husband's, posing a question in his I-think-you're-an-idiot-and-I-want-to-stump-the-chump voice. Afterward, I asked him if he had intended to sound so aggressive. He said he hadn't; nor had he realized that he had sounded that way. I offered my opinion that he might have had better luck chump-stumping if he had used a kinder tone—a point that's easier to identify when hearing another's tone than one's own.

If your tone conveys a blaming, arrogant, or you're-a-jerk-I'm-a-genius attitude, it's hard to fault those on the receiving end for dismissing not only the information, but the sender as well. The same is true of messages that convey weariness, boredom, or a lack of enthusiasm. For example, an IT vice president I hadn't met sent me an e-mail asking me to contact him. I called and reached his voice-mail. In his recorded greeting, he sounded lackadaisical and not very vice presidential. The attitude he conveyed was: I don't care. I wondered whether this was strictly his leave-a-message voice or whether it was how he really sounded, but I left my message anyway.

As I discovered once we spoke, he was outgoing, animated, and easy to talk to. I wondered why he hadn't created an outgoing message that would reflect these qualities.

---

[10] Richard Farson, *Management of the Absurd: Paradoxes in Leadership* (New York: Touchstone, Simon & Schuster, 1996), p. 58.

Notice How You Come Across to Others

Your voice is a powerful tool. You can use it to stifle interest, create animosity, and foster resentment—or you can use it to build trust, confidence, and respect. Consider the following statement:

> Well, if you think your way is better, let's give it
> a try.

Read this statement aloud several times, affecting in successive turns a tone of anger, frustration, fatigue, boredom, outrageous arrogance, and absolute certainty that the other party is dead wrong. Then, read it in your friendliest, most upbeat, enthusiastic, other-oriented, ready-to-lend-a-hand self.

See the difference? Subtle shifts in pitch, volume, and emphasis can dramatically impact the message the other party receives. People learn to affect these shifts at an early age; indeed, toddlers routinely employ them to appeal for what they want. As adults, we need to be conscious of how our tone of voice affects whether our message gets through.

In addition to tone, certain mannerisms can be off-putting, as a woman learned in one of my workshops. I had assigned groups of people to practice gathering information by holding mock interviews with "customers." Other members of this woman's group told her that she sounded impatient when she conducted the interview. She replied that she wasn't impatient, and said she couldn't understand their reaction. They explained that the deep breaths she took intermittently made her seem exasperated.

The "customer" confirmed this reaction, saying, "I felt that you were in a hurry to get it over with. I thought you might be upset if I asked any more questions." This feedback proved to be a major "aha!" for this woman, who explained that she simply liked to take deep breaths, and had no idea that it might be causing customers to shut down. With this awareness, she was able to improve her style of communication.

In Ken's situation, the wording used for the product screen might have conveyed an unintended attitude to customers, but he would have had a still-bigger problem if his customers had detected an off-putting attitude from the help-desk staff. If even just one staff member communicated with customers in an arrogant, offensive, or disinterested manner, customers could have reacted by ignoring the group's other messages.

ONE-SIDED MESSAGES

Along with a positive attitude, it's important that people communicate in a way that shows consideration of the other party's views. How you see things invariably differs from how others see them. But if you want people to come around to your view, then you have to consider their perspective. To do so, you may need to learn more about that perspective. Then, you can present your ideas in a way that indicates clearly that you are taking their concerns into account.

Learning about other people's perspective entails talking to them. The very process of your asking a question and then listening to the response may encourage people to listen to you in return. Ken's staff could have benefited from spending more face-to-face time with customers, separate from their product-support work, to learn about the customers' context. How do they use their software? What capabilities are most important to them? What concerns them about the products and the product standards?

By learning more about how the world looks from the customers' perspective, Ken's group would be in a better position to pitch product standards in terms that speak directly to their customers.

If you're in a similar situation, focus on how the other party will benefit from adopting your recommendations or standards:

- What do they stand to gain?
- How will their lives become easier?
- How will they save time, or turn out better work?
- How will their performance improve?
- How will they become more likely to be seen as successful in the eyes of their higher-ups?

By doing this background work, you'll discover how to communicate in a way that encourages people to be more open to your ideas. You may also find yourself becoming more open to theirs. Perhaps you can *each* adjust your thinking to create a meeting of the minds. In doing so, you'll discover that customers may do it your way because your way and their way have become the same.

UNEXPLAINED MESSAGES

No doubt, your policies, standards, and decisions are well-thought-out. However, in the absence of any explanation of how they came to be and why they matter, other people may perceive them as arbitrary and without rationale. If you appear to issue directives, orders, and mandates, people may decide consciously not to take in your message. By explaining the reasoning behind your decisions, you may make allies out of opponents.

Yet, it's not the policies, standards, and guidelines themselves that people resist; it's being confronted with rules without the whys and wherefores. If it's important that specific ideas be accepted, explain the reasoning behind them.

The experience of one group that had been wrestling with alternative approaches to solving a difficult problem illustrates the value of providing the reasons behind a decision. People in the group were incensed at the apparent arbitrariness of their manager's decision about how to handle the problem. Believing their views had been trampled on, group members demanded an explanation.

The explanation clarified a great deal. As the manager described his reasoning, group members learned that he had discussed the alternative approaches with a subset of the very group to be affected by the decision. In making his decision, he took into account the risks of each option, as well as the increased work load that might result. Did his explanation make everyone like his decision? No, but by increasing their understanding of what was behind it, they were willing to accept and support it.

Be Forthcoming with Your Reasoning

In situations like Ken's, those most affected by the standards that are set are rarely given information about the reasoning behind them. Explanations won't always change people's opinions, but sometimes they can show people how they may benefit from the standards—or even how the standards may have been designed expressly for their benefit.

In Ken's case, for example, the absence of product standards would have hurt his staff's ability to competently and rapidly support customers. Conversely, the presence of product standards meant that customers would receive faster response, quicker problem resolution, cost savings, and greater support for more complex software problems. Customers might not eagerly embrace these reasons, but knowledge of potential benefits might encourage more customers to accept the standard.

At times, the absence of an explanation can create a dilemma for both parties. A systems development director told me that he repeatedly asked his staff members to tell him about problems they encountered, but they kept ignoring his requests. He asked me what he could do to get them to keep him informed.

I suggested that a good first step might be to find out why they didn't do what he asked. Did they forget? Were they not taking his requests seriously? Were they afraid of what might happen if he knew more about the problems they were experiencing? He needed an explanation from them.

But it is very likely that they needed an explanation from him, too. Why did he want to know about their problems? How was he going to use the information? What were the consequences when he didn't have it? How would having it enable him to help them?

As their manager, he would be more likely to get their explanation by first offering his own—provided that the environment wasn't a punitive one. In general, people who are willing to convey the reasoning behind their own decisions, requests, and actions are more likely to enjoy successful two-way communication.

CONFLICTING MESSAGES

Sometimes, the message does get communicated, but it may not have its intended impact if the receiver detects a contradiction between the sender's words and actions. Contradictions between words and actions can be funny. I once considered trying bungee jumping, an activity in which you pay an outrageous fee that entitles you to plunge headfirst from a twelve-story platform toward the earth. Before making my decision, I asked the bungee operator, "Is this activity safe?" "Absolutely!" he said, "we've supervised more than ten thousand jumps without an accident or injury of any kind." So I paid my money. He then handed me a release form to sign that contradicted his verbal assurance. It read, "Bungee jumping is a high-risk activity in which you can sustain whiplash, . . . rope burn, . . . serious injury, . . . or death." Contradictions notwithstanding, I did sign, and I did jump!

Conflicting messages are common in technical-support groups like Ken's. If his group violates its own standards by supporting products that its standards claim it doesn't, it is communicating a conflicting message.

Whenever there is a contradiction between what you say and what you do, it's the latter that people notice. So don't expect others to comply with standards that define the boundaries of your services if *you* frequently overstep those boundaries.

Being responsive means occasionally making an exception. Just be aware of the message an exception communicates: "We may say one thing, but sometimes we do another." Be careful not to cross that fine line beyond which people will cease to trust you.

Do you assist customers even when that assistance violates your standards? Do your actions contradict your words? Don't be too quick to say no. If you're unsure whether you act in contradiction to what you've communicated, ask your customers. Often, your contradictions are blatantly obvious to them. If you discover that you're guilty of a pattern of conflicting messages, it may be time to reexamine the difference between your words and your deeds. Adjustments to one or both may be necessary to ensure they are in sync with each other.

BEFUDDLING MESSAGES

After all is said and done, the message has to make sense to the recipient. Do you ever mystify people with vague, convoluted, or ambiguous information? Do you ever offer explanations that befuddle people?

I experienced this kind of ambiguity-induced befuddlement at the gym while using the exercise machine that simulates climbing steps. When I selected the fitness-test option on one particular stepamajig, the digital display asked me to choose my "level" from a 10-point scale. Assuming the higher the level, the harder the exercise, I selected Level 6. Then, the machine asked for my age. Let's say I entered "27." Next, it asked for my weight. Well, um, I entered "96." The contraption directed me to exercise for three minutes, periodically urging me to step faster. As I climbed to what felt like the top of the Empire State Building, it kept shouting at me to step faster.

When the three minutes ended, the display panel informed me: "Your fitness is 44." What? Is that good or bad? I haven't a clue. Does it mean I'm a fine aerobic specimen, or that I'd better start upping my huffing and puffing? I wish I knew. Is "44" relative to jocks who use such machines regularly or relative to those who have revealed their statistical secrets to this specific machine? Or is it relative to a population of 96-pound 27-year-olds? I'll never know.

Generally, people who prepare written information want it to be understood. The problem is that they know what their information means, and can't conceive of its having any other meaning (or no meaning at all!) to others. Yet situations like my stepamajig experience are a reminder of how easy it is for messages to create confusion. Clients sometimes ask me to review the guidelines they send out to customers. As an outsider, I can quickly see writing that might confuse the intended audience. Having not written the material myself, I can review it objectively. As a result, glitches, goofs, and contradictions leap out at me. I can give valuable feedback as a result of my distance from the writer.

Get Feedback from Others

There's nothing like a second pair of eyes, and sometimes a third, or even a fourth, to improve the quality of written material. If you're preparing technical documentation, customer instructions, or other such material, try to read it from the perspective of the intended audience to see how it might be misinterpreted.

But don't stop there. Have material reviewed by content experts and prospective recipients. Both types of reviewers will suggest improvements that you might never have considered. A third category of reviewer—someone who has no connection to the material at all—is sometimes the most valuable of all. Such reviewers, totally removed from the situation, often find egregious errors that those close to it miss.

Despite your best attempts to communicate clearly, it's easy to cause confusion. No one is immune from using language that, although grammatically perfect and thoroughly spell-checked, is other than what we intended. And oh, what embarrassing errors we're capable of! I'll never forget the time when, if it had not been for reviewer feedback, I would have omitted a mandatory *not*, without which readers would have crowned me Idiot of the Year.

Don't trust your instincts to determine whether your policies, standards, procedures, instructions, and explanations make sense. Collaborate with others and become each other's reviewers. Or send it to me, and I'll let you know what I think. Keep in mind, though, that my feedback will represent the perspective of a 96-pound 27-year-old whose three-minute rating at Level 6 is a perfect "44"!

INFORMING AND INVOLVING

When I told Ken some of the reasons I believed his product information hadn't gotten through to his intended audience, he realized he didn't know for sure what the problem really was. And here is a key point: Neither did his customers, because they didn't even know that their requests for help with non-standard products were creating a problem. Very likely, they didn't know they were causing frustration for the support staff. How could they? They were never told. So, although Ken and his staff viewed their customers as the problem, they hadn't given them an opportunity to be part of the solution.

If you face a situation like Ken's, in which the message does not seem to be getting through, consider informing and involving your intended recipients. Informing and involving are key communication strategies. When people function in a manner other than what you'd like, it's risky to presume to understand why they are doing so. Instead, seek out their reasons for their actions. Sometimes their explanations will surprise you. Help them become aware of the impact that their actions have on you. Describe what you need from them, and invite their input.

Organizations that inform and involve those on the receiving end seem to have both fewer problems to solve and faster resolution of those that arise than organizations that fail to communicate. People who have a role in proposing and supporting solutions are more likely to endorse, promote, and take responsibility for their success or failure. And, when you're on the receiving end, you can improve the quality of the messages you receive by communicating with the sender about problems that arise and by suggesting ways to eliminate them.

You might also find it helpful to do a communication assessment, using one or both of the following approaches:

- Using the ten types of messages discussed in this chapter, identify situations associated with each in which your personal or organizational messages aren't getting through. Consider what you might do to change the situation.[11]

---

[11] Note that these ten types don't account for all the reasons that messages don't get through. Numerous other possibilities exist. For example, in *BusinessSpeak*, Suzette Haden Elgin describes how we each have a preferred sensory mode, such as sight, hearing, and touch, that influences the way we communicate: "I can't picture that" versus "It doesn't sound right" versus "It falls flat for me." She notes that during relaxed circumstances, people use all three sensory modes, but under stressful circumstances, they tend to become locked into their preferred mode. Therefore, she suggests that recognizing someone's preferred sensory mode and, when possible, matching it through your own choice of words can help to build rapport, increase understanding, and persuade others to agree with what you say. See Suzette Haden Elgin, *BusinessSpeak: Using the Gentle Art of Verbal Persuasion to Get What You Want at Work* (New York: McGraw-Hill, 1995), pp. 33–37.

- Analyze problems you're experiencing in which the person or group you're communicating with doesn't seem to be listening. Ask yourself: What actions, attitudes, or behaviors have been displayed that give me the impression that they're not listening? Could any of the types of messages in this chapter account for the situation? If so, what changes might encourage message recipients to listen?

Are frustration and grousing about others not listening really better than finding out what the underlying problem is and working to solve it? The next time you claim that others don't listen, *stop* and ask yourself how you might be contributing to the situation. Then decide what you can do differently to ensure that your messages get through.

3

Misinterpretations

How Messages Cause Confusion

My brother, Jess, is an enthusiastic cross-country skier. I'm addicted to downhill skiing. A few years ago, when he said he had become proficient on hills and wanted to go downhill skiing with me, I was delighted. As we got off the chair lift, he looked down the slope and exclaimed, "It's so steep!" Steep? This easy slope? That's when I realized that the word "hill" meant something different to him than it did to me.

That was my first experience with cross-country confusion. My second occurred just before a first meeting with staff of an East Coast software company. I had begun chatting with people as we assembled for our morning meeting, and one woman told me she had just arrived from the West Coast. Living in Massachusetts, I have suffered through many snooze-less, red-eye flights from the West Coast, and I was sympathetic. "How long did it take you to get here?" I asked. "Three hours," she responded. Only three hours? I wrote off her response as foggy thinking caused by travel fatigue. Partway through the meeting, I realized, with a jolt, that she was right. Not only were we on the East Coast of the United States, but we were on the east coast of Florida as well, a state with a west coast and one of the company's other offices a mere three-hour drive away!

Although the previous chapter described miscommunications created by the senders of messages, my cross-country confusion was a result of both the sender's and receiver's terminology. In this chapter, I focus on ways both the sender and the recipient may mislead and get misled by each other, despite seemingly familiar terminology.

TWO PEOPLE SEPARATED BY A COMMON LANGUAGE

When people converse in a common language, they assume that they're speaking the *same* language. Yet that assumption regularly proves false. While language helps to clarify understanding, it can also cause confusion, conflict, and unintended consequences when people attribute different meanings to the words they use.[1] We each speak in our own idiom, often oblivious to the possibility that our words might have a different meaning to others. And we interpret the messages sent our way without realizing they might have a different meaning to the sender than to us. As both sender and recipient, we're susceptible to misinterpretations, and in both capacities, the responsibility is ours to question, follow-up, clarify, and do whatever is necessary to ensure that we're in sync.

Let's be clear: I'm not talking about doublespeak, which, as described by William Lutz, is language that merely pretends to

---

[1] This is when we are at least nominally speaking the same language. Imagine the situation described in a May 1991 article by Jared Diamond in *Discover* magazine, about a region of New Guinea the size of Connecticut that has about twenty-five languages, each spoken by a hundred to a thousand people. One such language uses only six consonants and mostly one-syllable words. However, as a tonal language, its four pitches, three possible variations in pitch within a syllable, and different forms of each vowel result in more than twenty permutations. Thus, depending on the way it's spoken, *be* could mean mother-in-law, snake, fire, fish, trap, flower, or a type of grub. Diamond reports that his attempts to accurately repeat even simple names were a source of great amusement to the locals.

communicate and whose purpose is to "mislead, distort, deceive, inflate, circumvent, obfuscate."[2] No, what I'm referring to here are innocent, unintended differences in interpretations.

Cultural differences account for many of these misinterpretations. In *Fundamentals of Human Communication,* authors DeFleur, Kearney, and Plax describe four cultural factors that affect how we relate to one another:[3]

1. Individualism versus collectivism: This difference concerns whether people place value on emotionally independent, social, organizational, or institutional affiliations (individualism) or on close-knit, supportive, family-like affiliations in which collaboration, loyalty, and respect are prized (collectivism).

2. High versus low context: High-context cultures are ones in which information is communicated in a comparatively indirect and subtle manner, with reliance on nonverbal cues. Low-context cultures are those in which information must be communicated explicitly, precisely, and accurately. An absence of adequate facts, details, and examples in a low-context culture may muddle the message being communicated.

3. High versus low power-distance: This characteristic concerns how people within a culture distribute power, rank, and status—whether equally to all members or according to birth order, occupation, and class or status—and how this influences the way people communicate with each other.

4. Masculinity versus femininity: This factor pertains to whether the culture tends to be traditionally masculine—emphasizing success, ambition, and competitive-

[2] William Lutz, *The New Doublespeak: Why No One Knows What Anyone's Saying Anymore* (New York: HarperCollins, 1996), p. 4.

[3] Melvin L. DeFleur, Patricia Kearney, and Timothy G. Plax, *Fundamentals of Human Communication,* 2nd ed. (Mountain View, Calif.: Mayfield Publishing, 1993), pp. 153–58.

ness—or traditionally feminine—emphasizing compassion, a nurturing stance, and class or social support.

Adding to these complexities of culture are differing interpretations between people from two countries in which people speak ostensibly the same language. But even being alert to the probability of differences doesn't necessarily prevent confusion. That's been my experience each time I've presented a seminar in London.

Despite the fact that I know many of the differences between British and American English, time after time, I leave my hotel room, get in the elevator (I mean the lift!), and press "1." When the door opens, I peer out and wonder, "Where's the lobby?" having again forgotten that in Europe the ground floor is the one at street level and the first floor is one floor up—what we in the United States call the second floor. This difference isn't so hard to remember; yet habit compels me to press the button labeled "1" instead of the one labeled "G."

When I describe this experience to my British students, we invariably begin a discussion of the many differences. I recite some of the words that I know have different meanings in their English and mine. They delight in offering their own examples. Amused by the thought that an English-to-English dictionary might help me in my overseas travels, I created one. Here are some of my favorite entries.

British English	American English
Chemist	Pharmacy
Flat	Apartment
Bobby	Police officer
Automobile bonnet	Hood of a car
Automobile boot	Trunk of a car
Silencer	Muffler of a car
Left luggage	Baggage room
Roundabout	Traffic circle
Public school	Private school
State school	Public school
Underground	Subway
Nappy	Diaper
Dear	Expensive
Vest	Undershirt
Jumper	Sweater
Waistcoat	Vest

Given these differences, as well as the hundreds of others, I now open my London classes by telling students, "If I say anything during this class that doesn't make sense to you or seems inappropriate or offensive, please understand that this was not my intention. Most likely, I was speaking my English and not yours." I've come to believe that this might be a useful disclaimer for all communication.

TERMINOLOGY DISCONNECTS

When we talk with people from other English-speaking countries, we often joke about how we come from two countries *separated by a common language.* But differences in meaning exist not only between countries but also between regions within a single country. Language differences can also exist between professions, organizations, or even subsets of an organization.

Lutz writes in *The New Doublespeak* that "the 500 most frequently used words in the English language have more than 14,000 meanings."[4] Pick any common word and look it up in your dictionary; you may see as many as twenty, thirty, or even more definitions. The reality is this:

> Any two of us are two people separated by a
> common language.

And failure to identify and clarify differences in interpretation can have damaging effects upon projects, productivity, and relationships.

In theory, the way to avoid misinterpretation and misunderstanding would be for any two, say, English-speaking people to have their own specialized English-to-English dictionary. The same is true for people communicating in other languages. And, as some companies have discovered, a dictionary or on-line glossary is particularly helpful in interpreting acronyms and EMAs (easily misinterpreted acronyms, that is).

With 26 letters in the English alphabet, there are thousands of possible acronyms, so you wouldn't think we would use the same ones to mean different things. Nevertheless, select any acronym used in your company and you can probably find it being used elsewhere, and even within your own company, to signify an entirely different entity. And, in the world at large, EMAs abound. As a longtime member of the National Speakers Association (NSA), I often forget that, to many people, NSA refers to the National Security Agency.

For decades, technology professionals have been reminded to be judicious in using technical terminology with customers. Business personnel want those serving their needs to know *their* language ("business-speak," in other words) and to use it in presenting their explanations, justifications, and rationales. I vividly remember one customer who complained to me that members of the technical staff persisted in talking "network nonsense." "I don't know what they're talking about," she

---

[4] Lutz, op. cit., p. 38.

explained. "I work in a world of loans, appraisals, and mortgage applications; not cycle times, servers, and mips and blips."

Before the days of personal computing, computer techies took great delight in using technical jargon with customers every chance they got. That was the culture of the time. Using jargon when it was quite clear that others didn't understand it was a way to exert power, intimidate, and display expertise. It emphasized that it was "them versus us." Perhaps it was even doublespeak.

These days, technical professionals of all kinds are more aware of the importance of not baffling customers with jargon. However, there are still plenty of exceptions. In my book *Managing Expectations,* I related the story of the doctor who, before examining me, reviewed my medical records and declared me "unremarkable"! Just short of slugging him (verbally, at least), I realized that he was using medical terminology that meant that I was in excellent condition.[5]

In retrospect, this was a funny experience. Nevertheless, the doctor should have known that the word "unremarkable" has a different meaning in medical jargon than in everyday English. Yet our own jargon is so familiar to us that we often don't even realize it's jargon. To us, it *is* everyday English.

And that is the real lesson here: Be aware of using everyday terms that mean different things to different people. Merely having an English-to-English dictionary won't prevent misunderstandings because differing interpretations are often about much more than different definitions, as the following sections illustrate.

Project Terminology

In a company I visited, two recently merged software engineering groups discovered that they'd been using the same terminology to describe different things and different termi-

---

[5] Naomi Karten, *Managing Expectations: Working with People Who Want More, Better, Faster, Sooner, NOW!* (New York: Dorset House Publishing, 1994), pp. 23–24.

nology to mean the same things. One of their first tasks was to create a shared language so they could understand each other.

Precise terminology is an essential ingredient in the difficult process of defining customer specifications. Take, for example, the matter of what to call a product. As David Hay notes in *Data Model Patterns*, "In many industries, this is not a problem. A bicycle is called a bicycle by nearly everyone. In other industries, however, different customers may call the same product by different names, and all of these may be different from the name used by the manufacturer."[6]

It's easy to assume that two parties using the same terminology mean the same thing. When Pete, a project manager at Quality Coding Corp., undertook a software project for his client Carl, Carl asked for a weekly, written status report. So Pete delivered a status report every Friday. The project concluded on time, within budget, and to specification—successful by all conventional measures. Only by reviewing his company's post-project client-satisfaction survey did Pete learn that Carl was dissatisfied with the project. Among Carl's complaints: He never knew the project's current status.

Pete and Carl had different ideas about the type of information that should be contained in a status report, yet they neither discussed the topic nor took steps to uncover disparities. Because Pete had prepared status reports for many projects, he had no reason to suspect that Carl wanted something different. Seeking clarification never occurred to him.

Carl, however, did have something specific in mind when he requested the status reports, expecting information that would help him communicate project progress to his own management. Had Pete asked how Carl would use the reports or who else might want to view them, or had Carl voiced his dissatisfaction early in the project, the outcome should have been vastly different.

The fact is, it didn't have to happen that way. Pete should have assumed right from the start, that although he and his client were

---

[6] David C. Hay, *Data Model Patterns: Conventions of Thought* (New York: Dorset House Publishing, 1996), p. 103.

using the same words, they were speaking a different language. What Pete gave Carl each week was not the status report Carl expected, but what, in Carl's view, was a jumble of lines, arrows, and bizarre little symbols. Assuming that you and another person are speaking the same words but a different language rarely proves to be a false assumption. Pete was unaware of the important process of communicating about *how you're going to communicate:* spending time throughout a project discussing not just the deliverable, but also how the two parties will communicate while that deliverable is being created. You don't have to make the same mistake.

Meeting Terminology

Stan, a consultant, learned a similar lesson—although, fortunately, before any real damage was done. Two weeks before presenting a class to a group of software project managers, Stan received an e-mail message from his client Sue, requesting an agenda for the class. Stan was surprised. In the preceding months, he'd had several conversations with Sue about the objectives of the training as well as about how he would customize the class to address those objectives. Plus, he'd already given her an outline.

Everything had seemed to be in order. Now, Sue wanted an agenda. Why, Stan wondered, does she suddenly distrust me after so many fruitful conversations? Does she think I can't do the job? Has she for some reason become unsure that I can do what I promised? Stan's insides began to talk to him: "What a nuisance! I don't need this aggravation!" he thought. "Maybe I should back out and save us both a lot of wear and tear!"

But Stan needed the work. He delivered the agenda.

When he arrived at the client site, Sue greeted him and seemed glad to see him, but she also seemed nervous. What Sue said next put her request into perspective for him. Sue had recently been put in charge of training. Three weeks earlier, she had arranged a class for the same software group, the first class she had organized in her new role. Unfortunately, after a strong start, the instructor had gone off on a subject-matter tangent from which he never returned. The project managers were angry at having their time wasted, and Sue couldn't risk a recurrence. An agenda, which she hadn't requested for the previous class, would help her monitor the class as it proceeded, enabling her to take action if Stan went off track.

Now Stan understood. Sue's request for an agenda wasn't due to a negative reaction to him, but rather, to a negative experience with his predecessor that made her understandably nervous. Stan realized that what Sue wanted wasn't an agenda per se, but rather the assurance that the class would be conducted as promised. Thus enlightened, he offered to meet with her during breaks each day to review the progress of the class and to see whether she had any concerns.

Stan had fallen into an interpretation trap. Had he asked for clarification of Sue's request for an agenda rather than try to interpret it, she might have revealed her unsettling past experience much sooner, and he could have both met her need and spared himself distress.

Service Terminology

Not surprisingly, people interpret words in ways that fit in with their particular perspective. For example, when a tech-support group created a service standard stating that it would respond to reported problems within one business day, customers took "respond" to mean "resolve," expecting that within one business day, they'd receive an explanation of the problem and a solution. But what tech-support personnel meant by "respond" was "acknowledge." Within one business day, they'd let customers know when they anticipated they'd be able to address the problem.

Now, you might consider this use of "respond" to be so obviously ambiguous that support staff would clarify their meaning before issuing their service standard. But in reviewing the service standards of many organizations, I've frequently encountered instances of the word "respond" used without clarification. The people who create the standards rarely do so with the intent to deceive; they are simply oblivious to the potential ambiguity. The notion of ambiguous terminology has never occurred to them.

In addition to "respond," a considerable portion of other service terminology is ambiguous. For example, what does "resolve" mean? Well, it depends. A hardware vendor publicized the company's commitment to resolve customers' problems within four hours. Some customers interpreted this to mean four hours from the time the problem appeared. In fact, what the vendor meant was four hours from the time the problem was reported to the customer-service contact at the company.

I asked the vendor contact when most customers learned of this difference in interpretation. "Oh, the first time they call for help," he explained. Although customer misunderstanding was common, the vendor did nothing to clarify what was meant. A motivated ambiguity, I suspect, giving customers a good reason early on to take responsibility for obtaining clarification of all terminology pertaining to the vendor's hardware.

But simply clarifying the time frame for resolving a problem is insufficient if the parties haven't agreed to the meaning of "problem resolution." What determines that a problem has been resolved? Must the resolution be a permanent fix? Do workarounds count? What about temporary patches that'll keep the problem in check until the next release can eliminate it? Furthermore, who determines that the problem has been fixed? The vendor? The customer? Both? Who authorizes closing out the problem? The vendor? The customer? Both? Almost every word of such service commitments bears examination for potential differences in interpretation.

Clearly, these differences are not about mere dictionary definitions, but about how two parties interact. Before they reach closure on what they've agreed to, they should compare their understanding of the terminology they're using. Otherwise, surprises are likely, sooner if not later. Or both sooner and later.

Differing interpretations can occur with other service terminology as well. Take up-time, for example. When a vendor commits to 99 percent server up-time, does this mean 99 percent of the entire tracking period? Or does it exclude specified time periods, such as planned downtime for maintenance and customer-triggered outages? In addition, over what period of time is the calculation of 99 percent being made? Whether an eight-hour outage falls short of the commitment depends on whether service delivery is being tracked over a month or a millennium. Similarly, customers may view a 1 percent outage differently depending on whether it's a single outage totaling 1 percent of a given month's service or a month of random two-minute outages that total 1 percent.

These differing interpretations often surface only after customers discover, usually at an inconvenient time, that the standard didn't mean what they'd originally thought. By then, the damage is done: The customer is unhappy and the vendor has to scramble to resolve the problem—or the two parties enter onto the battlefield of "But I meant . . ." It is much more effective for the two parties to explicitly discuss differences in interpretation to ensure a common understanding of the terminology and its implications for service delivery.

Many organizations use a formal type of agreement called a service level agreement (SLA), which tackles these differences directly. One feature of the SLA is a glossary in which are listed agreed-upon definitions of terms that the parties have discussed and agreed to before service delivery begins. SLAs are an excellent mechanism for helping two parties communicate more effectively and achieve a shared understanding of what they've agreed to. The process of proactively discussing terminology is one of the things that makes an SLA so effective as a communication tool and as a way to avoid the misinterpretations that otherwise lead to conflict. The glossary serves, in effect, as an English-to-English dictionary between a provider and customer. (See Chapter 11 for a detailed look at SLAs.)

Business Terminology

Even terms as obvious as "customer" lend themselves to different interpretations. Is it possible for company personnel to not know how many customers the company has? Definitely. In one company, four departments disagreed about how many customers the company had because they defined customers differently and therefore counted them differently.

- One department counted the total number of customers in the database, regardless of their purchasing history.
- A second counted only those that had placed an order in the previous twelve months.
- A third excluded as customers those that had requested information but had never placed an order.
- The fourth excluded those whose payments had been deemed uncollectible.

Each of these definitions was appropriate to the particular business unit served, but oh, the problems that arose when they needed to make joint decisions or interact on behalf of those very customers. Meetings would become forums for debate over whose count was the True Count. And woe to those who requested customer information from any of these departments without first asking "How do you define customer?"[7]

In another company, three groups had conflicting definitions of "customer complaints."

---

[7] In a private conversation, Jerry Weinberg explained that he's found the general semantics technique of subscripting very helpful in these cases. Instead of arguing about the "true count" or "true definition" of customers, he tells them that there is perhaps a customer-sub-a and a customer-sub-b—using letters instead of numbers as subscripts, so as not to make a priority of one over the other. Alternatively, they can use the initial of the department name for the subscript, such as a for accounting, r for receivables, and s for sales, because it gives them a mnemonic device and some ownership of the definitions. He points out that helping the pertinent parties make as many definitions of "customer" as needed really cuts down on arguments.

- One group categorized a complaint as any customer who reported a problem.
- A second group evaluated the customer's tone in presenting the problem, classifying the tone as either a complaint or a request; the service rep taking the call made a subjective determination.
- The third counted as complaints those matters that could not be resolved within 24 hours.

Is it any wonder that the reports of these three groups appeared out of sync?

Of course, in situations like these, the definitions are often designed to make the group reporting the statistics look good to some judging authority. ("Complaints? Hardly any; just look at the numbers.") Such conflicting definitions suggest that if you are providing services to a company that based its business decisions on such "obvious" measures as number of customers or number of complaints, you'd be wise to find out how the company defined these terms.

And before you propose a partnership relationship with another party, keep in mind that people have different interpretations of the term "partnership." Some consider a partnership to be the ultimate professional relationship, with both parties sharing in the risks and rewards, and each party having a stake in the success of the other. For others, partnership means "Let's you and I agree to do things my way." I know of two business partners who, while writing a book on building a professional partnership, dissolved their own partnership because they were unable to make it work. Ask them publicly about partnerships and they talk a great line, but ask them privately, and you hear a very different story.

Everyday Terminology

The biggest culprit causing misunderstanding is everyday language. Some words are so much a part of our everyday vernacular that it never occurs to us that other people might define them differently. But often they do—sometimes with serious consequences. Misunderstandings and misinterpretation happen even with the use of simple, familiar words, such as "year." An amazed colleague once described to me the confusion that occurred when she insisted that she could complete her customer's requested analysis "this year"—after all, it was only February. The customer strenuously disagreed.

If you're thinking that one party to the conversation meant calendar year and the other meant fiscal year, you're so near and yet so far. My colleague did mean "this fiscal year," which ended in September. The customer, she finally discovered, meant "this fish-sampling year," which ended in May! The customer was a scientist, whose prime data collection was done between March and May. In his business, the year ended in May.

The challenge is to find these differences in terminology before it's too late. My colleague now recommends having an "interpreter" on a project team to translate between the scientist and the software engineer. That's not a bad idea between any two parties, as the following examples illustrate.

Involvement

A mega-corporation's network-management department (NMD) undertook the upgrade of networking technology used by its internal customers, many of whom were remote from corporate headquarters. These internal customers had experienced a long stretch of poor service and asked to be involved in the upgrade. To accommodate this request, and in hopes of reversing customer dissatisfaction, NMD staff periodically updated customers by phone, offered to visit them on-site, and requested their feedback in response to written reports. Yet when I interviewed the customers, they explained with frustration that NMD was ignoring their desire to be involved. Clearly, there was a communication gap between the two groups, but what was causing it?

I asked several customers what they meant by "being involved." One said he wanted to be invited to meetings at which key issues were being discussed. Another wanted to be able to ask for the reasons behind key decisions, and to get a clear and complete answer. A third wanted to be interviewed because (she said) her department had unique needs. The fourth said he'd be satisfied if NMD would just return his phone calls! Clearly, what these internal customers meant by "being involved" differed significantly from what NMD thought they meant. Perhaps NMD could have accommodated these differing wishes or perhaps not. But lacking awareness of these differences, NMD's attempts to be responsive were *adding* to customer dissatisfaction, not reversing it.

NMD at least deserved credit for trying, unlike one IT organization that conducted a strategic review of its policies and practices, and named its undertaking The Voice of the Customer—but didn't involve customers at all. This organization didn't need to worry about conflicting interpretations of "involve" because the very notion of involvement had not entered the thought process. The only voice the organization's management wanted to hear from its customers was the silent voice of total compliance.

Difficulty

At a conference I attended, Dale Emery, a specialist in transforming people's resistance to change, described the reasons people commonly cite when resisting a change to a new technology, a new methodology, or a new procedure. One common reaction is, "It's too difficult."[8] It's possible that the person quite literally means that adopting the new way is too difficult. However, what is usually meant is something else, such as, "I need to be able to set aside time to learn it." Or, "I need help in understanding it." Or, "If some adjustment could be made so that I have some time to tackle it, I could do so."

The same reasoning applies to other reactions to change, such as, "It's not worth using." Or, "I have no time." Taking people's words at face value during times of change can lead

---

[8] Dale Emery, "A Force for Change—Using Resistance Positively," Software Quality Engineering Software Management Conference, San Diego, Feb. 14, 2001. See also www.dhemery.com.

you to the wrong conclusion. Emery cautions that it's important to consider alternate interpretations of people's reasons for not embracing change; often, people mean something other than what they're saying. Your challenge is to inquire and learn more.

Communication

People frequently complain about insufficient or inadequate communication, yet the very word "communication" is subject to multiple interpretations. For example, one director I worked with conducted a survey to determine the cause of low morale among employees. One of his findings was that the employees desired more communication. Eager to put things right, he circulated a greater number of reports and memos than ever before, as well as numerous articles from periodicals. Morale, however, did not rise.

Why? Because when the employees said that they wanted "more communication," what they really wanted was increased attention and recognition. They wanted the director to wander by their desks more often to ask how things were going. They wanted to feel that he appreciated how hard they were working. They wanted to hear from him not just when they made mistakes, but also when they did things well. Yet, savvy though he was, the director never questioned either their interpretation of "more communication" or his own, so he couldn't understand why his good intentions changed nothing.

Both those who contribute to misinterpretations and those who fall victim to them usually have good intentions. They are doing the best they know how. But both parties to miscommunication too easily forget that although they are using the same words, they speak different languages.

The Sounds of Silence

Even silence can be ambiguous, especially if you're interacting or negotiating with people from another country or culture, or from another organization or social milieu. I remember reading a newspaper clipping that described a key point during the negotiation between two U.S.-based companies. As final settlement terms were put on the table, one party remained silent, intending to convey its dissent. Using silence to mean dissent was part of the cultural norm in that company, and its negotiating team took its meaning for granted.

The second company took the silence to mean agreement, believing that if members of the opposing party disagreed, surely they would voice their dissent. Tracing the subsequent disputes between the two companies to this difference in interpretation took some doing, and resolving the resulting mess took even more. Clearly, silence indeed can mean different things to different parties.

Fleeing Felines

Fortunately, not every misinterpretation is serious. Some of the most amusing ones occur when we hear something, interpret what we heard, draw a conclusion, and act—because the situation is so clear-cut that we have no reason to doubt our interpretation. One of my favorite examples of this kind of cause-effect interpretation is The Case of the Great Cat Escape. I was presenting a seminar at a client site when a secretary came and told Tara, a manager in the group, that her neighbor had called to report that Tara's cat, Panther, was running around in the hallway outside her apartment.

"Not again!" Tara exclaimed. She said the cat probably dashed out when her cleaning lady opened the door to her apartment. Fortunately, Tara lived only a few blocks away. Her secretary offered to go to Tara's building, retrieve the cat, and return him to Tara's apartment. Which she did—and didn't. That is, she *did* go to Tara's building. But she *didn't* retrieve the cat and return it. Why? It seems the cat wasn't Tara's. She'd met Panther before, and she knew this wasn't him.

Tara quite reasonably had assumed it was her cat. After all, Panther had gotten out of the apartment before, so she had no reason to question the situation. As a result, she didn't think to ask whether her neighbor had described what the cat looked like, or where, exactly, it was found, or if it responded to "Panther." The likelihood was that it was her cat—except it wasn't.

The fact that Tara lived nearby eliminated the need to analyze her interpretation of the situation. She lived only a few blocks away, and her secretary could just dash over to her building. If the cat *had* been hers, the problem would have been quickly resolved. But what if Tara had lived further away? What if her secretary hadn't been so accommodating? What if the temperature had been 30 degrees below zero or raining you-know-whats and dogs?

Misinterpretations are especially likely to occur during times of stress, and when they do, they may have less amusing consequences than in Tara's case. Taking a moment to challenge one's interpretation is rarely a waste of time.

CLARIFY, CLARIFY, CLARIFY

The preceding examples illustrate how easily circumstances as well as terminology can be misinterpreted. Strongly felt ideas about policies, processes, attitudes, and intentions influence the way people perceive each other and interact with each other. The words they choose frequently mean different things to each of the parties to an interaction. To assume that parties share the same interpretation and then to act on that assumption can have serious consequences. As the family therapist Virginia Satir observed, " . . . people so often get into tangles with each other simply because A was using a word in one way, and B received the word as if it meant something entirely different."[9]

Author and IT management consultant Wayne Strider notes that when someone disagrees with him, it's easier for him to handle the situation when he knows that his message has been understood. He points out that unless he is certain that his message has been understood, he has no way of knowing whether the person disagrees with his intended message or with some misunderstood variation of it.[10] The same, of course, applies when someone agrees with you: It is important to know that the person agreed with what you meant, rather than with some misinterpretation.

The way to prevent misunderstandings is simple in theory although tedious: Follow every word you write, sign, or speak with a clarification of what you mean, and follow every word you read, see, or hear with a request for clarification. To be absolutely sure that you are communicating exactly what you mean, you could diagram each sentence, the way my elementary-school teachers did when teaching me English grammar. To me, a diagrammed sentence was a hodgepodge of lines drawn at various angles, with each word snatched from its

---

[9] Virginia Satir, *Conjoint Family Therapy* (Palo Alto, Calif.: Science and Behavior Books, 1983), p. 81.

[10] Wayne Strider, private communication. Wayne is author of *Powerful Project Leadership* (Vienna, Va.: Management Concepts, 2002). For additional information, see www.striderandcline.com.

rightful place in the sentence and affixed to one of these lines. I could never understand why anyone would want to rip apart a perfectly good sentence in this way. But if it would improve communication . . .

Clarify Interpretations

If these approaches seem cumbersome, then try this: Make a commitment to become sensitive to the potential for differing interpretations. When customers, teammates, or others give you information, ask yourself this question:

Am I sure I understand what they mean?

If your answer is no, make it your responsibility to ask clarifying questions. Be as specific as possible, and ask for examples. Questions that might have helped to prevent some of the misinterpretations described in this chapter include the following:

Status report:

- What kinds of information would you find helpful in a status report?
- How will you be using the report?

Agenda:

- I'm curious about why you're asking for an agenda after we seemed to have everything in order. Can you say more about that?
- Since I've provided you with an outline, what additional types of information would be helpful to you?

Resolve:

- How do you decide that a problem has been resolved?
- What kinds of criteria can we establish so that we both agree that a problem has been resolved?

Involve:

- When you say you'd like us to involve you in this effort, I take that to mean you'd like us to call you periodically and request your feedback. How close is that to what you were thinking?
- What kinds of things do you have in mind when you say you'd like to be involved in this effort?

Communicate:

- What are some things that would help you feel we're doing a better job of communicating?
- What kinds of changes might help us eliminate the current dissatisfaction regarding communication?

In formulating questions, don't fall into the same trap as a director I talked with recently who requested customer feedback on material his group had prepared, and asked customers: Is the information clear and unambiguous? Think about that question. If you review material and find it confusing, you know you found it confusing. But if you find it clear and unambiguous, it may be that you misinterpreted it, but were clear that your (mis)interpretation was correct—which proves that it's ambiguous.

The risk of posing questions that can be answered yes or no is that the response provides little indication of the real situation. Notice that all of the clarifying questions listed earlier in this section require some explanation or elaboration. The additional information generated and shared through the ensuing discussion will reduce the likelihood of misinterpretation.

Whenever you are certain that you fully and completely understand the other party without benefit of clarifying questions, ask yourself this question:

> If I weren't absolutely, positively certain that I fully and completely understand, what would I ask?

Keep in mind that it's in situations of absolute certainty—situations in which you're *sure* you understand—that you're most likely to misinterpret. Make it your responsibility to clarify your own terminology to ensure that the other party understands you. As you provide clarification, use these questions as a guide:

1. What assumptions might I be making about their meaning?
2. What assumptions might they be making about my meaning?
3. How confident am I that I've exposed the most damaging misinterpretations?

The best policy is simply to try to heighten your awareness of the potential for misinterpretation. You probably can't catch all communication problems, but if you do the best you can, and don't allow yourself to feel too rushed or too intimidated to ask for clarification, you should find that you're in sync with the other party. If you're not, it's better to find out early on, rather than later when the consequences could be catastrophic.

Clarify Agreements

For informal commitments, these clarifying questions probably will suffice. But for more formal commitments, such as when you're developing products or designing services, it is important to put the details of the agreement in writing. Then go through the written document, discussing each important word or phrase, ensuring that you and the other party agree about its meaning. Consider creating a glossary of key terms to prevent misinterpretation by others who may later have responsibility for carrying out the agreement, but who were not involved in its creation.

In addition, communicate your expectations early and often. Never assume that you and the other party have the same understanding of what you've discussed. Ask questions. Check, and then double-check. State your understanding and ask if you've got it right. Be guided by a variation on two questions I previously mentioned:

1. Am I sure I understand what we agreed to?
2. If I were unsure, what would I ask?

Whenever the outcome of a discussion is that one or both parties have agreed to take some action, conclude with a restatement of what you've each agreed to do. Make sure both you and the other party understand your own and each other's responsibilities. Allocate time for this clarification process, so that if you discover conflicting interpretations, you can resolve them without feeling rushed. And if you do identify some differences, give yourself a pat on the back, because you caught a miscommunication early on that could have had serious ramifications if left undetected.

Set the stage for the clarification process by explaining its purpose. Point out the prevalence of ambiguity and comment on how easily misunderstandings occur. Offer real-life examples that will hit home and discuss how both parties can work together to minimize confusion and maximize understanding. Make a commitment to discuss disparities sooner rather than later.

By taking these steps and the others described in this chapter, you'll reduce the likelihood that misinterpretations will happen. In the process, you'll be improving your communication skills dramatically.

4

Untangling Tangled Interactions
Reaction of the Recipient

At my urging, Jim, a buddy of mine, attended one of my workshops. Given what an energetic, quick thinker he is, I was concerned that he'd be impatient with the slower, more reflective parts of the class. During day one of the class, he seemed focused and attentive. The next day, however, while I was presenting a key segment, Jim rose, went to the back of the room, leaned against a wall, and closed his eyes. My worries had come true; it was all he could do to stay awake. He probably felt trapped and upset with me for badgering him to attend. Why in the world did I invite him in the first place?

As we were gathering after lunch, I overheard someone tease Jim about his little snooze. He responded, "I didn't sleep well last night, but I really didn't want to miss Naomi's presentation. I figured that if I leaned against the wall, I could close my eyes and still be sure to stay awake."

I was shocked. I had interpreted Jim's shut-eye to mean he wanted to leave; he explained it as meaning he wanted to stay. Could I have been more wrong? "Anyway," he added, "Naomi has known me for years, and she knows I wouldn't miss a minute of her class." I do? Then why was my interpretation so far off? And why was I so sure about his intent that I had not a single doubt about it?

The reason is simple: I had a mental view of how things were, and I had interpreted what I saw to fit that view. This adjustment wasn't a conscious, analytical process, but rather an automatic, instantaneous response. Anyway, I knew I was right, so what was there to analyze? As Barry Oshry points out in *Seeing Systems,* in the absence of information about other people's worlds, we make up stories about them: "We create our myths about their motives, their competencies. And we don't see ourselves making up stories, we see our stories as the truth."[1]

That's exactly what happened here. I received a nonverbal message from Jim—"I don't want to be here"—that Jim didn't even know he had sent. If I hadn't overheard his explanation, I'd have remained certain that he disliked the class and was angry with me for cajoling him into attending. I'm sure I'd have interpreted everything he said and did during the rest of the class to fit this conclusion.

As a result of that experience, I've never again made the mistake of misinterpreting someone else's words or actions. Well, no, not really. That's just wishful thinking. As Chapter 3 illustrated, it's easy to misinterpret, and no one is immune. My discovery of the explanation for Jim's actions was a strong reminder that I should consider alternative explanations before leaping to a conclusion. The problem is that although it would be ideal to cautiously, logically, and dispassionately consider alternative explanations for someone's words or actions, sometimes I simply react. So do you at times, and so does everyone else. Sometimes, a word or phrase or gesture triggers an unanticipated reaction. But are we to be held hostage by reactions over which we seemingly have no control?

This chapter addresses that question, and presents a model that helps to explain the recipient's experience upon receiving a message. This model sheds light on how to resolve misinter-

---

[1] Barry Oshry, *Seeing Systems: Unlocking the Mysteries of Organizational Life* (San Francisco: Berrett-Koehler Publishers, 1995), p. 12.

pretations after they've occurred—and how to prevent them in the first place.

LET ME COUNT THE WAYS

Think about all the interactions that take place among employees during a typical day in your organization: the private chitchat, small group discussions, coffee breaks, meetings, lunchtime chatter, planning sessions, problem-solving sessions, requests for help, the grapevine, and so on. How many interactions do you suppose take place during a typical day?

If you're an equipment installer trapped by a raging snowstorm in a hut on a remote mountaintop in Alaska, the number might hover close to zero.[2] But if your company employs one hundred people, or a thousand, or several thousand, the number of interactions is large—and grows even larger when you include interactions with customers, vendors, and other outside parties. Add in the number of nonverbal interactions (a wink, a frown, a hand wave, a pat on the back), e-mail messages, and other written communications, and the resulting number would be well on its way to infinity. And that's just in a single day!

Consider how many of these interactions would have to go awry in order to seriously damage your organization. In these turbulent times, it's not inconceivable that just one would be enough. A *New York Times* article reported a 22 percent drop in a software firm's stock price within three days after the highly belligerent and blaming message sent by the CEO to company managers found its way onto the Internet.[3]

Fortunately, most communications have less at stake. Our daily interactions can withstand a vast amount of ambiguity without major repercussion. As Donald Norman points out in *Turn Signals Are the Facial Expressions of Automobiles*, both speaker and listener contribute to an exchange, ". . . the one

---

[2] This was the experience of a fellow named Joshua Caldwell, as reported in an article in *The Wall Street Journal* on Dec. 26, 2000.

[3] Edward Wong, "A Stinging Office Memo Boomerangs," *The New York Times* (April 5, 2001), p. C1.

clueing the other as to the amount understood and the points of real interest."[4]

Nevertheless, messages are constantly lost, misinterpreted, ignored, dismissed, or distorted. Spoken and written communication are full of opportunities for confusion. Listen in on somebody else's conversation, for example. The talk meanders all over the place. Pay attention to the way people give instructions and directions, and you'll hear imprecision galore. Notice how inattentively people listen to each other.

Communication is hampered when we can't rely on non-verbal cues (gestures, facial expressions, and the like), such as when we communicate over the phone or by means of written documents. Written communication, lacking the auditory emphasis and the *um*'s and *ya'know*'s of everyday speech, is especially prone to misinterpretation. We use symbols and special formatting to try to convey in written material what we can more directly communicate vocally, but this process is highly imperfect; who hasn't gotten tangled in a misinterpretation of an e-mail message?

Recipients, having read the wrong meaning into a spoken or written message, are often quick to take umbrage without ever bothering to verify their understanding or clarify their interpretation. What's amazing, really, is not how many tangled interactions occur, but how few, given the odds.

INGREDIENTS OF AN INTERACTION

Consider the interaction between Stan and Sue in Chapter 3. Recall that three weeks before Stan was to visit Sue's company to present a class to project managers, Sue requested an agenda.

> Sue: "I'd like you to send me an agenda for the class."
>
> Stan: "Okay."

---

[4] Donald A. Norman, *Turn Signals Are the Facial Expressions of Automobiles* (Reading, Mass: Addison-Wesley, 1992), p. 11.

But that response was hardly Stan's entire reaction. No matter how cleanly or quickly an interaction seems to happen, a lot is going on that causes the tangle. A valuable model for understanding the intermediate steps between the sending of a message and the response is called the Ingredients of an Interaction Model. Also known as the Interaction Model, this model is applicable in organizational settings and is one of many created and used by the family therapist Virginia Satir.[5] By using this model, you can become skilled at debugging an interaction that has gotten tangled—and at avoiding a tangled interaction in the first place.

How can the Interaction Model help to untangle Stan's reaction to Sue? The model divides an interaction into four major components:

1. Intake: what the recipient saw and heard
2. Interpretation: how the recipient interpreted the message
3. Feelings: how the recipient felt about that interpretation
4. Response: what the recipient communicated in response

When you use this model, you describe your intake, interpretation, feelings, and response. In conversations I had with Stan, he reported the following:

> **What Stan heard Sue say:** "I'd like you to send me an agenda for the class."

This statement is an exact replay of what Sue said. Ideally, the intake matches what we'd hear if we had taped the interaction, and in this situation, it does.

> **How Stan interpreted what Sue said:** "She's asking for something she really doesn't need. I already provided all the information she requested. I thought the class was a go. Why in the world does she now need to know what

---

[5] Virginia Satir et al., *The Satir Model: Family Therapy and Beyond* (Palo Alto, Calif.: Science and Behavior Books, 1991), ch. 6.

order I'll be presenting the topics in and how long I'll spend on each?"

This is the meaning Stan attached to Sue's request. Notice that the interpretation is different from the intake. Sometimes, when people are asked what they saw or heard, what they report is their interpretation of that experience. They've moved so quickly from intake to interpretation that they may have missed the intake altogether. As a result, they can't restate what they saw and heard, suggesting that they may be interpreting a distorted version of the actual intake.

> **How Stan felt about his interpretation:** Angry, frustrated, and nervous. "She seemed happy with me, but suddenly, for some reason, she no longer trusts me and I don't know why. Maybe she changed her mind and wants to scratch the whole thing. I really need the money and I know I can do the class, but now I'm wondering if I should just cancel. I'm feeling stressed. Maybe I really *can't* do what she wants."

This was Stan's visceral reaction—how he felt when Sue uttered her request for an agenda. Stan didn't consider any other possible explanations.

> **How Stan responded:** "Okay."

Stan responded grudgingly, and with suppressed anger, shaken by his sudden uncertainty about his ability to meet Sue's expectations.

This is a lot to have happened in an instant—yet it's exactly what often happens, especially when those who receive a message have an emotional reaction to what they see or hear. As a result, a disconnect occurs in the infinitesimally short period between the time one person says something and the other person responds. Just as quickly, a gap can begin to form in the relationship, as confusion surfaces and then grows.

Not until Stan was on-site did he discover the true motivation behind Sue's request: It wasn't that she distrusted him, but that an unsettling experience with a previous instructor had made her cautious. His erroneous interpretation had triggered a strong internal reaction related not to Sue's request, but to his own fears and vulnerabilities.

Stan was fortunate; he had the opportunity to learn Sue's actual meaning. Often, though, the recipient never discovers the sender's real intent; indeed, even Stan wouldn't have found out if Sue hadn't volunteered the information. However, if he had asked her for additional information when she requested the agenda, his response ("Okay") might have been the same, but his internal experience might have been very different, and much less distressing.

To see another example, think back to Jim's snooze in my class. Notice that in this interaction, the sender didn't even know he was sending a message. The experience was entirely the recipient's (which is to say, mine). Here's what I experienced:

> **What I saw:** "During the class, while I was speaking, Jim stood up, walked over to the wall, leaned against it, and closed his eyes."
>
> **How I interpreted Jim's behavior:** "He's having a hard time staying awake because he's so bored. He doesn't want to be here. He wishes he hadn't come to this class. He's angry with me for persuading him to attend."
>
> **How I felt about that interpretation:** "I made a mistake in inviting him, and I should have known better. I'm so stupid to have allowed this to happen. What could I have been thinking? I'm going to have an awfully hard time facing him the rest of the class."
>
> **How I responded:** "I was in the midst of presenting to the class so I didn't say anything. I

hope my presentation masked the sinking feeling I had. It's possible my internal dialogue showed in my tone of voice or facial expression and was noticed by others in the class (except Jim, of course, who had nodded off by that point!)."

In both of these examples, the sender was unaware of the receiver's internal reactions. But in some situations, the sender's message may inadvertently push the recipient's buttons, eliciting such a strong or inappropriate reaction that it can't be missed. When that happens, the parties can use the model to help them untangle their interaction.

For example, during a high-pressure project, Ann, the project manager, checked in with team members to see how they were doing. She asked one team member, Joan, "How are you feeling?" Joan replied, "I'm fine!" An appropriate response, except that Joan said it in a go-away-and-leave-me-alone tone of voice.

The next day, I asked Joan to use the four components of the Interaction Model to describe her reaction to Ann's comment. She reported the following:

> **What Joan saw and heard:** "Ann came over to my cubicle and asked, 'How are you feeling?'"

> **How Joan interpreted Ann's words:** "She's being thoughtful and caring, which is just like her. She wants to see how I'm doing."

> **How Joan felt about that interpretation:** "I suddenly felt angry. At the time, I didn't know why. But in thinking about it overnight, I realized that I want to be valued for my ideas, not my feelings. She was asking me the wrong question. I wanted her to ask how my work was progressing. For some reason, hearing her ask how I was feeling really bothered me, and I snapped."

How Joan responded: "I said, 'I'm fine.' I said it harshly. I may have shouted it."

I then asked Ann to use the model to describe her reaction to Joan's response. She reported the following:

What Ann saw and heard: "Joan said, 'I'm fine.' There was a certain intensity to her voice. She wasn't smiling."

How Ann interpreted Joan's words: "Something about the way she said it made me feel she wasn't fine. She didn't seem to want me around."

How Ann felt about that interpretation: "I was confused. I was trying to do the right thing in showing my employees that I care about them. I want to be a good project manager, but what I was doing wasn't helping. I didn't know what to do. I felt helpless."

How Ann responded: "I think I said, 'Good,' and left."

Notice that in this example, both Joan and Ann had an internal reaction to what the other had said. As a result, each felt puzzled, Joan by her strong reaction to Ann's well-meaning question, and Ann by both Joan's reaction to her inquiry and her own uncertainty about what to do about it.

Discussing their experiences provoked further introspection. Joan became curious why, even given her preference for having her ideas valued, she reacted so strongly to Ann's caring comment. In further discussions, she realized that her reaction actually had little to do with Ann, whom she admires, but rather was a "then and there" reaction to something from earlier in her life. This kind of reaction isn't unusual; many of us are occasionally propelled back in time as the result of something we hear, and we react in the current interaction as though it occurred at that previous time.

Ann, in turn, learned that despite her caring intentions, people have different reactions to how those intentions are expressed. This interaction prompted her to learn more about these differences (such as those described in Chapter 6), and to see whether she could tailor her expressions of caring to the intended recipient.

The Interaction Model provided a structured way for Joan and Ann to review what transpired. If they had not examined the interaction, the feelings stirred up might have left behind a residue of confusion that could have damaged their relationship: Joan might have toned down future responses to Ann, so as to avoid an outburst. Ann might have kept her distance from Joan.

Clearly, no matter how brief a communication seems, a lot can happen internally. Let's look further at the individual components of an interaction.

INTAKE: CANDID CAMERA, WITH A TWIST

Before you make meaning of a message or have an internal reaction to it, you have to see or hear it. Yet people fail to see or hear accurately for numerous reasons. For example:

- The listener may hear poorly, be distracted by noise, be preoccupied, be absentminded, or be unfamiliar with the language.
- The speaker may have a cold, a thick accent, or a tendency to speak so quickly or in sentences so long that listeners stop paying attention.
- A person may misread a written message due to poor eyesight, dim lighting, blurred writing, tiny type, or assumptions about what the message says.

In other words, aspects of oneself, the other party, the message, and the context can all contribute to an incorrect intake.

Donald Norman reminds us that we deceive ourselves even with events that we remember with great clarity, and that what we recall as an accurate memory may in fact differ significantly from what actually happened.[6] Even with the best of intentions, people often get the message wrong. Recall the game of Telephone, in which children whisper a message, presumably verbatim, one by one, around a circle. Invariably, by the time the message gets around the circle, it's a distant, distorted third cousin to the initial message.

Adult interactions are like the game of Telephone. People are remarkably poor at restating what they've just heard or at seeing what's right in front of them. In *How We Know What Isn't So*, Thomas Gilovich addresses this issue, citing research that demonstrates that people rarely convey messages verbatim, and noting, "The limits of human memory and the implicit demand that the listener not be burdened with too many details constrain the amount and kind of information that is transmitted. What the speaker construes to be the gist of the message is emphasized or 'sharpened,' whereas details thought to be less essential are de-emphasized or 'leveled.'"[7]

It's easy to understand why some intake distortions occur. For example, I posed a question about French poetry to Yvonne, a colleague visiting from Paris. Although fatigued from jet lag and immersion in English, she reached for her pad and started drawing some elegant curves. I didn't know what she was doing, but then I suddenly realized: Yvonne had heard me say "French pottery," a subject she knew well, and she was sketching some examples for me. I was glad I discovered this error before she spent her hard-earned francs to buy me some "poetry" from an expensive craft shop nearby.

Other mistakes are less amusing. People frequently misspell my street name as Woodlawn Parkway rather than Woodland Parkway, even when it's is in large type right in front of them. This would be inconsequential—except that a half-mile north is Woodlawn Road. And a half-mile south is Woodlawn *Street!* You can understand why I get nervous when someone tells me the check is in the mail.

---

[6] Norman, op. cit., p. 4.

[7] Thomas Gilovich, *How We Know What Isn't So: The Fallibility of Human Reason in Everyday Life* (New York: The Free Press, 1991), p. 91.

Unfortunately, intake errors can have devastating consequences, as revealed by experiments such as those conducted
in law school classes to demonstrate the fallibility of eyewit-
nesses. In one experiment, the professor secretly arranges for
an accomplice to dash into the room unexpectedly, create a
commotion, grab an item, and run out. Afterward, the "surprised" professor asks the students what happened. Their
descriptions of the intruder's appearance are strikingly different from each other's as well as from the person's actual
appearance—differences as extreme as tall versus short, red
jacket versus blue jacket, and black hair versus blond hair.
Equally striking differences characterize what they say they
saw happen.

These scenarios confirm how readily what we see and hear
becomes distorted. Yet distortion is a natural process, occurring because we process what we see and hear through filters
that modify the message our senses deliver. These filters
derive from our upbringing, recent history, habits, prejudices,
moods, hopes, dreams, fears, vulnerabilities, and maybe even
whether the car started right up this morning. The intake
resulting from the message passing through these filters is the

first ingredient of an interaction. Is it any wonder that interactions get so tangled?

INTERPRETATION: MULTIPLE MODIFIED MEANINGS

Given these filters, we each view the world as we are, not as it is. That view shapes and even defines our experiences and the meaning we make of the messages we receive. Thomas Gilovich attributes responsibility for this to "the tendency for people's preconceptions to bias their interpretations of what they see."[8] Indeed, believing is seeing.

Yet this fact is extraordinarily difficult to remember in the moment. The ease and speed with which people draw erroneous conclusions is fascinating and, at times, unnerving. Just as our filters influence our intake, so too do they influence the meaning we make of that intake. In *The Power of Nice*, authors Shapiro and Jankowski comment on people who listen through a negative filter. "They suspect what is being said; they're skeptical of motives. It can't be good; it's someone trying to get the better of them."[9]

Such errors can be deadly—as one fictional example reminds us. In a Chris Bohjalian novel, a patient asks a specialist what would happen if he took a small dose of a certain remedy. The specialist answers, "Nothing," meaning, "It won't help you." The patient, however, takes this response to mean, "It won't hurt you." The devastating consequence for the patient is disturbing, even in fiction.[10]

When you encounter misinterpretations that others have made, it often seems obvious that they should have noticed the ambiguity or asked a few questions. But when it's you,

---

[8] Gilovich, op. cit., p. 15.

[9] Ronald M. Shapiro and Mark A. Jankowski, with James Dale, *The Power of Nice: How to Negotiate So Everyone Wins—Especially You!* (New York: John Wiley & Sons, 1998), p. 55.

[10] Chris Bohjalian, *The Law of Similars* (New York: Vintage Books, 1999). I'm deliberately being vague about the details of what transpired, so as not to ruin the story for you.

somehow it's much harder to slow down and consider other possible interpretations. As project-mastery guru David Schmaltz observes about the behavior of others on a project team, "Because we are not others, our meanings, our interpretations, are most likely to be wrong if we ascribe *our* meanings to *their* behavior."[11]

One way to become more skilled at considering multiple interpretations is to practice with hypothetical situations or with real situations that you analyze after the fact. You might be surprised at all the possible interpretations. Take the case of two help-desk groups, a Level One group that was the first point of contact for callers with problems and that resolved as many problems as possible, and a Level Two group that handled more complex problems referred by Level One. The responsibility of both groups was to help employees with their technical problems, but their spirit of cooperation with each other was less than optimal.

Level One staff automatically escalated to Level Two certain urgent problems that seriously disrupted employees and that required immediate attention. Level One staff members then would drop by the Level Two work area to check on the status of the resolution. But whenever they dropped by, they found Level Two staff kidding around and giggling. Giggling! Employees were unable to do their work, and those in charge of fixing the situation were having a good old time, and not taking it seriously at all. At least that was the interpretation of the Level One group.

When we used the Interaction Model to analyze this experience, Level Two personnel explained that their behavior had been misunderstood: "We take such situations *extremely* seriously. But they are stressful, and our way of relieving tension is to laugh. This reaction doesn't mean we're not giving the problem our full attention, but just the opposite; it relaxes us and allows us to be more productive." This explanation

---

[11] David A. Schmaltz, *Coping with Fuzzy Projects: Stories of Utter Ignorance, Theologic Wars, and Unseen Possibilities* (Portland, Oreg.: True North pgs, 2000), p. 66. For additional insights on the behavior of project team members, see www.projectcommunity.com.

enabled the Level One staff to see the giggling in a positive light.

Multiple interpretations are also possible when physical cues, such as someone's body language or facial expression, lead us to read into the situation something other than what is there: A certain curve of the lips could be a smile or a grimace. A furrowed brow could signify deep thinking or total confusion. The facial expression that accompanies laughing can be similar to the one for crying.[12] Every facial expression or bodily orientation has multiple meanings, and some of those meanings are the opposites of each other.

Therefore, start with the most generous interpretation you can of the other party's intentions. As the Level One support group learned, the explanation may actually be more positive than you might have imagined. By starting with the most generous interpretation, you will be more likely to ask questions, consider alternative possibilities, and respond in a way that does the least damage to the interaction and the relationship.

FEELINGS: WHAT HAPPENS ON THE INSIDE

Despite the way most workplaces function, pretending that feelings don't exist will not make them disappear. Without acknowledging the reality and impact of our feelings, we stand little hope of communicating congruently and of understanding how to resolve or avoid miscommunication.

As I've presented it thus far, the Interaction Model indicates that the feelings associated with one's interpretation of a message lead to a response. But the model actually includes some other ingredients that get triggered by strong feelings. According to Satir, *feelings* lead to *feelings about the feelings*,

---

[12] Daphne du Maurier captures this point perfectly regarding two characters recovering from a fit of laughter in her short story "The Pool": "Deborah, the first to recover, wondered why laughter was so near to pain, why Roger's face, twisted now in merriment, was yet the same crumpled thing when his heart was breaking." See Daphne du Maurier, *The Breaking Point* (New York: Avon Books, 1959), p. 142.

which trigger a *coping mechanism*, which activates one's *rule for commenting*, which influences the ultimate response.[13]

This complex interplay of ingredients that lead to a response is triggered by "then and there"—some prior time in your life, whether yesterday or when you were six—and the response that results is disconnected from the message the sender intended. As Jerry Weinberg notes in *Quality Software Management, Vol. 2: First-Order Measurement*, "Obviously, any time my response has little to do with what you said, it isn't likely to be helpful. For a response to be helpful, it should be coming from the 'here-and-now-and-you,' not a different place, at a different time, with different people. When I respond as if I were in a different situation, my response is incongruent—that is, it doesn't match."[14]

The model identifies the following ingredients:

> **The feeling:** As a result of your interpretation of a message, you might feel upset or angry or happy or excited or depressed or impatient or any of a variety of other emotions.

> **Feelings about feelings:** This ingredient refers to your internal reaction to the feelings provoked by the message. Feelings about feelings are typically triggered by what you learned while growing up about what is acceptable to feel and what's not. The feelings you have about your feelings are an important indicator of your emotional health. For example, if you are told that you're being transferred to another department, away from your friends, you might feel upset. If, as a child, you were scolded when you became upset or you were led to believe that you

---

[13] Satir et al., op. cit., pp. 124–28.

[14] Gerald M. Weinberg, *Quality Software Management, Vol. 2: First-Order Measurement* (New York: Dorset House Publishing, 1993), p. 209. I highly recommend this entire volume for its in-depth look at the Interaction Model in the context of software organizations.

should never feel upset, you might feel angry with yourself about feeling upset. Conversely, if you learned that it's normal to occasionally become upset, you wouldn't think less of yourself for feeling that way.

Coping mechanisms: How do you cope in response to the feelings you have about your feelings? What behavior do you exhibit as a defense? How do you protect yourself when these feelings strike? Coping mechanisms come into play automatically when you experience vulnerability, low self-esteem, insecurity, incompetence, or lack of self-worth. Some common coping mechanisms include lashing out at others, giving in and going along, distorting what's being discussed, or changing the subject. At times, it could be a combination of all of these—and others.

Rules for commenting: These are rules that influence what we say or refrain from saying in various circumstances, and especially when we feel stressed. We all have rules, many of which are subconscious, about what's appropriate or inappropriate to say in a given situation. Typically, we acquired these rules during childhood. As we mature, we discard some that are no longer useful. But most of us retain rules about expressing, or refraining from expressing, what we're thinking and feeling. Such rules include, "If I can't say anything nice, I shouldn't say anything at all," and "I shouldn't contradict people in roles of authority." In the workplace, "I mustn't reveal my feelings" is a particularly damaging rule.

Given this expanded description of the Feelings portion of the model, let's revisit Stan's interaction with Sue:

What Stan heard: "I'd like you to send me an agenda for the class."

How Stan interpreted what Sue said: "She's asking for something she really doesn't need. I already provided all the information she requested. I thought the class was a go. Why in the world does she now need to know what order I'll be presenting the topics in and how long I'll spend on each?"

How Stan felt about his interpretation: Angry, frustrated, and nervous. "She seemed happy with me, but suddenly, for some reason, she no longer trusts me and I don't know why. Maybe she changed her mind and wants to scratch the whole thing. I really need the money and I know I can do the class, but now I'm wondering if I should just cancel. I'm feeling stressed. Maybe I really *can't* do what she wants."

How Stan felt about his feelings: "I was really upset with myself for feeling angry, because I didn't think I should feel that way. Why do I keep letting these things get to me?"

Stan's coping mechanism: "In my mind, I blamed Sue for suddenly asking for an agenda. Yet at the same time, because I needed the money, I placated by convincing myself that her request wasn't that important."

Stan's rules for commenting: "Don't make a fuss. Don't be a pest. Don't let on that I don't understand. Don't let anyone know how I feel. Just do what I'm asked to do."

How Stan responded: "Okay."

This entire scenario plays out, often at an unconscious level, in every interaction that pushes an emotional hot button.

Similarly in my interaction with Jim, the wall-snoozer:

What I saw: "During the class, while I was speaking, Jim stood up, walked over to the wall, leaned against it, and closed his eyes."

My interpretation: "Jim is having a hard time staying awake because he's so bored. He doesn't want to be here, and wishes he hadn't come to this class. He's angry with me for persuading him to attend."

How I felt: "I made a mistake in inviting him, and I should have known better. I'm so stupid to have allowed this to happen. I'm going to have an awfully hard time facing him the rest of the class."

How I feel about this feeling: "I really hate feeling stupid."

My coping mechanism: "I'll get through the class somehow (placating), but I'd better stay out of Jim's way (avoidance) so I don't have to face the fact that he's unhappy. Afterward, I'll just steer clear of him (placating *and* avoidance)."

My rule for commenting: "I can't let Jim know how I feel or that I know how he feels."

How I responded: "I was in the midst of presenting to the class so I didn't say anything. I hope my presentation masked the sinking feeling I had. It's possible that my internal dialogue showed in my tone of voice or facial expression and was noticed by others in the class."

In actuality, these ingredients don't necessarily follow such an orderly path. One's feelings about one's feelings can trigger a rule for commenting, which activates a coping mechanism, which triggers another rule for commenting, which stimulates other feelings, and so on. In analyzing your own tangled interactions, you might encounter this type of circuitous path—all in a fraction of an instant.

HOW TO PUT THE MODEL TO USE

This model can help you consciously consider multiple interpretations, better understand your feelings, and exert more choice over your responses. Using the model to prevent or analyze tangled interactions isn't difficult. The challenge is to *remember* to use it, and to make using it a habit. Fortunately, most interactions don't warrant a side trip through the Interaction Model to figure out what happened. It's those other times when one party or another responds in a puzzling way that the model can help make sense of what happened.

The Interaction Model can be applied to avoid or prevent tangled interactions. Six uses for which the model is especially effective are listed below, with elaboration in the sections that follow:

1. to untangle problems with a previous interaction
2. to untangle problems with an interaction in progress
3. to untangle problem interactions among others
4. to untangle patterns of behavior
5. to untangle patterns of response
6. to untangle common personal traps

Application #1: Untangling a Previous Interaction

Sometimes, a puzzling interaction takes place so quickly that it's not until later that you try to untangle it. Fortunately, it's almost always instructive to try to figure out what took place, even if the other party is no longer present.

For example, it was several weeks after an exchange had occurred before Sandy realized what probably had happened between herself and her colleague Kate. The interaction had taken place during a project retrospective facilitated by Sandy. At lunch on the first day, Kate had asked Sandy, "How is it going for you?" Sandy said, "Great—but I know what's coming next." Kate responded, "Well, that sure sounds like a power play!"

Kate's reply seemed odd to Sandy, but the conversation quickly moved on and Sandy forgot about it. Weeks later, it came to mind and in thinking about how she sounded as she answered Kate's question, Sandy could see how Kate might have interpreted her comment to mean, "*I* know what's coming next and *you* don't."

Was that what Sandy meant? Not at all. As Sandy worked to untangle this past interaction, she explained that when Kate asked how it was going for her, she was instantly transported back several years to the start of her own career and a stressful retrospective that had followed a battleground of a project. At the exact same time—lunch on the first day of that earlier retrospective—she had been nervous about what the facilitator was planning for the afternoon. So while Kate may have thought what Sandy meant was, "I know what's coming next and you don't" (a Sandy-versus-Kate response), what Sandy actually meant was, "I know what's coming next, and I like that feeling much better than during that first retrospective years ago when I had no idea" (a Sandy-then versus Sandy-now response).

As happens in situations like this, the exchange occurred in an instant. Neither Sandy nor Kate stopped the discussion to explore the many possible interpretations of each other's comments, and there were no noticeable, immediate repercussions. However, puzzled by what had initially seemed like a strange response, Sandy found it personally instructive to contemplate what might have transpired.

Application #2: Untangling an Interaction in Progress

When you're in the midst of an interaction that seems to be getting tangled, try to slow it down enough so you can seek clarification before going any further. For example, if you've received a puzzling response, think of the model and try to clarify the person's intake and meaning. You might say, for example:

- I'm wondering if you heard me correctly. What I was saying was . . .
- Might you have misunderstood me? What were you thinking I meant?
- I have a feeling I said something you misinterpreted. My point was . . .

Similarly, if you find yourself about to respond in a way that seems inappropriate, s-l-o-w down and ask yourself, "What was my intake? What did I see or hear?"

If you're unsure, clarify what you heard by asking questions:

- I'm not sure I heard you correctly. Could you repeat that?
- Did I understand correctly when I heard you to be saying XYZ?
- Did you say XYZ? Or did I hear you incorrectly?

Ask yourself, "What meaning am I making of what I've heard? Is that the only possible meaning? What would be the most generous interpretation?"

These questions might lead you to ask the other person:

- Could you clarify what you meant when you said XYZ?
- I'm puzzled by that comment. Could you explain what you had in mind?
- I'm confused because it sounds as if you mean ABC. Is that correct?

If you notice that you're experiencing a strong reaction, ask yourself, "Am I reacting to what's happening here and now, or has my reaction come from some other place and time?" If possible, request a time-out or excuse yourself so that you can reflect calmly on what you might be experiencing.

These questions are examples of what you might ask if you need to clarify potential misunderstandings, but don't be bound by my words. Choose and use your own wording. However you phrase your questions, be mindful of your tone of voice. A tone that conveys that you genuinely seek clarification is far better than one that finds fault before the answer has been given.

Application #3: Helping Others Untangle Their Interactions

The Interaction Model is a wonderful tool to use to help others untangle an interaction. If you witness a misunderstanding unfolding, you can gently ask the same questions that you would ask if you were one of the parties involved in the interaction:

- What did you notice?
- I'm curious about what you heard her say?
- What do you suppose he meant?
- Can you think of any other possible interpretations?

You can also invite the parties to restate what they said and what they meant, so that each person can determine whether a misunderstanding occurred. But don't be intrusive; unless specifically asked to help out, refrain from going beyond an offer to assist. Take your cue from the response you get.

After the fact (and similarly, only when asked to intervene), you can serve as a guide to help each party to a tangled interaction step through the model, with each person's response serving as the other person's intake. In doing this, make sure that what people report as intake is really intake. Sometimes, people report their interpretation rather than the intake itself, such as, "He was angry with me." Or, "She thinks I never do anything right!" Sometimes, too, people report their feelings instead of their intake: "When she said she was taking me off the project, I felt depressed."

In providing guidance to others, be sure to have them start by reporting the exact words they heard and, for face-to-face interactions, the nonverbal cues they saw. At times, an erroneous intake can account for the tangled situation, so don't hesitate to ask again, "What was your intake? What did you see or hear?"

Application #4: Untangling Patterns of Behavior

The model can also be used to analyze a pattern of behavior that has played out over time. I've found it particularly helpful in groups that want to improve their relationship with specific colleagues or customers, or that seek new ways of working (or playing) together. That was the experience of the Level One group members described earlier in this chapter who misinterpreted the giggling they heard from the Level Two group. Using the model, the Level One and Level Two groups worked through this pattern of interactions together.

In another situation, team members worked among themselves to identify possible explanations for the blaming behavior of a customer whom they'd dubbed Hostile Holly. In discussing her behavior, they realized that their interpretation—that she was trying to goad them into doing things her way—might have been wrong. A more generous interpretation would be that she needed to have her views acknowledged. They speculated that this need may have been driven by her own feelings of inadequacy or her frustration at not being listened to by her coworkers (or even her caretakers, when she was growing up!).

The team members decided to modify their own responses to Holly, agreeing to give her the freedom to tout her ideas and vent her problems. In carrying out this plan, they listened to her carefully, asked questions, and empathized. Over time, her aggressiveness diminished, and then vanished; in addition, she started becoming attentive to the pressures *they* were facing and, for the first time, empathized with *their* challenges.

The result: A stressful and adversarial relationship became strong and positive. One unanticipated benefit was that Holly began to alert the team to upcoming business changes that they'd need to support. Previously, the team had not been advised of change requirements until it was too late for them to plan adequately.

There's no guarantee that your analysis of a pattern of behavior will help you transform all the Hostile Hollys in your midst into Helpful Hollys, but it's worth a try. The most generous interpretation may open many doors for you, enabling you, too, to replace a troubling relationship with one characterized by collaboration and mutual respect.

Application #5: Understanding the Absence of a Response

What is the meaning of no response? Suppose you leave a phone message for someone, or send an e-mail message, and despite the passage of time, you do not receive a response. If you are like many people, you find yourself becoming angry, frustrated, or upset. How you react to this absence of a response can be viewed through the lens of the Interaction Model. What you learn can help you modify your behavior and make your communication efforts more effective.

For example, I recently tried to reach a fellow who had invited me to give a presentation to a management group. I called the bank where he worked, reached the switchboard, and was transferred to his line. The phone rang what seemed like 27,000 times. I hung up, waited a few minutes, and then tried again. And again, and again, and again. Does this sound familiar?

I was particularly disappointed because I knew that this manager directed a customer-service area, and I expected responsiveness to have been second nature to him. I wondered why he didn't have voice-mail, or someone else to answer his phone. I blamed him for being unreachable. (Blaming is one of my favorite coping mechanisms!) In this situation, my rule for commenting was: Don't let him know how miffed I am!

When I met him at the hotel where I'd be speaking, I told him that I had tried calling him several times, but couldn't seem to reach him. "Oh," he said, "we had a problem." Here it comes, I thought. The Grand Excuse. The Alibi. The Passing of the Buck. I could scarcely wait to hear what his excuse would be. "I'm sorry I wasn't able to take your call," he said, "but the bank burned down."

The bank burned down? That was a new one. But, indeed, it had burned down, the day before I called. Up in smoke. Poof. Just like that. Because the bank was in a city located more than 1,500 miles from my front door, it wasn't surprising that I hadn't heard about it. But who had answered the switchboard when I called?

He explained that I hadn't reached the bank's switchboard. It seems that at the first sign of the fire, the bank put its disaster-recovery plan into motion: Bank managers set up an emergency phone service to receive incoming calls and reroute them to temporarily relocated staff. But since disasters rarely happen according to plan, everyone was busy attempting to restore order and keep bank business as close to normal as possible. During the frenzy, some phones went unanswered. If I had tried a day later, I probably would have reached him and never would have known the scorching truth.

The lesson? When you don't receive a reasonable level of responsiveness, refrain from assuming the worst about the silent party. More often than not, there's a perfectly acceptable explanation.

Application #6: Untangling Common Personal Traps

The Interaction Model can help you better understand the ways in which you contribute to tangled interactions. Although the entire interaction, from intake to response, happens almost instantaneously, many people seem to spend more time at the intake, interpretation, or feelings ingredient than at one of the other ingredients—and some people seem to spring directly to the ingredient that comes most naturally to them.

For example, some people excel at seeing or hearing the intake. They function well in videotape mode, accurately restating what they saw or heard. Some people head directly to meaning. They may take in some of the intake, but as the saying goes, they don't let the facts stand in the way of a good opinion. Some people dash toward feelings, sometimes short-changing both intake and interpretation; they may be quicker than others to have a visceral reaction to someone else's comments. And some (perhaps all of us at one time or another) leapfrog over intake, meaning, and feeling—and simply respond.

No timepiece exists that can record how much time people spend at each of these stages. Whatever that amount of time, one thing seems clear: When people's emotional buttons get pushed, they typically become blind to the intake and meaning, and follow a trajectory directly to feelings. Then, their feelings about their feelings, their coping mechanisms, and their rules for commenting take over and trigger their response. Sometimes, they can barely say what they saw and heard and how they interpreted it. Their insides are too busy playing hopscotch.

By keeping these patterns in mind as you observe your own behavior, you can improve your message-processing skills dramatically. For example, when you get into a tangled interaction, is it because you saw or heard something inaccurately? Do you often make interpretations that prove to be flawed? Do you have strong emotional reactions that seem out of proportion to the intake?

By becoming aware of your own particular traps, you can gain control over them and choose a more congruent response. Ask a close colleague or friend to help you by questioning you about your intake, interpretation, and the other ingredients while you're in the midst of an interaction. This trusted person can also help you by guiding you in reflecting on an interaction that has ended and by pointing out instances in which you seem to get stuck.

My own challenge is to remember to question my interpretation, especially when the context tricks me into heading in the wrong direction. (Notice how I blamed the context for my own misinterpretation!) I was reminded of this challenge recently when I reacted to an e-mail message I received from Rudy, a fellow who had done work for me from time to time, but whose work quality had declined over the previous several months. The subject line of his e-mail message read, "New Address."

Upon seeing this subject line, my mental monologue sprang into action: "Gee, and he just moved into a new house a few months ago. How sad. I thought things were good with his wife, but I doubt he'd tell me if they weren't. This situation would certainly account for all the errors he's been making. He must be awfully stressed. Maybe I shouldn't have heaped one more thing on him by telling him I was dissatisfied with his work. I know he's trying. But maybe I'd better just find someone else. . . ."

These thoughts tumbled through my mind in the time it took me to load the e-mail message. When I read it, I discovered that the "new address" he was alerting me to was a *new e-mail id.*

A FEW MORE GUIDELINES AND SOME WORDS OF CAUTION

In facilitating the use of the Interaction Model, try to adapt it to fit the context. For example, when I help people untangle an interaction in a corporate setting, I may refrain from directly referring to feelings and instead refer to that ingredient as "significance." I may ask, "What is the significance for you of your interpretation of the intake?" Using the terminology most familiar in the organization may make people more receptive to what the model offers.

Furthermore, in some settings, I may ask people to describe their feelings about their feelings, their coping mechanisms, and their rules for commenting—but I will do so without using these terms. For example, instead of asking people about their feelings about their feelings, I might say, "How is it for you when you become angry?" or "What's your reaction to becoming angry?" Instead of asking about someone's rules for commenting, I might ask, "When you have this type of reaction, are there certain things you say to yourself that you don't say out loud?" Based on the response, I can help people understand their feelings about their feelings or their implied rule for commenting.

In certain situations, I focus on the four ingredients of Intake-Interpretation-Feelings-Response, omitting the other ingredients altogether. In fact, if you are just learning to work with the Interaction Model or have little experience in applying it, I'd urge you to stick to these four ingredients. Unless you're using the model in a setting in which people feel a strong sense of safety—and few organizational environments have such a setting—it's wise to bypass feelings about feelings, coping mechanisms, and rules for commenting.

Finally, a few words of caution: This model is both easy to use and, at times, risky to use. There's a critical line between being a helpmate and playing "therapist." A person's "then and there" reaction, which can be triggered surprisingly easily and with little forewarning, can sometimes be intense and emotional. Unless you have the requisite training and skills to handle such situations, limit your use of the model to the four main ingredients—or defer use of the model altogether until you have the opportunity to attend training sessions or to gain experience under supervision.[15]

---

[15] My source of training was the Year-Long Satir Systems Training workshop offered by Jean McLendon and the Satir Institute of the Southeast. For more information, see www.satirsystems.com.

Section 2
Gaps in Building Relationships

One of the predominant reasons why communication gaps occur is the failure of the parties involved in a given relationship to communicate early and often. Early in the relationship, they neglect to communicate sufficiently to build understanding, trust, and respect. And thereafter, when they should be strengthening the relationship, they give little attention to assessing how they're doing, to evaluating whether they're in sync, to resolving their conflicts, or to discussing how they want to proceed. In short, they suffer from too little relationship-focused communication.

Of course, on occasion, less communication can be better than more, as I was reminded when I visited my dentist. The occasion was a root canal, and with it, the opportunity to help put my dentist's kids through college. First, he pumped me full of anesthetic. Then he filled my mouth with all manner of dental hardware. Explaining that the offending tooth was a tough one to reach, he had me crank my head around to an angle not designed for human cranking. And then he told me not to move. "Keep completely still," he said, "and don't try to say anything."

As he began to work, he did what must be a prerequisite for the dental profession. He started talking. And periodically, despite the fact that I was incapable of articulating a single word, he asked me questions. He clearly had mastered The Art of the One-Way Dialogue.

It would have been bad enough if his questions required merely yes or no answers. I mean, *you* try it. Open your mouth as wide as you can, tilt your head to whatever angle hurts the most, and then while pretending that you're under anesthesia, try saying "yes." Then "no." See what I mean? All you can do is grunt. And a yes grunt sounds much like a no grunt.

The worst of it was that my dentist seemed to favor questions whose answers required the use of the letters *m, p, f,* and *b.* But all I could do was grunt. Periodically, he asked me if I had any questions. "Yes," I thought. "Why do you keep asking me questions when I can't answer them?" I tried to say this, but it came out sounding like a yes grunt. He took it for a no grunt, and happily resumed his one-way dialogue.

In defense of my dentist, I should point out that at the end of my first visit, he explained in detail what he had done and what he would do next. His explanation came complete with pictures that he drew for me. Most were pictures of teeth, but one was a picture of a nutcracker, which he used to illustrate the different amounts of pressure needed to chomp down on something, and how this can damage teeth—and maybe nut-crackers, as well, though he didn't say.

On my second visit to my dentist—the one that funded his second born's freshman year—he instructed me to resume my position in the chair, and was quickly off and yakking. Giving him the benefit of the doubt (and being too cowardly to stifle the mutterings of anyone performing a root canal), I told myself that he was just trying to be amiable and help me pass the time.

My dentist's technique, however, turned out to be very helpful, because it led me to rethink the importance of two-way, relationship-building communication. This kind of com-munication is especially useful for helping people build rap-port, find common ground, establish group norms, resolve dis-putes, and discover communication preferences. Described below, the chapters in Section 2 focus on the importance of effective communication in building and maintaining relation-ships.

- Chapter 5 addresses the crucial issue of setting the stage: taking steps early in a relationship to build a foundation of understanding, trust, and respect.
- Chapter 6 describes key differences in how people com-municate and what they communicate about.
- Chapter 7 explains how people can improve their understanding of the other party's perspective.
- Chapter 8 suggests ways to maintain and strengthen an existing relationship.

5

Building a Strong Foundation

It is never too soon to start building a foundation for a strong relationship, as my colleague Gary's first days working at a new company demonstrated. Without waiting for anyone to arrange an introduction, Gary went to the technical-support group office and introduced himself to the staff members. They chatted for a while and had a few laughs. In the process, these support staff members came to know him before he needed their help; they, in turn, had a chance to explain their services to him. Members of the group later commented to me that this was the first time anyone had ever come by just to meet them. Usually, they explained, employees ignored the support group until they had a problem. Urgency was the defining attribute of most employees who contacted them.

By connecting with technical-support staff members as people first and as sources of support only later, Gary developed an excellent relationship with them. He came to appreciate their issues, pressures, and priorities. They, in turn, were eager to provide him with help when he needed it, even when they were overloaded with other demands. Unlike many people, Gary recognized that win-win relationships develop neither automatically nor instantaneously. He appreciated that a relationship stands a better chance of developing smoothly and amicably if the first contact between the two parties isn't in the form of "Gimme, gimme!" or "I need it yesterday!" or "I'm stuck! Come help me. Now!"

In this chapter, we'll see how early and frequent use of direct communication can help people work together successfully. It is in this part of the process that the important foundation for strong relationships is built.

WORKING TOGETHER, TOGETHER

While writing this book, I had a dream about another book— or, more accurately, about a book cover. The cover was red, with the title written in crisp, white, elongated, cartoon-like letters. It looked like this:

$$\textbf{Working}$$
$$\textbf{Together,}$$
$$\textbf{Together}$$

In the dream, I really liked this title. I liked it even more when I woke up and realized that the title had real meaning in the context of this chapter. Indeed, we will be more successful in working together if we work together at working together. (I woke up before I noticed who the author was. I like to think it was me.)

"Working together, *together*" involves collaboratively and proactively taking steps that will facilitate cooperation. To be successful, relationships must be built on a foundation of understanding, trust, and respect—factors that make it possible to persist and triumph amid the changing priorities, unceasing uncertainties, and confusion that are inevitable in any important undertaking.

Disagreements are rampant in the workplace—how many have you experienced just since Tuesday? But although some amount of conflict is normal in any relationship, and is inevitable in complex efforts, any undertaking can be derailed by prolonged, excessive, or unresolved conflict. Conflict is likely to occur more frequently and to be more difficult to resolve in the absence of a strong foundation. And, difficult as it is to believe when deadlines loom large and the ticking of the clock sounds like a jackhammer, developing a strong foundation takes far less time than repairing a relationship damaged by its absence.

The experience of a project team I corresponded with not long ago typifies what happens so often: At the start of a major project that I refer to as Ramp-Up, each of the dozen team members knew some of the others but only a few knew everyone. Given their shared history in the company and their related project experience, they felt a sense of connection with each other even though they'd never worked together as a team of twelve.

Driven by their enthusiasm for developing the product, all twelve team members dove right into the project, taking no time to compare expectations, find common ground, establish norms, or clarify how they wanted to function as a team. Conflict quickly surfaced, with heated disagreements arising about both the project and the way team members were interacting in carrying out their responsibilities. Tension mounted, increased, and then intensified. These people, who truly cared about each other and about their work, at no point took time to discuss what was happening, how they could learn from it, and how they might proceed differently.

Despite this nearly intolerable experience, the team completed the project on time and, judging from customer feedback, the product was a huge success. But most team members found the experience extremely distressing and one they wanted never to repeat. How different their experience might have been if they had focused on building a foundation to ensure that their relationship would succeed along with their project.

FOUNDATION-BUILDING TAKES TIME AND EFFORT

Trust, respect, and understanding among colleagues don't develop overnight, but the earlier in a relationship you start trying to create them, the fewer overnights they'll take. Trust, especially, helps to build the foundation, but building the foundation can also strengthen trust.

I learned some unforgettable lessons about trust and strong foundations when my husband and I decided to build a small ski house in a rural Vermont town that had a neighborly way of doing business. Although we planned to do most of the construction ourselves, we hired a local fellow to put in the foundation. As a child, I had the concept pounded into me that having a contract is a must for such work, but our builder didn't present us with one. When I asked him, "Don't you think we ought to have a contract?" he said, "That's okay, I trust you." Here I was, wondering if we could trust him, and he thought we were concerned that *he* didn't trust *us*. Putting our big-city nervousness aside, we proceeded without a contract. In the end, both the foundation and the relationship were perfect.

Normally, of course, just as building the foundation for a house takes time and energy, it takes time and energy to build the foundation for a relationship. We might have built our Vermont house on the cold, damp earth, but it wouldn't have been long before we'd have needed to put in more time, effort, and expense for repairs to an unstable house than we needed to build the house in the first place. Similarly, undertaking an important venture without building a foundation seems expeditious until conflict and excessive tension disrupt both the effort and the relationship. For both houses and relationships, a foundation confers stability and longevity.

Building a foundation for a relationship is worthwhile even for interactions that are transient, trivial, or infrequent. People who invest in future relationships stand to benefit, as Gary did when his need for technical support materialized. And sometimes, that investment requires little more of a person than stopping by to say hello, as Gary did, or showing someone some thoughtful attention. While taking little effort, such gestures often have a huge impact on those on the receiving end.

Early in my career, a wise colleague advised me, "Be nice to everyone; you never know who your next boss will be." How valuable this advice proved to be when a major reorganization at the company where I worked created unimagined combinations of reporting relationships. For months thereafter (or so it seemed), most of us walked around saying to each other, "I know that either I work for you or you work for me, but I'm not sure which." Those who had previously taken some small steps to develop understanding, trust, and respect had an advantage in coping with the new organizational relationships.

BUILD THE FOUNDATION WHILE BUILDING THE HOUSE

When building a wood-frame house, sequence matters: First, you build the foundation; then, the house. Happily, with relationships, you can build a foundation while doing the work—which is fortunate, since priorities invariably intervene and leave little time at the outset for foundation-building. Even if you wanted to, you couldn't complete a relationship foundation before work begins, because it's the very process of working together that helps to firm up that foundation. Indeed, for many group members, the work they do together *is* their foundation-building.

In other situations, though, the people involved in a work environment gradually and imperceptibly (or, in some cases, quickly and visibly!) become mired in faultfinding, blaming, and other incongruent behavior. When that happens, gaps between what people hope for and what they experience on a project emerge sooner, become bigger, and take longer to close. Even if people achieve their project goals, their sense of gratification is often diminished by the turmoil they experienced—as the Ramp-Up team learned firsthand. It is precisely to avoid this turmoil that starting the foundation-building as early in the effort as possible is just plain good sense. If you're already in a relationship that's immersed in conflict, "as early as possible" means now.

One of the flaws in the Ramp-Up project was that team members didn't appreciate the *importance* of creating a foundation. Because they weren't complete strangers when they came together, they erroneously assumed that they could just dive into the project—and perhaps they could have if their first project had been a simple Donut Acquisition and Distribution effort. But they had never even tackled a trivial project together, let alone a complicated one. They had never worked—or even played—as a group.

Don't fall into the trap of believing that your next group undertaking can avoid misunderstandings, conflicts, and serious stress in the absence of a foundation. It's not impossible that you can do so, but it *is* unlikely.

At the heart of foundation-building is communication that helps the parties do the following:

- Make contact.
- Find common ground.
- Laugh together.
- Build rapport.
- Establish group norms.
- Manage expectations.
- Develop understanding.
- Make time to talk.
- Meet face-to-face.

Depending on the nature of your work, your foundation-building efforts may focus on all of the above, or just a few.

Select the ones that fit your unique circumstances, and you'll be well on your way to creating a strong foundation.

Make Contact

Imagine an oversized duffel bag in which you store details of your past history, your current expectations and fears, and your hopes and dreams for the future. This duffel bag is enormous, but it and its contents are visible only to you. Everywhere you go, you drag your duffel bag with you. When you interact with others, some of the contents of your duffel bag spill out and pile up, interfering with your ability to see matters clearly and sometimes getting in the way of your ability to connect meaningfully with others. Imagine further that the people with whom you try to connect have their own duffel bags, invisible to you but just as much a factor in your interactions as your duffel.

These imaginary duffel bags can help us grasp the complexity of establishing meaningful connections. In her writings, the family therapist Virginia Satir emphasized that connections must be made in a way that enables understanding, trust, and respect to emerge within a *context of safety*. To provide a starting point for creating meaningful connections, Satir offered three questions that are readily adaptable to organizational settings and that serve as a catalyst for "making contact":

1. How did you happen to come here?
2. What do you expect will happen here?
3. What do you hope to accomplish here?[1]

Notice that the first question elicits information about events from the past; the second, the present; and the third, the future. All three questions provide a starting point to help you determine what's important to the person or group with whom you're trying to communicate.

---

[1] Virginia Satir, *Conjoint Family Therapy* (Palo Alto, Calif.: Science and Behavior Books, 1983), p. 141. See also Virginia Satir, *Making Contact* (Millbrae, Calif.: Celestial Arts, 1976) and www.satir.org.

What appeals to me about these questions is that they allow people to reveal as much or as little about themselves as they wish while establishing, at the least, a rudimentary connection. For example, suppose that a group of people who have never met before are waiting for a class to begin, and someone asks, "How did you happen to come here?" One person might explain that he has applied for a new job that requires the kind of background this class could supply. Another might talk about a major life-transition that made this the right time to attend the class. A third, not wishing to disclose personal information, might simply say, "United Airlines, by way of Chicago." People can respond to the questions based on their own level of comfort and safety.

These questions can be adapted to fit a variety of situations. For example, suppose you're a new member of a team and you are trying to connect with your teammates. In chatting with one or another of them, you might ask,

1. How did you come to join this team?
2. What is it like being part of this team?
3. What are you hoping the team will accomplish this year?

If you're already comfortable with a teammate, you might ask more probing questions that elicit deeper insight into the person and the context, such as,

1. What surprised you most when you first joined this team?
2. What's the best part of being a member of this team?
3. Is there something you'd like to see this team achieve that you doubt will ever happen?

Keep in mind that these questions are only intended as a guide. You can skip some, add your own, ask them in any sequence, or pick just one and let the conversation flow from there. If you find these questions helpful in initiating dialogue, use them; whatever emerges creates an initial connection and may also provide the context for extended discussion.

You can also pose these questions to customers you're meeting for the first time, such as by asking,

1. How did you come to be in this department?
2. What is it like doing this kind of work?
3. What will be your biggest challenge during the next few months?

Such questions are part of people-first relationship-building; they show your interest in the customer as a human being, and many customers respond enthusiastically to this attention. As a result, these questions can help to build a connection before the more formal work-related communication begins.

To gain insight into a customer's mindset at the start of a project, you might ask,

1. What kinds of experiences have you had with projects of this nature?
2. How is it for you to be undertaking this project?
3. What concerns do you have about this project?

Granted, these might not be the questions you would want to lead with in your first conversation with a customer, but when the time is right, these questions can help you understand the customer's history with past projects and fears regarding the current project. Knowing of a troubled history might suggest a different way of proceeding so as to improve your chance of succeeding with the current effort.

You can also adapt the questions for use in assessing customer satisfaction. For example:

1. How would you describe the service you've received from us this past year?
2. What are you currently most pleased about and most frustrated about in working with us?
3. Can you identify something you'd like us to keep the same and something you'd like us to change over the next year?

The Ramp-Up team might have begun its project by holding a discussion revolving around these three questions:

1. How did you come to be on this team?
2. How is it for you to be part of this project?
3. What are your expectations and concerns about this project and your involvement in it?

Find Common Ground

When immersed in squabbles and stress, people sometimes become so focused on their differences that they forget all about their similarities. They may believe they have some things in common—they work for the same company, take the same commuter train, or experience similar challenges as parents, for example—but that's it. Or is it?

In some of my classes, I use a quick exercise to demonstrate how much people have in common. I invite participants to form groups of four-to-six people. I then give each group ten minutes to come up with at least three nonobvious things that all members of the group have in common. The more clever and creative, the better.

At first, people look stunned at the thought of detecting anything at all in common in *only* ten minutes. Then they get to work, noisily comparing notes on their favorite foods, movies, hobbies, travel destinations—you name it! They later report similarities such as obstreperous kids, a fondness for take-out, an addiction to auction Websites, or exasperating experiences with their Internet-service providers. I remember one group whose members said they all spoke at least one language. Another reported discovering that none of them could sing on key (I challenged them to prove it, and they were right!). My favorite was the group of five people who each had feared my seminar was going to be a dreary, lecture-oriented class—no one was happier than I when they confirmed their fears were unfounded. Whew!

In only ten minutes, these groups identified numerous shared interests and experiences—both serious and zany—as well as many more things that were interesting, even if not common to everyone in the group. Although I challenge people to find three things they have in common, most groups come up with many more than the three. When put to the test, people accept the challenge. They abandon their defenses and strive to find ways in which they're alike. The very process of being silly together gives them something in common.

Invariably, while searching for what they have in common, people learn a lot they didn't know previously about each other—even if they'd been coworkers for years. How amazing it is that people who work together can be so connected, yet remain so disconnected. Discovering similarities helps not only in building or strengthening good relationships, but also in repairing damaged ones. What do you have in common with the person at the next desk? the managers with whom you interact? your least favorite customer? You probably have more in common than you think. Find out, and watch your foundation develop.

Laugh Together

Laughter, in my opinion, is underappreciated as a means of communication; it can serve as a relationship icebreaker and a door-opener. Bernie DeKoven, a speaker and workshop leader known professionally as the Guru of Fun, notes, "When you find yourself playing and laughing with other people, you find yourself feeling healthy and safe: good about yourself, about other people."[2] People who laugh together can accomplish amazing things—*together.* Conversely, a relationship in which the parties rarely laugh together is likely to get bogged down in conflicts that are especially difficult to resolve.

Laughter is very high on my list of ingredients that are essential to building strong relationships. Indeed, a workweek without some fun, playfulness, and lightheartedness will strain even the most committed worker. In the right atmosphere, laughter can make communication easier even among strangers, as I observed during a Weinberg & Weinberg "Problem Solving Leadership Workshop" that I led with Jerry Weinberg.[3] As everyone sat in a circle during the opening segment, a participant commented on the difficulty he had remembering other people's names. Jerry suggested we try a memory technique, and asked the person to his left to state his name and something he considered interesting about himself. Then Jerry asked the person sitting to the left of the first speaker to repeat what had just been said, and then to add her own name and a tidbit about herself, and so on, around the circle. Get the picture? Each successive person had to repeat what each preceding person had said and then add his or her own information until the last person had repeated the names and interests of everyone in the circle—and then added her own.

This delightful technique provided a quick way for strangers to learn about each other. Without it, I might never have known that this group included a wind surfer, a wine connoisseur, a soccer dad, a painter, and a motorcycle enthusiast.[4] But as it turned out, this technique did much more than

---

[2] Bernie DeKoven focuses on the art of bringing more fun to work and play. See www.DeepFun.com.

[3] Problem Solving Leadership (PSL) was a week-long experiential workshop designed by Jerry and Dani Weinberg, of which I was a faculty member for many years.

[4] My thanks to the PSL class of September 2000 for a memorable experience.

merely help people identify names and hobbies. An amazing thing happened. We began to know each other, laughing with each other as we learned about each other. By the time we had gone around the circle, we were no longer strangers. We felt connections that we didn't have at the start.

This experience could easily fit in several of the other sections in this chapter—it illustrates a way to make contact, find common ground, develop understanding, and so on. But this is a section on laughter. And I'll never forget all the laughing we did that week. I don't mean an occasional giggle or chuckle. Laughter filled the room during our opening go-around and continued throughout the entire week. With no prodding on Jerry's or my part, this group had made levity a defining characteristic. Participants may not have viewed that laughter as communication, but it was. Furthermore, not only did the heightened levity not diminish learning, it seemed to enhance it. At the end of the workshop, participants described how deeply they had learned important lessons about themselves, about problem-solving, and about leadership.

The laughter that characterized this unplanned opening activity contributed greatly to the ability of this group to connect quickly, to interact readily, and to build trust rapidly. We had created the beginning of a foundation on which to spend the week together. Did this activity prevent conflicts, disagreements, and personality clashes? Certainly not, but foundation-building entails doing a variety of things, and this one thing called laughter contributed to a remarkable experience.

When you laugh with a stranger, you begin to know each other. When you laugh with a friend or colleague, your relationship deepens. And when you laugh with a person you're angry at, it's difficult to hold onto that anger.

Build Rapport

Connections strengthen when people start to know each other beyond the roles they play and the persona they reveal at work. Yet, as valuable as good rapport is to business success, building it sometimes requires time and effort. This was the case when I began a consulting engagement with a new client, and met Max, a networking director, who had been on the job for about six months. At my first meeting with him, he welcomed me into his office, but he answered my questions in an abrupt and cursory fashion. Despite the fact that the work his boss had hired me to do would ease Max's burden, he was reserved and aloof, a stark contrast to the friendly, open manner of the others I'd talked to in his division.

While we were chatting, I noticed that Max's walls featured several framed photos of little kids happily engaged in little-kid activities. I stopped probing for details about the work challenges he was facing and asked, "Who are all these adorable kids?" Instantly, his demeanor changed from cool and distant to warmly paternal as he transformed from a serious professional into a proud papa. Max beamed as he told me that two of the kids in each photo were his (of course!); the rest were cousins, neighbors, and friends. He loved kids, he told me with a broad grin (the first smile I'd seen from him), adding that he hoped in the not-too-distant future to find a way to work with them, instead of being trapped in what he referred to as "a stifling corporate dungeon."

This glimpse into the human side of Max gave me insight into what he cared about, and that information helped us to connect. From time to time thereafter, I inquired about his kids, sent him articles about interesting kid-doings, and pointed out clever kid-toys that I'd discovered. He remained reserved, downplaying the challenges he faced at work, but any mention of kids—especially his own—brought a huge smile to his face that told me where he really lived.

Building rapport is often as simple as looking around, noticing what you see, and commenting on it. Some people know intuitively how to do this. If you do, you have a powerful communication tool at your disposal. But even if you aren't lucky enough to have this intuitive sense, just keep in mind that people love to talk about the things that matter most to them. Give them the opportunity to do so, notice how their eyes light up, and you'll know you've connected.

Establish Group Norms

Group norms focus on an extremely important gap-prevention measure: communicating about how you're going to communicate. Group norms concern how people will interact, behave, and conduct themselves as members of the group. Norms help people agree on how they want to get along with one another before circumstances arise that might otherwise prevent them from getting along.

The process of establishing group norms at the start of a major undertaking is crucial in foundation-building because it allows people to express what's important to them. Conversely, when groups neglect to establish norms, they lack the context for discussing concerns about individual and group behavior—and they suffer the consequences. Jean McLendon, a therapist and trainer in the teachings of Virginia Satir, notes, "If we don't set norms up front, we tend to not do them later on till there's a crisis. Without norm-setting, disconnects occur, feelings are not recognized, vulnerabilities are not accepted, and more dysfunction occurs in the group. We must learn to do this work on the front end *before* we get into trouble."[5] It has been my experience as well that establishing norms as early in the relationship as possible is a key to its future success.

Some people use terms such as "ground rules" or "guidelines" rather than "norms." My own preference is norms. To me, the term "ground rules" sometimes sounds like a mandate, a way that people must be; whereas "norms" suggests a way that people will strive to behave—a desired state rather than a must-do command. And guidelines, for me, seem akin to a list of how-to's. In your own context, use whatever term fits best; you'll have a better chance of successfully introducing and implementing processes such as this one if you adapt the terminology to fit your own culture.

---

[5] Jean McLendon, Year-Long Satir Systems Training, March 30, 2001, sponsored by the Satir Institute of the Southeast (www.satirsystems.com).

A group can create norms in several ways. For example, one approach is to have each person in the group identify a norm to be listed on a flip chart, going around to each person as many times as needed until no one has any other norms to suggest. Another approach is to split the group into teams of two or three people and have each team create its own list, which later can be compiled into a master list. A third approach is for each person to prepare his or her own list of desired norms to be submitted to a facilitator for compilation and posting.

It's important that group members create their own list from scratch rather than relying on another group's list. Using a preexisting list may make group members feel that the norms have been foisted on them rather than selected by them. In any case, the process of creating norms together is a valuable team-building activity.

One typical list of norms created by a group I worked with included the following:

- Respect each other's views.
- Withhold judgment and hear each other out.
- Try to resolve problems without blaming.
- Let everyone have a say.
- Don't interrupt while someone is talking.
- Start and end on time.
- Ask for help if you need it.
- If you don't understand, ask questions.
- Offer help if you think it's needed.
- If asked to do something you'd rather not do, feel free to say no.
- If you have an issue with someone, address it directly with that person.
- Appreciate others for their efforts.
- Notice what we've done well, not just what we've done wrong.
- Accept all group members' views as real and important to them.

Norms such as those listed above are appropriate in most group settings. You may also want to identify norms that are unique to your own situation. Writing about his determination to banish jokes and teasing among colleagues during end-of-project review sessions, *Project Retrospectives* author Norman Kerth notes, "Sometimes, humor can be used to communicate endearment, but sometimes it is used to humiliate. As a facilitator from outside the organization, I can't always tell the difference. Furthermore, there may be times when someone in the retrospective is feeling vulnerable and even gentle kidding might be taken as an insult."[6] Therefore, when working with members of a retrospective group to establish norms, Kerth adds to the list an item about refraining from using humor at someone else's expense, and invites everyone's cooperation.

After collecting everyone's proposed norms, group members can discuss their reactions. In addition to eliminating redundancies, they also may note some items that seem to be contradictory. In one group, for example, one norm stated,

> We'll respect and adhere to the agenda we've set.

Another one said,

> We will not cut off the resolution of important issues simply in order to stick to the agenda.

Discussion of this apparent contradiction revealed that the two people who had suggested those norms weren't as far apart as they had thought. The fellow who wanted to adhere to the agenda was tired of meetings in which the direct route through the agenda regularly gave way to side trips, detours, and rest stops. The woman concerned about resolving important issues had just come off a project in which discussion of such issues was repeatedly cut short simply to preserve the schedule.

After the two described their concerns and the experiences they didn't want to relive, they agreed to combine the two

---

[6] Norman L. Kerth, *Project Retrospectives: A Handbook for Team Reviews* (New York: Dorset House Publishing, 2001), p. 21. See www.retrospectives.com.

norms to read: "We'll adhere to our agenda, provided we don't arbitrarily cut short the resolution of important issues." In subsequent meetings, when the schedule was occasionally scrapped in the interest of resolving important issues, no one was upset. They had established a norm that permitted them to both honor their schedule and allow for exceptions to it.

Contradictions among norms can often reveal people's individual preferences. For example, during the first meeting of a particular project team, one attendee said that when he appeared to be distressed, he wanted help from others in reducing his distress. Another person quickly responded that when *she* was upset, she wanted to be left alone to work it out for herself. She asked that people *not* try to help her unless she requested their help. In effect, one person was saying "Help me when I'm down," while the other was saying, "Don't help me when I'm down."

The discussion that followed created awareness that asking others to identify their preference is better than assuming that what they want matches your own preference. A group can post seemingly contradictory norms, recognizing that they represent the views of different people. After noticing several norms that seemed to contradict each other, members of this particular group posted one final norm: "Let's remember that we are unique individuals with unique perspectives and preferences."

In practice, people can often lose sight of these norms. But the very process of establishing them enables group members to publicly acknowledge and remind each other of the behavior they value. Furthermore, the very existence of these norms—particularly if they are posted as a reminder to all—gives everybody in the group permission to gently point out any deviation. Changes and additions may be made at any time, as long as the entire group agrees to them.

Manage Expectations

People sometimes think that "managing expectations" means getting other people to do things your way—but it doesn't.

Managing expectations is about talking to each other to understand what each party realistically needs and what each can reasonably deliver.[7] Expectations management inevitably entails a compromise between oneself and others, so as to reflect the most important concerns of each party. I once heard someone say that reaching an agreement is a matter of each party going away just a little bit unhappy. I prefer a positive rephrasing of this idea: If each party can give up a little of what it wants, together they can succeed.

The most serious flaw I see in the way people manage expectations is that they don't. That is, people move forward without talking about what is expected from and by each person involved, and why. Down the road—sometimes *far* down the road—they discover that they've embarked on different, even conflicting, missions. No amount of communication will help people become 100 percent in sync if they're determined to remain apart; even in the best of cases, 88 percent might be as good as it gets. But if the parties are unable to create shared, or at least compatible, expectations, they'll be much better off if they discover this fact early on.

In one scenario that I observed, two groups—let's call them WeHaveIt and WeWantIt—were surprised to discover how far apart they were in their vision of a joint venture they had agreed to undertake. WeWantIt had a desire to implement in its domain a product that WeHaveIt had developed for a domain very different from that of WeWantIt. To use the product successfully required extensive training and experience, a requirement met by none of WeWantIt's personnel. Nevertheless, driven by enthusiasm about its potential, WeWantIt immediately focused attention on logistics: the implementation date, the selection of the initial users, the design of a pilot, even the rollout to a larger user base once the pilot was complete.

The WeHaveIt representative had a very difficult time focusing the dialogue on WeWantIt's expectations. It eventu-

---

[7] For more on the subject of expectations, see my book *Managing Expectations: Working with People Who Want More, Better, Faster, Sooner, NOW!* (New York: Dorset House Publishing, 1994).

ally became clear that WeWantIt envisioned a financial and ownership arrangement that the WeHaveIt management had no interest in offering. It also became clear that WeWantIt seriously misunderstood the customization, marketing, sales, and support implications of implementing the product in its domain. No wonder the members of WeWantIt were so focused on logistics; they believed the product's implementation entailed little more than deciding where to plug it in. The two groups had vastly different expectations about what was feasible, desirable, and achievable. Fortunately, they discovered their irreconcilable differences before spending real money, although the effort had cost them in terms of time. Not everyone is so lucky.

Comparing expectations at the outset of a new relationship can be difficult. The context may not be well enough understood to allow you to even know what to ask. But even in such a situation, there are some questions you can ask that can help you compare expectations, such as,

- What will you be looking for when this work is completed so that you feel it's been successful?
- What is the most important aspect of this product for you?
- What is important to you about how we work with you on this project?
- What do you expect of us?
- What are your criteria for success?

People don't often consider these questions before embarking on an effort, but visiting and revisiting them can help you determine whether people are able to work together. It's equally important for people within an existing relationship to discuss their expectations before setting forth on a *new* venture. Otherwise, they may discover, after they're well on their way, that they differ both on the goal and the process they want to follow to achieve it.

Managing expectations isn't just about responding to the needs of the other party; it's also about what *you* want, need, and hope for from the effort, both professionally and personally. It's hard to meet the expectations of others if you can't meet your own. Writing in *Coping with Fuzzy Projects* about being powered by objectives that excite him, David Schmaltz notes, ". . . I am not so depleted by my effort to conquer them. When I forget to dedicate the effort to my own best interest, these encounters just exhaust me."[8]

Develop Understanding

As the WeWantIt example illustrates, communication leads to understanding. What's more, understanding develops best when both parties seek to understand and be understood. That was the case with an information-technology division that was to begin supporting a new client division as a result of a corporate reorganization. The division managers wanted the groups to have a foundation on which to build their new relationship. To help build this foundation, I was asked to facilitate a two-day get-together. An off-site meeting would have been ideal; a change of location and the opportunity for people to interact in a nontraditional context can have a freeing effect on their readiness to communicate. As it turned out, however, an off-site location wasn't feasible and so we assembled in a large meeting room.

A key to success in foundation-building is for people to begin to know each other outside the context of their daily responsibilities. Accordingly, the activities and discussions I scheduled for the first day were designed to allow the participants to work in various groupings to compare ideas, solve problems, and laugh together. These sessions enabled individuals to connect with people they didn't know and to strengthen their connection with those they did, including, as is common in these sessions, coworkers they knew, but knew little about.

---

[8] David A. Schmaltz, *Coping with Fuzzy Projects: Stories of Utter Ignorance, Theologic Wars, and Unseen Possibilities* (Portland, Oreg.: True North pgs, 2000), p. 14. See also www.projectcommunity.com.

On day two, I focused attention on ways to foster a deeper level of communication, emphasizing what the participants could do to strengthen their ability to work together. Midday, I invited the information-technology personnel to form one group and their clients to form a second group, and then instructed the two large groups to divide into smaller groups to discuss the following questions with regard to the other division:

- What don't you understand about their policies, responsibilities, and activities?
- What puzzles you?
- What have you always wanted to ask, but never had the occasion?

I then invited each subgroup to report back to the entire group and to engage in whatever discussion the reassembled IT and client personnel thought appropriate. What followed was fascinating. For each item that the clients described as puzzling or confusing, someone in the IT group eagerly offered an explanation, clarification, or source of information. Similarly, the clients willingly responded to the IT group's questions and sources of confusion. If you were a fly on the wall, you would have heard people saying things like, "I can explain that," or "Let's schedule some time next week so I can step you through the procedure." In a few cases (and usually with a laugh), people said, "It's no wonder you don't understand—we're pretty confused about it ourselves."

For the first time, it became permissible to publicly admit that they didn't know everything about the other's environment—or even their own. Within a strikingly short period of time, members of both groups felt safe revealing to each other the things they had always wanted to know about the other, but felt too uncomfortable to ask. Their rule for commenting had changed from "Don't reveal what you don't know," to "If you don't know, ask." In short order, both asking for and offering help became unspoken norms.

I posed another question for them to discuss in their sub-groups and then report to the full group:

- What can you do to help them better understand your policies, responsibilities and activities?

The responses of the IT and client groups were remarkably similar. For example, each group invited members of the other group to attend their staff meetings and visit their department to observe work in progress. Each offered to review their procedures with the other, to set aside time to answer nonurgent questions, and even to pair up so that anyone who needed clarification of a particular issue could call on a designated member of the other group for help.

Furthermore, some major insights surfaced regarding each division's priorities. For example, when an IT project manager challenged the client's responsiveness, he was shocked to learn the reason as the manager of the client group replied, "Information technology is one-hundred percent of what you do. But it reflects only ten percent of what we do. We have many other priorities that you're not aware of." What an eye-opener! This revelation led to a discussion of ways the IT division could work to make better use of the client's limited time. Such a discussion would have been most unlikely in the normal course of events. But now, even though no one told them to do so, the two groups began to communicate on how they could work together more efficiently.

In fewer than 48 hours, the two groups made great strides in building a foundation for a strong relationship. A year later, the division managers reported that the foundation stood strong. I firmly believe that all groups have it within themselves to do the same.

It's difficult to build or strengthen relationships amidst the projects, problems, and chaos of daily work life. It's even harder to fix a broken relationship while the parties are bogged down in troubleshooting, priority-juggling, or crisis resolution. At such times, the immediate need is to respond to the situation. But most people would really prefer to get along with each other rather than do battle, and when given the opportunity, they will find ways to help each other. In the process, they are likely to find ways to help themselves.

Make Time to Talk

Even when people work in close proximity to each other—say, an elevator ride away or a short walk down the hall—they rarely take time to talk about anything other than job-related tasks. Yet taking advantage of systematic opportunities to get together to talk informally about whatever interests them—and to listen—is essential to building a strong foundation and to maintaining that relationship as the work proceeds.

When I suggested using this type of informal communication to a group I was working with, a network specialist said he didn't have time to meet with all his customers. His point was indisputably true if the idea was to meet with every customer every day, or even every week or month. But did he have time to meet with one or two customers each week for a brief conversation? He certainly did! His office was located on-site at the customers' plant, barely a one-minute walk from their desks!

A manager in one of my conference workshops voiced a similar concern. He said he already worked nine-hour days. How could he possibly find any additional time to spend with his customers? I put the question to the rest of the group: "Can he afford to spend time with his customers?" The response was immediate: "He can't afford not to."

The network specialist and the manager had valid concerns: Who among us has an abundance of free time? But they didn't understand that checking in periodically with customers and spending time with them is an investment in a relationship that ultimately *saves* time. And happily, the challenge isn't to do a lot of it, but to do a little of it systematically and regularly. In building relationships, every little bit helps.

How much time together do the parties to a relationship need? In the essay "Life as a Software Architect," Bob King offers a way to think about this question: the Visibility Ratio.[9] King describes this ratio as the time you actually spend with a given party in comparison to the time you *ought* to spend. You are the judge of the latter. At the start of a relationship, you might not know how much time is appropriate, and certainly, this amount of time is likely to vary over the course of a project or the delivery of a service. But if you're spending an hour a month when you ought to be spending something closer to one day a week, the disparity ought to attract your attention. What is the ratio in your situation?

King notes that the Visibility Ratio can also help you gauge whether you are spending time with the "wrong" people, relative to your responsibilities, or whether you are failing to spend time with the "right" people—customer management, for example, rather than with frontline users; or with your teammates rather than with your superiors. Let this Visibility Ratio be your guide.

Not only do people rarely take the time to talk with each other when they are discussing problems and projects, they rarely take the time to talk about anything *other than* the project

---

[9] Bob King, "Life as a Software Architect," *Amplifying Your Effectiveness: Collected Essays,* eds. Gerald M. Weinberg, James Bach, and Naomi Karten (New York: Dorset House Publishing, 2000), pp. 48–49. See also www.rc-king.com.

or problem. As a result, communication gaps form as each individual or group feels misunderstood. Yet something magical happens when people cease to view each other strictly as roles and titles, and start to view each other as people who have needs, fears, and hopes much like their own.

This kind of magic occurred among three groups I worked with. All three needed to interact with each other to support their customers, but they were mired in conflict. Members of each group saw the other two groups as major impediments to their ability to get the job done. To help them improve their relationship, I had them split into small groups, with each made up of people from the three original groups. Their assignment was to discuss various issues that I specified that revolved around their support challenges, and then to reunite to discuss the topic as one group.

The behavior of these three groups was fairly typical: Once people started talking, they came to see that the problems they'd been experiencing were due, at least in part, to the fact that they had never before spent time together to share and compare perspectives. They realized that they had much more in common than they had differences. They also discovered that there were valid explanations for many of the problems they had blamed on each other. Furthermore, some of these problems could be quickly and easily resolved; others required more effort, but were far from insurmountable.

For their final small-group activity, I suggested that they discuss what they saw as their next steps. Members of each subgroup independently decided that they wanted to continue their conversations on their own. In a full-group debriefing session, they compared ideas on how to make that happen.

The initial discussions among the three groups marked the starting point in smoothing the bumps in their relationship. Despite the success of their discussions, one fellow in the group lamented, as he left, "We spent all this time together and all we did was communicate." Indeed, if only more groups would spend time together in which all they do is communicate!

Meet Face-to-Face

A foundation of understanding, trust, and respect is harder to build when the parties to a relationship work in locations that are remote from each other. Ellen Gottesdiener, author of *Requirements by Collaboration* and a specialist in requirements identification and analysis, emphasizes the importance of bringing all parties together at the outset of a project, especially when they will thereafter work out of different locations. In numerous conference presentations, she has emphasized, "Build trust before meeting in a virtual space."[10] This initial gathering is especially important if interaction will be primarily through e-mail messages.

In the absence of trust, a relationship can become adversarial before it has ever had a chance to become mutually supportive. Unfortunately, this is an exceedingly common scenario. For example, a customer group had a nagging problem that could be eliminated by means of some straightforward programming modifications. When I asked group members why they didn't just contact their IT group for assistance, they unleashed a stream of invectives to describe the IT group. In their view, the IT folks were untrustworthy, undependable, disagreeable, and for the most part, inconsiderate, incompetent ignoramuses.

Granted, these customers had experienced a significant amount of frustration in their interactions with the IT group. Nevertheless, to hear them tell it, the IT group did everything wrong and nothing right. But this reaction was merely the symptom of a larger problem. When I inquired further, I discovered that most of the people in this customer group had never met anyone in the IT organization. Some of them had communicated with IT personnel by phone, fax, and e-mail, but because the IT group was located several states away, face-to-face meetings between most of the people in the two groups had never occurred.

---

[10] Ellen Gottesdiener, *Requirements by Collaboration: Workshops for Defining Needs* (Boston: Addison-Wesley, 2002). See also www.ebgconsulting.com.

Still, the vehemence with which customer group members spewed negatives made me wonder whether their description could just possibly be accurate. I began to visualize a group of people aggressively plotting to make their customers' lives difficult. That was my image, at least until I visited the IT group myself. Fearful of what I might find, I arrived wearing an emotional coat of armor, just in case these folks decided to be as nasty to me as they'd apparently been to their customers. I looked around cautiously. Where were the nasty people? Where were the plotting masses?

I met numerous members of the IT organization. They were good, decent, hardworking people who wanted nothing more than to do right by their customers. They admitted that their service quality had slipped badly following a wallop of a reorganization, and that the impact on both humans and technology had indeed been colossal. "Our service stinks," one member of the IT division told me frankly.

Yet, even when they had corrected some of their blunders, they never heard a positive word from their customers, nor did they ever get recognition for what they did well. They felt dispirited. As I listened, they poured out their own litany of negatives about their customers, calling them demanding, unyielding, unappreciative, and on and on. Both parties suffered from the same problem. Although some of them had communicated with each other by phone, fax, and e-mail, they had ever met face-to-face. As a consequence, each group saw the other in the worst possible light.

This tendency to view those you've never met and whose faces you've never seen as being responsible for what has gone wrong is a familiar human pattern. Once conflict has emerged, people tend to see those who are located elsewhere as being at fault. It doesn't matter whether that location is the opposite side of the globe or down the street; when something goes wrong, many people's instantaneous reaction is, "It's *their* fault." This faultfinding seems most acute when the parties have never met. Conversely, when people finally meet face-to-face, they usually discover that the other parties aren't the mean and malicious monsters they might have seemed to be.

Obviously, geographic distance can make face-to-face meetings difficult. And yes, travel can be both time-consuming and expensive. But even when the parties are located far apart, they would do well to arrange to meet face-to-face at least once, because the time and expense required to repair a damaged relationship are always greater than the cost of building a strong relationship at the outset. Perhaps in the future, as technology increasingly enables virtual face-to-face contact, people will cease to be strangers to each other. For the present, people must make the effort to arrange to meet face-to-face.

In the situation of the IT organization and its customers, the introduction of face-to-face contact both helped them repair their damaged relationship and strengthened their understanding of and empathy for each other. They began to visit each other's sites, tour each other's facilities, and engage in direct conversations. Establishing this personal contact was a necessary step in building the foundation for a relationship that they had failed to build at the start.

Start Anywhere

Clearly, these nine foundation-building steps that I describe in this chapter overlap considerably. And that's exactly the point. Start with any one of them and you'll be going a long way toward building the foundation for a strong relationship. The book whose vibrant red cover came to me in a dream is still only a dream, but by accepting the challenge of following whatever steps in this chapter make sense to you and your colleagues, you'll only *think* you're dreaming when you find yourselves

Working
Together,
Together.

6

Appreciating and Benefiting from Communication Differences

While traveling by train some months ago, I overheard four people talking. Three of them were soft-spoken and reserved, while the fourth, an engaging and energetic conversationalist, spoke loudly and dominated the conversation. She earned a mention in this book when I heard her say to one of her companions: "You have a lot of ideas for such a quiet man."

Have you ever fallen victim to this misconception—that a quiet person lacks ideas? It's an easy mistake to make. After all, if a person has ideas, he or she would share them, right? Well, not necessarily.

Virginia Satir observed that we connect with one another based on our similarities and that we grow based on our differences. But for growth to take root, we must become aware of our differences. And for growth to thrive, we must appreciate, respect, and accommodate these differences.

Sadly, however, when we notice differences between ourselves and others—say, in how we communicate—one person being gregarious, for example, while another is reserved—we often judge those who are unlike us. At times, we find fault not only with their communication style, but also with the content of their communication. In the process, we associate traits

135

with the person's communication style that have nothing to do with that style, as the woman on the train did in associating verbosity with quantity of ideas. Yet such a connection is as farfetched as if the quiet fellow with the many ideas had assumed the woman to be empty-headed because she spoke so engagingly, energetically, and enthusiastically.

Our ability to accommodate communication differences, and indeed to benefit from them, can significantly affect our success in building a strong foundation. When forging relationships, carrying out projects, seeking buy-in, and selling ideas, communication differences can distance people as easily as they can bring them together. This chapter focuses on some key personality differences that are observable in how people communicate, when they communicate, and what they communicate about. An awareness of these differences can help you choose how to interact with others—and how you express what you need from them—so that you can work with them amicably and productively.

As you read this chapter, ask yourself: How can I take personal responsibility to accommodate these differences between myself and others? Can we discuss these differences, enjoy them, and use them for our mutual gain?

A FRAMEWORK FOR DISCUSSING COMMUNICATION PREFERENCES

Numerous personality instruments offer insight into how people communicate. One of the best, in my opinion, is the Myers-Briggs Type Indicator.[1] Known as the MBTI, this indicator sheds light on how people take in information from the outside world and how they operate on this information to make decisions and form conclusions.[2]

---

[1] The Myers-Briggs Type Indicator™ and MBTI™ are registered trademarks of Consulting Psychologists Press, Palo Alto, California.

[2] Note that I'm referring to the MBTI as an instrument or indicator, not as a test. The MBTI does not test people and provide a grade, but rather offers information that will help people to better understand themselves and others.

Taking the Myers-Briggs Type Indicator is not a prerequisite to reading or understanding this chapter. Rather, this chapter is intended to help you notice differences in communication style so that you can use these observations to close or prevent communication gaps. This awareness can help you work more effectively with people with different communication preferences.

The MBTI focuses on four differences—called preferences, in MBTI language. A preference refers to a natural inclination: how you do things when you're being yourself, rather than functioning in the manner that's expected of you in your personal and professional relationships. It's what is referred to as your "shoes off" self. These preferences focus on the following areas:

- Where you get your energy: a preference for introversion (I) or extraversion (E)[3]
- How you take in data from the outer world: a preference for sensing (S) or intuition (N, since "I" is already in use for introversion)
- How you use that data to make decisions: a preference for thinking (T) or feeling (F)
- How you relate to the world: a preference for judging (J) or perceiving (P)

Combining these four categories yields sixteen possible types, or letter combinations—ISTJ, ENTP, INFJ, or ESFP, for example. Each letter indicates one aspect of an individual's communication preference. Each preference influences and is influenced by the other three preferences; for example, although ESTJs and ENFPs are both Extraverts, what, when, and how they exhibit that quality will be influenced by the other three type indicators.

---

[3] This spelling of "Extravert" is not an error. In everyday English, it's spelled "extrovert." However, in this context of psychological type, it is spelled "Extravert."

According to type theory, which derives from the work of the psychologist Carl Jung, psychological type is inborn.[4] According to the premises of type theory, you *are* a certain type, although your upbringing and life experiences may steer you into behaving as another type. No type is better than any other. Each type has strengths and potential weaknesses, and any important work effort benefits from the participation of many types. The following sections describe how people of different types can communicate more effectively with others.

WHERE YOU GET YOUR ENERGY: EXTRAVERSION (E) VERSUS INTROVERSION (I)

A colleague of mine threw herself a fortieth birthday party. She told me she invited one hundred of her closest friends and was disappointed when only sixty showed up. I, by contrast, don't even like *going* to parties. More often than not, I end up at a side of the room, looking at books on the bookshelf. If I go out in the evening, in those infrequent instances in which I *do* go out in the evening, I'd rather spend it with a few close friends. I trust you can tell which of us is the Extravert and which is the Introvert!

But don't jump to the wrong conclusion. Both Extraverts and Introverts can talk your head off. And both need quiet time for reflection. The two differ, however, in where they get their energy, whether from other people or from inside themselves. Where the energy comes from can make a huge difference in communication style.

Extraverts get their energy from interacting with other people and tend to be more animated and expressive than Introverts. Introverts get their energy internally—much of their communication takes place within themselves, in a quiet and private place not accessible by others. Thus, they are often less talkative, less animated, and less expressive than their Extravert counterparts. Extraverts tend to enjoy talking, sometimes if only for the sake of talking; Introverts tend to talk when they have something to say.

---

[4] C.G. Jung, *Psychological Types* (New York: Harcourt Brace, 1923).

In introducing types, I have deliberately used qualifiers such as "tend to," "generally," and "often" because two people of the same type can be dramatically different. It is essential to remember that we are all multidimensional, and are influenced by many factors in addition to our MBTI type.

Consider some of the key communication differences between Extraverts and Introverts. Extraverts gain energy from interacting. Many Es, after talking with people all day long, can still enjoy a large social gathering in the evening. Introverts, by contrast, lose energy from interaction. Talking— or even listening—for an extended period can deplete an I's energy. Thus, whereas Extraverts enjoy being with lots of people, Introverts have a greater need for "cave time" and generally prefer conversing one-on-one or in small groups.

The E's gain in energy and the I's loss of energy are not consciously motivated. They are somehow hardwired; someday, someone will invent a talk-o-meter that will produce graphs and charts confirming these changes in energy levels.

This difference in their sources of energy influences the way Es and Is think. Extraverts think out loud. When you listen to an Extravert, what you hear is the thought process in action. Es quite literally think outside the box—the cranial box! Introverts process their thoughts internally and often need time to reflect before speaking.

It is said of Es that they don't know what they're thinking until they say it out loud. Conversely, it is said of Is that they don't know what they're thinking until they process it internally. Thinking out loud, something Es take for granted and do naturally, can be uncomfortable for Is. However, if Is have time to reflect, they often express themselves more articulately than Es because their utterances have been through several rehearsals and are ready for show time. Actually, as one who knows, I'll admit that the process sometimes entails having a thought, reflecting on it, reviewing it, revising it, rehearsing it, modifying it, editing it, rehearsing it once more, and then saying it aloud—maybe.

Given these differences, it's not surprising that Es and Is some-times get into conflict with each other. William Murray points out the dilemma in his humorous portrayal of type, *Give Your-self the Unfair Advantage:* "Obviously, both are liable to mis-communicate the importance of a problem because when an Introvert signals importance by putting it in writing, the Extravert assumes that it wasn't important, or he would have called about it. The Extravert calls about something urgent, and the Introvert may assume it's not important—or it would have been put in writing!"[5]

Taken to an extreme, the Introvert wonders whether the Extravert will ever shut up, and the Extravert wonders if the Introvert is dead or alive. Is this a huge communication differ-ence? Absolutely! And unless we really work at under-standing this difference, it can lead to conflict, frustration, or confusion.

Even listening styles are different between Es and Is. My extraverted friends tell me that interrupting an Extravert is a sign that you're listening; one friend actually urged me to interrupt her when she was talking. I tried, but it felt rude—maybe because to Introverts, interrupting is a sign that you're *not* listening. To further complicate matters, you can interrupt

---

[5] William D.G. Murray, *Give Yourself the Unfair Advantage: A Serious Prac-tical Guide to Understanding Human Personality That Will Have You Rolling in the Aisles* (Gladwyne, Penn.: Type & Temperament, 1995), p. 31.

Introverts even when they're totally quiet, because they're often busy processing ideas internally.

It is important to note that conflict, frustration, and confusion can occur not only between Es and Is, but also between Es and between Is. That is, when an Extravert is speaking, it can be just as difficult for another Extravert to know when the speaker has reached a final thought as it is for an Introvert. We'd all benefit from a visual signal that says, "I'm done thinking out loud and I've reached a conclusion."

Similarly, Introverts sometimes confuse other Introverts. When a person is especially quiet, both Introverts and Extraverts can fall into the trap of wondering if anyone is home. An Introvert's visual signal might say, "Processing in progress."

Helping Yourself and Each Other

What can Es and Is do to accommodate each other? If you're an Extravert who interacts with Introverts,

- Give Introverts information in advance, preferably in writing, and allow them to reflect on it before asking for feedback. For example, if you're planning a meeting, send out an agenda or a list of questions beforehand, so Introverts have time to think about the plan.
- Allow opportunities for quiet time. Some Introverts will go stark, raving bonkers if they don't have at least a brief period of quiet time every day.
- Try not to foist too much of your extraverted energy on Introverts at one time without checking to see how they are reacting. Sometimes a break in the conversation, a time-out in the meeting, or an opportunity to converse one-on-one instead of in a large group enables Introverts to recharge.
- Recognize that an Introvert's silence doesn't mean that the person isn't participating. More often than not, the person is fully engrossed—but because this involvement is going on inside the person's head, his or her

interest may not be apparent. If you want to know what Introverts are thinking, ask. Otherwise, they may not tell you.

If you're an Introvert who interacts with Extraverts, consider the following:

- Recognize that Extraverts truly do think out loud. This means that what they say is often a work in progress, not a final thought, as it may be for you, so don't take it as a conclusion without confirming that that's the case.
- When Extraverts are speaking, show some expression on your face, like a smile, a curious expression, or even a frown, and offer an occasional utterance. Even "uh-huh" will help; if you nod your head at the same time, even better. In general, be as responsive as you can. Extraverts thrive on signs of life.
- Recognize that Extravert's often prefer to interact face-to-face or by phone, rather than strictly by e-mail. Direct interaction energizes them; impersonal forms of communication drain them.
- Allow Extraverts to do the talking that's essential for them to come to an understanding of an issue. For Es, printed information often doesn't come alive until they've had a chance to discuss it out loud.

Most importantly, both Introverts and Extraverts can speak on their own behalf about what will be helpful to them. That's where an understanding of this difference really helps. Extraverts can remind their introverted colleagues (as well as their fellow Extraverts) not to mistake the ideas they are expressing as their conclusion; they're still processing their ideas. Introverts can remind their extraverted buddies (and their introverted friends as well) that they need a time-out, a break, or a week alone in Hawaii.

I offer this last little quip deliberately to emphasize the point that people who understand E/I differences and can talk about them with their counterparts can enjoy the playful implications associated with these differences. I can readily accuse my MBTI-conversant extraverted friends of competing for the gold in the Yap-athon. And they can quite justifiably accuse me of not knowing which end of the telephone is for talking into.

Remember, though, that you can't always determine from someone's behavior at work whether that person is an Introvert or an Extravert. Behaving like an Extravert is required to get along in the world, and many Introverts are skilled at it. I was a manager when I first took the MBTI along with several other managers. Every one of us, myself included, assumed that all the other managers were Extraverts. In fact, as we discovered, most of us were Introverts; we extraverted because the job required it, and clearly we excelled at it. This revelation was an important lesson: Do not confuse talkativeness with introversion or extraversion. Both types are capable of filling the airspace with plenty of conversation when the job requires it.

People frequently express surprise at learning that an Introvert can be a seminar leader and a professional speaker who feels energized from speaking in front of an audience of a thousand or more. Yet that's what I regularly do—and *love* doing. And it is an undeniable fact that Extraverts can and do write books, an activity that may require both introspection and isolation. Extraversion does not mean a person lacks the ability to be introspective and reflective. Some Extraverts are shy and some Introverts are aggressive. Whatever the case, it's best to guard against stereotyping anyone—Extravert or Introvert.

Whether or not you positively know that someone is an E or an I, the best approach to building a strong foundation for communication is to discuss preferences as early in your relationship as possible. Talk about what communication style is most comfortable for each of you. Collaborate on how you can communicate with each other in a congruent fashion, maintaining respect for each other's preferred style without sacrificing your own. And let it be part of your foundation-building effort to give each other explicit permission to raise issues about how you communicate so that—both as individuals and as a team—you can adjust communication styles in support of your relationship.

As I think back to my train ride and my thoughts at over-hearing the energetic talkaholic, my wish is that she may someday learn that neither talkativeness nor silence is indica-tive of the quality or quantity of a person's ideas. We *all* have lots of ideas; we just express them differently.

HOW YOU TAKE IN INFORMATION: SENSING (S) VERSUS INTUITION (N)

I once participated in a class exercise that dramatically illus-trated two different ways in which people take in information. The instructor divided the class into two groups and told us she would project an image on the screen for fifteen seconds, after which time we should discuss what we saw with the others in our group.

Up went the image. I tried to grasp what it was, but as quickly as it was projected, it was gone. It was just as well. It was a strange image, and I didn't like it. It struck me as other-worldly and eerily futuristic. My group-mates and I compared reactions. We agreed that the man in the image seemed car-toonish rather than human, and that there was something robot-like about him. He was carrying a container of balls or fruit or maybe the objects were rocks, although the idea that he was carrying rocks seemed odd. There were also some creepy bugs, reminiscent of pre-special-effects movies in which the monsters didn't look quite real but appeared menacing nonetheless.

When the time allotted for discussion was up, the instructor asked my group to report what we saw. We described what we had seen and conveyed how uncomfortable we felt. Then, she asked members of the other group to describe what they had seen. They reported an image with three people in it, describing a man, roughly in the center, facing out; a woman at the top left of the image, looking upward; and another man, off-center to the right, facing back and to the right. They said the man facing forward was car-rying a basket of yellow fruit, but they couldn't be positive whether the fruit was grapefruit or lemons, or both. They noted that there were several insects in the image, saying that some looked like tarantulas and some like centipedes that were missing legs. As they finished speaking, people from my group looked at each other in amazement: three people? grapefruit? centipedes missing legs?

This exercise provided a striking—and amusing—illustration of the differences in what people pay attention to and what kinds of information they gather. We get information in two ways: through the five physical senses, and through intuition, sometimes described as a sixth sense. We all use both ways, but we gravitate toward one or the other, and the one we favor influences how we communicate.

Some people tend to be detail-oriented, like my grapefruit-observant classmates. These people are known in MBTI terminology as Sensors (Ss). They are tuned in to what they see, hear, smell, taste, and touch—that is, to what they take in with their senses. They have an orientation to the here-and-now and a tendency to trust what they can experience firsthand. They tend to see details before they see the big picture, so it's not surprising that in only fifteen seconds, they noticed the number of people, the size and color of the fruit, and whether the centipede had all its legs.

Other people tend to be more like those who were in my group during the class exercise. Known in MBTI circles as Intuitives (Ns), I and the others in that group gravitate toward the big picture (recall that, to us, the image seemed otherworldly), toward impressions (the composition gave me a creepy feeling), toward possibilities (the container may have held balls or possibly fruit or even rocks), toward interpretations (the presence of rocks seemed odd), and toward associations between things (the man looked robot-like). We often miss details, at least at first glance; it's the gestalt that captures our attention. In short, Ns tend to see the forest; Ss tend to see the trees.

I'm not saying that Sensors don't form impressions, or that Intuitives are incapable of observing details. Given more than fifteen seconds to view the image, our reactions would have overlapped to some degree. But in taking in information, the starting point for Ss tends to be facts and details, and their communication reflects this perspective. Being grounded in reality, they are often more comfortable when an idea is supported by concrete examples; the idea by itself may be harder for them to grasp in the absence of an example.

For Ns, on the other hand, the starting point tends to be the idea, impression, or thought. Examples can help to ground the idea, but are less critical than the idea—and sometimes Intuitives overlook examples altogether. Discussing matters at a hypothetical level comes more naturally to Ns, often to the exclusion of attention to facts and details. For example, a group of Intuitives was discussing how to pitch a product to prospective customers. When the group received an e-mail message from the sales staff with a recommendation it didn't quite understand, group members began to speculate about what the sales staff meant: "If they meant this, then here's what we should do. But if they meant that, then we should do this other thing. On the other hand, . . ." Relishing the hypothetical and enjoying if-then's, they never considered simply going to the sales personnel and saying, "Please explain what you meant."

Sometimes, Ss and Ns differ in their speaking style. Ss tend to speak in shorter sentences about down-to-earth facts. They focus on what is practical, real, concrete, and explicit. They tend to be literal, saying what they mean and meaning what they say. Conversely, Ns often speak in generalities and possibilities, voicing metaphors, theories, analogies, abstract terms, and wordplay. They sometimes confuse other people (including other Ns) by talking in long, meandering, circuitous, winding, maze-like, seemingly endless sentences—a style I know a lot about because I have been known to speak (and write) in sentences so long and winding that even I get lost partway through and wonder what it was that I was trying to say in the first place. Okay, you know what I'm saying. Fortunately, by practicing my sensing skills, I can sometimes tell by the puzzled look on people's faces that I've lost them!

Ss and Ns often give directions in very different ways. In *LIFETypes*, authors Sandra Krebs Hirsh and Jean Kummerow offer a delightful example of how an Intuitive gave a Sensing friend directions to a mountain lookout. The directions entailed heading east on a particular route, then turning north just beyond a fountain landmark, then continuing to the tree line, and finally turning west and following a road to the lookout point. These directions seemed precise enough—at least to the N—but the S friend got hopelessly lost on a dirt road. Fortunately, she managed to find her way back to her hotel.

As the N discovered—when her friend later called her—she had omitted some important details concerning the where-abouts and appearance of key landmarks. It seems the fountain spouted only five minutes every hour and was otherwise flush with the ground and indistinguishable from the surrounding landscape. The tree line, which clearly *looked* like a tree line from a distance, wasn't recognizable as such from close up. As a result, the friend didn't know where to turn or when she had gone too far.[6]

Details omitted from directions can be a problem, but the reverse can also be troublesome, as I personally experienced when Judith, a Sensing friend, gave me directions to her house: "Turn right immediately after the See's Candy sign," she said. Easy enough. But when I came to the sign, there was no right turn. The next right turn was onto a road a half-block away. I drove back and forth past the See's sign three times trying to find the turn until I discovered there was a *driveway* immediately after the sign. I turned into the driveway, and it led me to a road that took me right to her front door. When I teased her about her directions, she pointed out that she had said to turn right *immediately* after the sign. I resolved to follow her directions precisely from that point on.

Unlike Ss, who tend to trust their senses, Ns are more likely to trust their intuition. They are less likely to let the facts stand

---

[6] Sandra Krebs Hirsh and Jean Kummerow, *LIFETypes* (New York: Warner Books, 1989), p. 29.

in the way of a good opinion. Because their focus is on the abstract, they may miss what's right in front of them, such as the exact wording of an e-mail message, or even an object so big it blocks their path. I once walked into my hotel room on the third day of a stay and noticed a huge potted plant near the entrance. "Where'd that come from?" I wondered. Of course, it had been there all along.

Ss and Ns often have different reactions to change. Ss, being present-oriented, tend to prefer the status quo. To them, stability is good; if it ain't broke, don't fix it. What's here and tangible and real is what can be trusted. Ns, being future-oriented, are more open to change. To them, too much of the same bores them, whereas something new is seen as fun, instructive, or a source of fresh possibilities. If it doesn't work out, something else will.

The difference between Sensors and Intuitives can pose communication challenges in the workplace, such as the following:

- An N manager may describe an assignment in abstract, conceptual terms, leaving the S employee, who prefers more concrete detail, unsure about what to do. An S manager may give so much detail that an N employee experiences it as micro-managing.
- An S may resist a proposal presented by an N unless there's tangible proof that the N's idea has merit. An N may speak in metaphors that an S finds difficult to decipher.
- An N, having jumped back and forth between possibilities, may become frustrated at an S's methodical step-by-step approach. An S may get just as frustrated by an N's meandering approach.
- A team of all Ss may do a great job of identifying the details of a project (the how), while neglecting the big picture (the why and what). A team of all Ns may have a lot of great ideas (the why and what), but may inadequately consider the details of implementation (the how).

Remember, however, that both Ss and Ns can excel at detail work. And both can do big-picture work. And at times, Ns can be shortsighted and Ss can be careless. What's most important is not whether a person is a Sensor or an Intuitive, but how that person functions at work and how you accommodate that orientation in the way you communicate.

Helping Yourself and Each Other

What can Ss and Ns do to accommodate each other? If you're a Sensor working with Intuitives, you can take the following approach:

- Don't try to solve problems for Intuitives. Present the problem or need or assignment, and allow them to use their imagination and originality to figure out a solution.
- In tackling a project, take advantage of the N's natural skill in generating alternative approaches and innovative alternatives.
- Pay attention to the N's big-picture ideas, recognizing that most important efforts require their vision skills as well as your own implementation skills.
- Help Ns see the details they may miss, or the facts they may forget to check, before drawing a conclusion.

If you're an Intuitive working with Sensors, keep the following in mind:

- Recognize that Ss will more readily grasp your ideas if you incorporate specifics, such as examples, illustrations, stories, and firsthand accounts.
- Try not to get so carried away with your far-reaching ideas that you resist the pertinent details Ss are likely to bring to the decision-making process.
- Remember that Ss tend to communicate literally. Don't overload your communication with metaphors, hypotheses, or the like.

- Appreciate the S's ability and practical approach to implementing ideas; Ss provide an important balance to your visionary thinking.

Most important, both Ss and Ns can speak on their own behalf about what will be helpful to them. That's where an understanding of this difference really helps. Sensors can remind their Intuitive colleagues of their preference for the real, the practical, and the concrete—and they can provide an example of what they mean in order to help Intuitives understand the importance of examples. Intuitives can remind Sensors of the trust they place on their imagination, and they can ask Sensors to tolerate a certain amount of jumping nonsequentially from idea to idea.

HOW YOU MAKE DECISIONS: THINKING (T) VERSUS FEELING (F)

In MBTI terminology, Thinking and Feeling are the terms used to describe how people make decisions. These terms derive from Jung's work, but, unfortunately, as translated into English, they convey a meaning altogether different from what is intended. It is *not* the case that people with a preference for Thinking don't have feelings, or that people with a preference for Feeling can't think. Rather, this difference pertains to *what people focus on* as their starting point when they make decisions or form conclusions. Thinking-deciders tend to start with their head and feeling-deciders with their heart.

People with a preference for Thinking tend to be logical and analytical in the way they go about making decisions. They focus on pros and cons, cause and effect, logical consequences, and objective reasoning. As a result, the way they communicate their decision-making process or advocate the benefits of a certain course of action may come across to their Feeling colleagues as cool and insensitive.

People with a preference for Feeling, by contrast, tend to focus on personal values in making a decision. They are more likely to begin decision-making by considering how it will affect the people involved. This is a more subjective approach than the one used by those with a preference for Thinking, so it often strikes the latter as illogical.

In *People Types & Tiger Stripes*, Gordon Lawrence aptly captures the difference between Ts and Fs: ". . . thinking types believe an issue should be settled when they produce an objective, impersonal and logical argument, while feeling types don't want it settled until the reasoning gives adequate weight to the human, personal consequences of the decision."[7]

In their drive to be logical, Ts sometimes forget to consider the impact their actions or decisions may have on the people involved. Fs often come across as warmer, friendlier, and more diplomatic than Ts. When two Ts debate an issue, they may appear to their F counterparts as if they're engaged in a vociferous argument. However, what appears to be a brutal battle may actually be a lively exchange that they are actually *enjoying*. Fs prefer harmony to divisive differences of opinion, and prefer to refrain from entering into disputes. When a Feeling friend overheard a decidedly heated discussion between my husband and myself (we are both Ts), she apologized for having asked the question that triggered it. She said she felt bad and hadn't meant to start anything. "Start what?" I responded. "We were just doing some friendly jousting."

Fs tend to be more forthcoming with praise, acknowledgment, recognition, and feedback (matters that are often thought of as feelings-related). They may empathize greatly with another person, even when that person's actions are wrong or inappropriate at some logical level. Ts tend to give praise less often than their F colleagues, and to be more uncomfortable when they do give it.

Ts can and do care about people; and Fs can and do make a logical case. The fact is that most important decisions benefit from both a logical analysis and an assessment of the impact on the people involved, and both Ts and Fs can handle both approaches. But thinking-deciders and feeling-deciders start from very different places in the way they most naturally go

[7] Gordon Lawrence, *People Types & Tiger Stripes*, 3rd ed. (Gainesville, Fla.: Center for Applications of Psychological Type, 1993), p. 100.

about making decisions and forming conclusions, and the differences can be frustrating when the two types interact.

For example, a Thinker was trying to persuade his Feeling colleague to agree with him on an issue that was important to both of them. Logical though his ideas were, the colleague wasn't convinced. The Feeling fellow explained that on matters of great importance to him, logical arguments didn't stand a chance. He said that, in fact, the more his colleague appealed to his sense of logic, the less likely he was to be won over. The reverse can also be true—an F attempting to make a case to a T without using logic is likely to come across as just plain illogical.

This difference also affects what people want to be valued for. Recall Ann, the project manager in Chapter 4 who took great care to check in and ask how her team members were doing during a project. One team member, Joan, expressed dissatisfaction with Ann's asking how she was feeling. Joan explained that she wanted to be acknowledged for her ideas, not her feelings. When the two reflected on their MBTI differences, they realized that Joan was a T and Ann was an F. Most people appreciate praise and recognition; however, as this experience illustrated, they may differ in why they want to be praised and recognized.

These examples suggest that if you want to successfully present your case to someone who takes a logical approach to things, use logic to make your point. Focus on the ideas and issues. Present the pros and cons. Describe the advantages and disadvantages. List some alternatives and the trade-offs of each.

Conversely, if you want to persuade someone whose orientation is people-focused, stress how the people involved will be affected. Express empathy, consideration, and concern for those who will be affected. Show concern for human issues, demonstrating how your case will take them into account. Express appreciation for the perspective of the person you're trying to persuade.

The difference between these two decision-making approaches can play out dramatically during times of change. Ask a group of Ts and Fs what is important to them during times of change. Certainly, many of their responses will overlap. But Thinkers are more likely to report that they want to understand the reasoning behind a change, to know that it is driven by a plan, and to be kept informed of the status. They want an idea of the historical data behind the change. They want to have a sense of the parameters of the change. Being treated honestly is very important to them.

Fs are more likely to emphasize their desire to know how the change will affect people, how they can prepare for it and help with it, what will be different for themselves and others as a result, and how they can minimize the resulting stress. They want to know how others have dealt with the same situation, and who they can talk to who has been through it before. They want to know that someone is in charge of what's happening. Being treated with compassion and empathy is very important to them.

As you'll see in Section 4 (which treats the topic of gaps in managing change), a successful change effort requires communication that recognizes and acknowledges both Thinking and Feeling types. To emphasize one at the expense of the other may leave many people unhappy and unproductive.

Helping Yourself and Each Other

What can Ts and Fs do to better accommodate each other? If you're a thinking-decider who interacts with feeling-deciders, you might take the following approach:

- Present your ideas to your Feeling colleagues in terms of the impact they will have on people, especially if you're trying to be persuasive.
- Acknowledge and appreciate them for their contributions. Offer praise. Let them know that their efforts are valued.
- Don't overwhelm them with logical ideas and analyses. Ts sometimes inflict information on others, whether or not they want that information, and this tendency can be especially off-putting to Fs.

- Even if you're uncomfortable displaying emotion, be open to its presence in others.

If you're a feeling-decider who interacts with thinking-deciders, try some of the approaches noted below:

- Present your ideas in a logical, objective fashion.
- Recognize that Ts often focus more on the product than on the people. How people get along isn't unimportant to Thinkers, it's often just not as important as getting the job done.
- Encourage and allow Thinkers to express their natural skepticism and to question new ideas. Their views have merit, even when they seem to be presented in a hard-hearted way.
- Don't overwhelm Thinkers with too much caring. Heaping help—whether work-related or personal—on others can be off-putting to Ts.

Both Ts and Fs should communicate their preferences about what will be most helpful to them as individuals. Those who prefer Thinking can remind their Feeling colleagues of the pluses and minuses, pros and cons, and advantages and pitfalls of a decision. Those who prefer Feeling can remind their Thinking counterparts of the high value they place on people's emotional well-being and communicate that they will be more likely to see the merits of a case if it accommodates these values.

HOW YOU RELATE TO THE WORLD: JUDGING (J) VERSUS PERCEIVING (P)

This discussion of MBTI type categories wraps up with a story: A couple was to set out on a multi-destination sightseeing trip. Knowing they'd have only a limited amount of time in each location, the husband, prior to departure, created a list of the places he wanted to see. He felt that having a list would ensure that they wouldn't miss anything important. The wife, however, didn't like his list. "How can we know what we'll find interesting before we even get there?" she complained, explaining that she wanted to remain open to possibilities that might prove to be more interesting than what was on his list.

They had other differences as well. She especially enjoyed chancing upon interesting detours that would take them off the beaten track. He usually found these side trips interesting, but he was frustrated because they diverted him from his plan.

He insisted upon making hotel reservations in advance so they'd be sure to have a place to stay each night. She felt constrained by having accommodations already arranged, pointing out that a place to stay always seems to emerge when you need one. "Anyway," she reasoned, "what is the worst that could happen if we don't arrange everything in advance?"

She disliked his certainty that he knew the best way to plan things. He felt annoyed with her relentless impulsiveness and her inability to make a decision that they could stick to.

At the same time, they were able to see something positive about each other's point of view: He admired her ability to adjust to the unexpected with relative ease. She admired his ability to create a plan and then follow it.

This couple's experience illustrates two ways that people go about organizing their lives and their work—and also, as this example shows, their play. The two ways, in MBTI terms, are Judging (J) and Perceiving (P). As with other MBTI terminology, these terms have different meanings in everyday English than they do in MBTI context.

Let's consider Js first. People with a preference for Judging favor closure and control. For such people, "closure" means having work done, decisions made, issues settled, and things in their place. "Control" means having control over one's own actions and activities; it does not mean having control over others (although it may translate into this at times). Judgers like to have a plan, whether for the project, the trip, or the day—and maybe even for the weekend and the vacation. They like to be organized. Schedules and time frames are important to them. Judgers tend to be more interested in reaching the destination than in enjoying the journey; they often focus more on achieving the goal than on the *process* of achieving the goal. Getting things done is sometimes more important to Js than getting the *right* thing done.

Completing tasks is important to Js. In fact, to-do lists often reign supreme in their lives. Many Js get great satisfaction from not only having a to-do list, but also from checking off items once they're done. (As a J, I'm not beyond writing "Check off this item" on my to-do list so I have something to check off first thing each day!) Uncertainty and surprise can make Js uncomfortable; after all, a surprise signifies a departure from the plan. Given these traits, Js are often very good at getting things done. One possible problem, though, is that Js can drive Ps crazy.

Perceivers see things very differently. For Ps, the journey is what's most important, and if new options and opportunities arise along the way, well, they're probably more interesting anyway. Perceivers tend to favor spontaneity and to be comfortable with open-endedness. A J friend of mine described an outing with her P husband as being like the flight of a bumblebee. For Ps, exploration is more important than planning; after all, plans change. When I told my friend David that I rarely give exactly the same presentation twice, he pointed out that he rarely gives the same presentation even once. Spoken like a true Perceiver!

Unlike Judgers, Perceivers aren't averse to surprises, because a surprise is just one more possibility. Ps may make to-do lists, as Js do, but they aren't as likely to use them; indeed, they may lose them or forget about them. They usually dislike being forced into making a decision too soon because they want to remain open to new options. Ps resist routine, may work best under pressure, and tend to be comfortable with change, viewing it as just another possibility. Perceivers can be very inventive in seeing new ways to do things. Just as Js can drive Ps crazy, Ps can drive Js crazy.

The differences between Perceivers and Judgers are very real, and relationships can break down when people don't appreciate the existence of these differences or haven't found ways to talk about them. In *Type Talk at Work*, Otto Kroeger contends that this Judging-Perceiving difference is the biggest source of interpersonal tension at work, with numerous problems traceable to the difference between the Judger's need for "an opinion, a plan, and a schedule for nearly everything" and the Perceiver's ability to be "spontaneous and easygoing about everything short of life-and-death issues, and sometimes even about those."[8]

As with the E/I, S/N, and T/F differences, both Ps and Js bring enormous strengths and potential liabilities to their work. Too strong an emphasis on either P or J can be damaging to a relationship; the challenge is to strike a balance between the two. As Kroeger notes, "Js need Ps to inspire them to relax, not make a major issue out of everything; and Ps need Js to help them become reasonably organized and to follow through on things."[9]

Communicating about these differences is key to working together. Ps and Js may decide to divide up the work so as to draw from the strengths of each type. Communicating successfully may also entail compromise, with Js and Ps each giving up a little of what they prefer in order to work together amicably.

---

[8] Otto Kroeger, with Janet M. Thuesen, *Type Talk at Work: How the 16 Personality Types Determine Your Success on the Job* (New York: Dell Publishing, 1992), p. 42.

[9] Ibid., pp. 42–43.

Ultimately, each type can benefit from becoming open to the other's approach and even trying it out. Despite being a J, I find the idea of being more spontaneous very appealing, and I'm working on it. Every Wednesday at 3:00 P.M., I try to do something completely spontaneous!

Helping Yourself and Each Other

What can Ps and Js do to better accommodate each other? If you're a Judger who interacts with Perceivers, incorporate some or all of the following steps into your daily routine:

- Try to resist the natural J tendency to express yourself with strong judgments, quick opinions, and emphatic decisions. Try to be open to as-yet-unconsidered possibilities.
- Accept that from time to time, Perceivers will head in a direction other than the one you had expected and anticipated.
- When a P's efforts take you in a different direction than you had planned, try to find the positive aspects of the experience; often, there will be more than you might think.
- Strive to build a solid-enough relationship with your P associates that you're willing to trust them despite the surprises they may spring.

If you're a Perceiver who interacts with Judgers, consider trying the suggestions listed below:

- To alleviate the J's discomfort with uncertainty about when you'll reach a decision that you can stick to, be willing to give a date by which you'll have made the decision—or at least a date by which you'll provide that date.
- Try to give advance notice to Js who travel with you that you are likely to change direction, even if it's just a warning when you set out that you may end up going in a different direction. This procedure can also work

for changes in business strategy and even for a change of mind.

- Try to appreciate a J's attention to schedules and time. If it appears that circumstances will prevent you from ending a meeting on time or getting to an appointment when you are expected, ask the J's permission to deviate from the plan.
- Focus on communicating expectations and clarifying intentions. Judgers who have some clue as to where you're heading are likely to be more comfortable with taking a circuitous route to get there.

Both Perceivers and Judgers need to articulate what will be helpful to them. Judgers can remind their Perceiving counterparts of their discomfort with postponing decisions indefinitely. Perceivers can remind Judgers that they'd like to leave matters open for as long as possible. Finally, the two can try to draw from the strengths of each in order to achieve a mutually successful outcome.

IT TAKES ALL KINDS

Although the MBTI helps us describe ourselves in terms of four letters, our behavior and communication styles are so much more than the sum of the descriptions of each of the letters. Each of the four preference categories—E/I, S/N, T/F, and J/P—interacts with the other three in complex and subtle ways that require entire books to explain and even more books to teach type identification. Every one of us is similar in some ways to people whose four letters match ours—and different in other ways. And each of us sees all other types through our own eyes, and we express what we see using a communication style that's natural to our particular type.

We are multidimensional beings. Type is an important dimension, but it's only one of many. Each of us brings tremendous strengths to our professional lives; and for each of us, a strength overdone can become a liability. If we allow ourselves to, we can find ways to draw from all of our strengths to succeed together in the workplace.

7

Understanding the Other Party's Perspective

I cringe when I see books and classes with titles like *Dealing with Difficult Customers* or *How to Cope with Difficult People*. The premise of these offerings, at least judging from the titles, is that it's the person who is difficult, not the situation the person is in. These titles suggest that the people deemed difficult are unjustified in their behavior and that those with whom they interact are in no way part of the problem.

The fact is that most people want to get along. They want to do their job and to be acknowledged and treated with respect. They want to meet their goals and to be seen as successful by those who control the direction of their career path. They want to go about their daily rounds with minimal hassle.

Granted, people sometimes behave in contrary ways, such as by being grouchy, argumentative, obstinate, withdrawn, or short-tempered (you can insert the adjective of your choice). People sometimes act in ways that make you wish they'd find the nearest bridge and jump off it. At times, you might even be willing to give them a gentle push. But are they truly difficult people? Rarely. Usually, they're people dealing with difficult, unusual, or stressful circumstances.

That was the case with Brian, an IT director who was judgmental, argumentative, and confrontational, at least during the first few months of our acquaintance. Gradually, though, this behavior abated and he became more relaxed and less contentious. Observing the "new" Brian during an informal meeting between the two of us, I commented on how much more relaxed he now seemed. He gave me a pained look and said he wanted me to know the cause of his previous behavior. He explained that the challenge of managing employees on two shifts in four locations had been much greater and more complex than he had anticipated when he took the job. Furthermore, he had had difficulty filling some key positions, and two longtime employees who had hoped to have his job had been overtly resisting his key initiatives. Compounding these pressures, customers were growling, dissatisfied with the service they were receiving.

That was the work side of Brian's story. He added that, on top of everything else, he'd been pursuing an advanced degree in the evenings and had barely had time for his coursework. His family resented the work and school schedules because it meant he was rarely home. Yikes!

As he adjusted to his responsibilities and the demanding schedules for both work and school, he was able to spend more time at home with his family and his manner softened. As I had suspected, his former aggressiveness reflected not who he really was, but who he was when he felt super-stressed. He'd been through an extremely tough time, and the stress manifested itself in the form of aggressive behavior. It could happen to anyone.

When people behave in contrary ways, it's natural to want to dismiss them as troublemakers. But a better approach, one with little to lose and much to gain, is to try to understand their perspective. Taking their viewpoint into account may help you choose more effective ways of interacting with them.

Ideally, you would simply ask the contrary person to describe his or her view of a particular situation. However, if you can't or prefer not to, then other methods may help you better understand the reasons behind confrontational or unco-operative behavior. This chapter describes methods you can use to reduce communication gaps between yourself and others, showing you how to consider what their perspective might be, and in the process, helping them to better understand your perspective as well.

ON USING A PERSPECTOSCOPE

When people act in a manner that strikes you as contrary or counterproductive, it could be that they're being deliberately obstreperous. But it could also be that their attitude and actions are as well-founded as your own, when considered in the context of their particular view of the world.

One way to gain an understanding of another person's per-spective is to use a clever tool I've invented called the Perspec-toscope, a device that looks much like a kaleidoscope. To operate it, you point it at the person whose perspective you'd like to better understand. Then you look through the eyepiece and, voilà, you see the world as that person sees it! In becoming aware of the person's attitudes, actions, and behavior, you can choose ways of interacting with the person that may be more effective than those you've used up to that point.

This perspective-enhancing tool would provide the ideal solution to the problem of how to see things as others see them, but at the moment, there's one slight obstacle in the way of its widespread use: Perspectoscopes don't exist. I'm hoping to announce a working prototype any day now, but until then, the next best thing is the imaginary Perspectoscope. Any of the several techniques that follow can serve as an imaginary Perspectoscope to help you gain insight into another person's perspective.

START BY SCRAPPING YOUR LABELS

Labels that identify a person's predominant personality type or attitude offer a handy means of characterizing that person. Unfortunately, labels can also distort perceptions and create obstacles to understanding. Take, for example, some critters I once saw at a zoo. There, pink as could be, were two kinds of flamingos. The taller birds, according to the sign, were *flamingos;* the shorter birds were called *lesser flamingos.* Imagine being named as an imperfect version of another member of your family! You may laugh, but how would you like to go through life as a lesser flamingo? That could very well affect how you view yourself, and it could certainly affect how others treat you (other flamingos, at least).

The Constraining Influence of Labels

What you call something—whether it's an animal, an object, or an idea—influences how you perceive it, refer to it, and interact with it. This label can reflect perceptions and attitudes that often have negative consequences.

For example, once you label someone as a "difficult customer," you are likely to see that customer as difficult thereafter. You'll be quicker to find evidence of difficult behavior to support your label, rather than evidence to support more positive attributes. You'll also be more likely to describe that person to others as a difficult customer rather than as a person with whom you have had a difficult interaction. And you may very well pay more attention and provide better service to other customers—those you don't view as difficult—than you do the difficult person, and, in the process, perhaps exacerbate the very situation that led you to declare the customer difficult in the first place.

The author and authority on creative thinking Edward de Bono calls this tendency to label others "our category habit" and warns us to be alert to its impact on our perception. As he points out, "All 'criminals' are seen first as criminal."[1] While labels can serve useful purposes, de Bono suggests that they contribute to constrained and clichéd thinking. To counter this tendency, he proposes that people challenge the labels by asking what they really mean: What does it mean to call a customer "difficult"? He suggests trying to do without the label as a means of looking at a situation in a new way and perhaps discovering what exists when the label is removed. For example, what else do you know about this individual? What other attributes can you use to describe the person?

As an alternative to doing away with the label, de Bono suggests establishing new labels to escape the distorting and polarizing effects of the old ones.[2] For example, how might your experience differ if you referred to the customer as a cooperative customer? Might the way you react to that person change? Might you actually start to see instances of cooperation that you might have previously dismissed or ignored? Contemplating how a change in labels would influence your view of the other party is an excellent way to begin using your imaginary Perspectoscope.

In *Conjoint Family Therapy*, Virginia Satir offers a clinical perspective of labeling that applies to organizational settings as well. She notes that when therapists label a person in terms of a particular condition, they may then base their prognosis on preconceived ideas about that condition and identify the person with the label. As a result, therapists may shut their

---

[1] Edward de Bono, *I Am Right—You Are Wrong* (London: Penguin Books, 1991), p. 43.

[2] Edward de Bono, *Lateral Thinking: Creativity Step by Step* (New York: Perennial, Harper & Row, 1990), pp. 214–17.

minds to the possibility of other interpretations that different evidence might point to. Satir cautions clinicians to view any labels that they use as applying *at the present time, in the present place, and in the current context.* As she emphasizes, "Future times, places and contexts may show something quite different."[3]

Transform Irate Customers by Transforming Yourself

When managers ask me how they can help their staff deal with irate customers, my first suggestion is that they banish that word "irate" from their vocabularies. Although customers sometimes express extreme irritation or display anger or outright hostility, to brand them as "irate" suggests customers who are unreasonable and whose displeasure is unfounded—that is, people who unjustifiably are a nuisance, an irritation, or an interruption. In truth, their grievances may be as valid and as worthy of your attention as the grievances of your other customers.

---

[3] Virginia Satir, *Conjoint Family Therapy* (Palo Alto, Calif.: Science and Behavior Books, 1983), p. 133.

In fact, it could be because their problems were treated as *not worthy of your attention* that these customers became angry in the first place. Banishing negative, generalizing terms, like the term "irate," is a critical step in reducing communication gaps with customers.

Along with "irate customers," try to discard other overused labels, such as "resistant employee," "problem team member," "demanding vendor," and "unreasonable manager." Then toss such derogatory descriptors as "slacker," "troublemaker," and "liar." Jerry Weinberg gets at the heart of the matter in *An Introduction to General Systems Thinking:* "In common speech, we apply the name 'liar' to anyone who tells a single lie—yet we have no word for someone who invariably tells the truth."[4]

Once you characterize people with labels like these, you may become less inclined to try to understand the reason for their behavior—circumstances that might drive anyone (even you!) to react in exactly the same way. And you are likely to respond to those you've already classified as problems with a defensive, get-rid-of-'em attitude—even when they're behaving in a meek and mellow manner.

When someone's behavior leads you to negatively characterize him or her, a technique known as "reframing" may be used to reorient your perspective so you see that behavior in a positive light. In *A Complaint Is a Gift,* authors Janelle Barlow and Claus Møller encourage service providers to reframe the notion of a complaining customer.[5] They note that a complaint is a customer's way of describing an expectation that has not been met. The complaint gives the receiving organization an opportunity to correct a problem and to create a satisfied customer.

---

[4] Gerald M. Weinberg, *An Introduction to General Systems Thinking: Silver Anniversary Edition* (New York: Dorset House Publishing, 2001), p. 207.

[5] Janelle Barlow and Claus Møller, *A Complaint Is a Gift: Using Customer Feedback As a Strategic Tool* (San Francisco: Berrett-Koehler Publishers, 1996), p. 11.

PONDER FACTORS THAT INFLUENCE OTHER PEOPLE'S BEHAVIOR

An excellent technique for examining other people's perspectives is to consider their "logic-bubbles." As described by Edward de Bono, a logic-bubble helps to explain why other people see things differently from how you see them. A logic-bubble, he explains, is that bubble of perception within which a person is acting. When you analyze someone's logic-bubble, you're asking: What could be causing that person to act that way? Under what kinds of circumstances could that person's actions be viewed as completely logical?[6] Contemplating those circumstances helps you to consider that person's behavior differently. And it might just lead you to admit that in similar circumstances, you'd act the same.

Note that de Bono isn't saying that people *always* act logically within their logic-bubble. This technique is just one of the many that de Bono offers to help you challenge your thinking. The idea is to avoid the trap of automatically classifying others as stupid, obstinate, or difficult simply because they don't see things your way. Instead, consider other possible explanations for their behavior.

When you consider other possible explanations, you are doing three positive things for yourself:

- You are avoiding the trap of automatically judging people based on what you see on the surface.
- You may come to see people in a different light, and thus become open to other ways of interacting with them.
- You may discover a way to apply a generous interpretation to their behavior.

A TECHNIQUE FOR CONSIDERING THE POSSIBILITIES

To identify as many reasons as possible for difficult behavior, select a person whom you and your colleagues have found

---

[6] Edward de Bono, *de Bono's Thinking Course* (New York: Facts On File, 1982), pp. 93–95.

troublesome. Brainstorm with them to generate a list of factors that could account for the person's behavior. Then, select one or two items from the list and discuss how you might interact differently with the person in light of the newly identified possible explanations for his or her behavior. Can you imagine a better working relationship as a result of such interactions? Do you hold the person in higher regard as a result of the possible explanations?

When I was a systems development manager, one of my project teams undertook the development of a highly complex system for a division run by a manager I'll call Mr. Tough Guy. Although the project was on time and on target, Mr. Tough Guy was far from appreciative. Indeed, he struck just about everyone on my staff as mean-spirited, arrogant, aggressive, distrustful, demanding, pushy, constantly on the offensive, and resistant to ideas that weren't his own. I wrote him off as an impossible customer and a truly nasty person.

Many years later, after I began writing and leading seminars, I wrote a case study using Mr. Tough Guy to illustrate the technique of considering other possibilities. I asked seminar participants to imagine what might have accounted for Mr. Tough Guy's behavior. Here are some of the possibilities they suggested:

- He feared a lack of control over his work.
- He was passionate about his work and unintentionally came on too strong.
- He felt uncomfortable about his limited technical knowledge, and used a belligerent style to mask his insecurity.
- He was really a sweet, lovable guy who just didn't realize how he came across.
- He was ambitious, and saw this behavior as the means to an end.
- He expected to receive a big bonus as the result of driving everyone hard.
- Beat-'em-up behavior was the norm at his previous company, and that style had become a habit.

- He modeled his behavior on that of his superior, Mr. High-Level Tough Guy.
- He was raised to believe that if you don't use a domineering style, people won't listen.
- His prior experience with systems development teams that missed deadlines left him highly distrustful.
- He had a troubled childhood that made him quick to find fault with others.
- Contending with his teenage children affected his behavior at work.
- He didn't like working with women and considered them a threat.

In other words, the possibilities were numerous, but many other possible reasons could have been listed. The point of the exercise is that although you may never know which ones truly account for someone's behavior, the process of acknowledging the possibilities will, if you're open-minded, lead you to explore alternative ways of interacting with that person.

Unfortunately, I didn't come to understand Mr. Tough Guy's behavior until long after the project ended (successfully, by the way) and he had moved to another division. One day, after no contact with him for many months, I saw him in the train station. He looked calm and at ease. He actually smiled—the first time I'd ever seen him smile—and he seemed pleased to see me. I asked him how things were going. "Fine," he said, "absolutely fine."

He then related his saga of the politics, pressure, and priority-juggling that plagued his previous division. Describing how he faced huge demands with unyielding deadlines mandated by external authorities, he told me that the system my team developed was only a tiny piece of what he'd been responsible for. The IT organization my department was part of didn't have the best reputation, and he confessed that he was genuinely scared that we wouldn't deliver on time. He said the stress he experienced was overwhelming and he was so happy to finally be in an area where he had some control over his existence.

Mr. Tough Guy? No way. I could now see that he had really been Mr. Nice Guy Under Pressure, a warm and friendly fellow who'd had to contend with circumstances that made him act tough. The entire time I was suffering in reaction to him, he was suffering as well, never realizing how his behavior affected everyone around him. His situation didn't justify inappropriate, aggressive behavior, but it did help to explain it.

If I'd thought back then to consider the possibilities, I might have changed the way I interacted with him to better understand his situation and to help relieve some of his (and my) stress. I might have tried harder to create a foundation of understanding, trust, and respect. At the least, I might have given him the benefit of the doubt.

Improving Relationships with Other Parties

I've found this technique of considering the possibilities invaluable in helping groups improve their relationships with other parties. To try the approach, get together with your team members and select a manager, a service provider, or a customer whose behavior irks you. Generate a list of things that could account for that person's behavior. As in the case of the manager formerly known as Mr. Tough Guy, the list might include a wide range of possibilities, such as corporate politics, lack of information, fear of failure, demanding deadlines, or a history of negative service experiences.

Then, as a group, consider alternative ways of working with the individual based on some of the possibilities you've come up with. Don't be surprised if, as a result, the annoying aspects of the person's behavior disappear, and the relationship becomes as positive as it was once negative.

That was the experience of a team that speculated that one possible factor causing an overly aggressive member of another team to act that way was a need to have his views acknowledged. Since their work required regular contact with this other team, they decided to give it a try. In subsequent interactions, team members gave him ample opportunity to offer his views, and they listened and acknowledged his perspective. Over the course of a few months, his aggressiveness diminished significantly; to their amazement, he started becoming attentive to the problems *they* were facing.

The result: The stress the team members had felt in their interactions with this individual vanished, and the negative relationship they had with him turned positive. That's the beauty of techniques like this: When you become more open to considering the perspective of others, they tend to become more open to considering yours as well.

Prerequisite to Considering the Possibilities

This technique works only if people are willing to *truly* consider the possibilities, rather than simply nodding an acknowledgment that they exist. Unfortunately, that willingness is not always forthcoming. In one particularly discouraging situation, a fellow named Al whom team members had found to be argumentative and nitpicking on two projects was given a lesser role on the next project. Although Al genuinely meant well, he sometimes came across as self-righteous, making points in a "my way or no way" tone. On the new project, Al's diminished role and his reputation for being an impediment to productivity caused his ideas to be discounted even when they were on target. Having labeled him as difficult, Al's teammates closed their ears and minds to his ideas.

For the duration of the project, Al's teammates were quicker to find fault with his ideas than with the ideas of other team members, even when the same ideas were voiced. The unfortunate short-term result was that the project experienced numerous squabbles and struggles that his recommendations could have prevented. The long-term ramifications were even more serious: The project fell woefully short in selling its benefits to prospective customers, resulting in a financial loss to the company. Sadly, this situation is hardly unique; few people excel at honoring the sound ideas of someone on whom they've heaped negative labels. And in this situation, neither party ever stopped to consider the other's logic-bubble.

It's not necessary to wait for conflict to erupt before you consider another party's logic-bubble. The approach can be applied effectively in almost any situation in which individuals or teams need to interact to achieve shared goals—that is, it is universal in its usefulness.

OBSERVE POSSIBILITIES FROM DIFFERENT PERSPECTIVES

Another way to consider the possibilities is to examine multiple perspectives. As a group of IS managers discovered in an exercise designed to disclose the nature of the adversarial relationship between their division and their internal customers, the results can be enlightening. In the exercise, managers were divided into two groups. Members of each group were asked to work together to prepare two lists: The first group of managers was instructed to list adjectives that describe how they viewed themselves and then to list how they viewed their customers. The second group was asked to imagine themselves in the role of their customers and to prepare their two lists from their new perspective: that is, they needed to describe how they (as customers) viewed themselves and how they (as customers) viewed the IS staff. The managers in the first group described themselves:

> We (IS) view ourselves as: responsive, technically competent, having limited resources, more aware of corporate needs than our customers, hardworking, service-oriented, essential, inundated with requests, skilled, trying too hard to please, excessively structured, inadequately managed.

> We (IS) view our customers as: unrealistic about system complexity, having a tendency to over-automate, unable to specify requirements accurately, demanding, unforgiving, needing services, not knowing what they want, not being satisfied with what they get, thinking everything is easy.

The managers in the second group, acting as customers, described their role:

> We (in the role of customers) view ourselves as: responsive, responsible to our external customers, wanting a good and responsive product from IS, adaptive to business trends, knowledgeable about our work, compromised by the inability of IS to meet our needs, trying to do our job, forced to depend on IS more than we would like, under outside pressure, insufficiently recognized, caught up in politics.
>
> We (in the role of customers) view IS as: incompetent, overpaid, unresponsive to our needs, behind schedule, overly complex, insensitive, concerned only with technology, quick to say no, slow to deliver, poor communicators, bogged down in paperwork.

The lists proved that human nature influences our ability to be objective in an adversarial setting. *Both groups* viewed themselves in positive terms and saw the other side in negative terms. You are likely to discover the same proclivities if you try a similar exercise with your own staff. Try to look through your customers' eyes: You will undoubtedly identify much that is complimentary but if you see yourself as incompetent, insensitive, and unresponsive, you might want to take immediate action to understand the source of these perceptions and what you need to do to change them.

In *Getting It Done: How to Lead When You're Not in Charge,* authors Roger Fisher and Alan Sharp suggest a similar but more structured approach, which they call "escaping your biases." Fisher and Sharp suggest looking at important issues from three different positions: your own side, the other side, and a neutral third party's side.[7]

---

[7] Roger Fisher and Alan Sharp, with John Richardson, *Getting It Done: How to Lead When You're Not in Charge* (New York: HarperBusiness, 1998), pp. 85–88.

From your own perspective, ask yourself questions about how things look to you: your opinions and biases, the data available to you, your priorities, your emotions, and so on. Fisher and Sharp caution: "You want to be aware of the extent to which looking from your position shapes the data."[8]

The second position investigates the view of key people with whom you interact. What are their worries, standard approaches, and biases? Imagine how it would feel to actually be that person. What decisions would you (as that other person) have to make to go along with your own perspective (as yourself)? Fisher and Sharp state that adopting this perspective will help you become aware of different aspects of the situation you're both in.

The third viewpoint is one Fisher and Sharp call "high in the stands." This perspective helps you imagine how the situation might look to a spectator—that is, to someone who is not actively involved. This "fly on the wall" perspective helps you to stand back and see the big picture, giving you a better chance to consider information that you could miss if you focus strictly on your immediate involvement.

BECOME TRULY EMPATHETIC

As these techniques illustrate, it's not necessary to personally experience what another person has experienced in order to appreciate that person's perspective.

Some years ago, I viewed a televised program about Dr. George Blackburn, a Harvard professor and leading obesity doctor who wondered how feasible a prescribed daily diet and exercise regimen was for his seriously overweight patients. Like his peers, Dr. Blackburn had routinely given his patients advice long considered sound, such as: "Take a walk every day." "Limit your intake." "Use the stairs instead of the elevator." "Ride an exercise bicycle."

Curious about how readily his patients could adhere to his advice, Dr. Blackburn designed what he called an Empathy Suit, a cumbersome outfit that distributed twenty-five pounds

---

[8] Ibid., p. 85.

of additional weight over a person's frame. Wearing the outfit, he tried to follow the advice he'd so frequently given to patients. He discovered that just getting around was difficult, and that even the simplest form of exercise left him breathless. For the first time, he realized that his instructions, rather than helping overweight patients to lose weight, were probably discouraging to them and demeaning as well.

The doctor began to use the Empathy Suit in his work with primary-care physicians, encouraging them to wear the suit so they could try to walk a mile in their patients' shoes. The result: They couldn't. Armed with this new awareness of the reality of their patients' lives, doctors changed both their advice and their empathy to acknowledge their patients' reality.[9]

What would it be like if more of us could spend time in an Empathy Suit—one specifically designed to help us better understand the reality of those we so easily dismiss or discount? Whether the suit gave us insight into another person's physical reality, personal plights, or professional pressures, the experience would help us to better understand the context behind that behavior.

This notion of an Empathy Suit nicely complements Edward de Bono's logic-bubbles. The logic-bubble approach asks: What factors drive another person to function as he or she does? The Empathy Suit approach asks: How would it feel to actually be that person?

Unfortunately, none of us has a closet full of Empathy Suits that we can put on so as to better appreciate the plight of others. But sometimes, circumstances in the workplace enable us to achieve the next best thing. In *Managing Expectations,* I describe the experience I had as a manager striving to improve the negative attitude held by a group of internal customers about IT. As an experiment, I set aside space in our department within which customer team members could conduct acceptance testing on a series of major modifications we had made to their system.

---

[9] See www.usatoday.org/life/health/diet/lhdie144.htm and other Web listings for more information on Empathy Suits.

Early on the first day of the experiment, the members of the customer team showed up, eager to complete the job and depart. However, as they worked side by side with us, they came to see how readily what they had viewed as simple changes could have a significant impact on the rest of the system. They began to appreciate the complexity of the debugging process, and saw firsthand the seriousness with which my staff members tackled the job of making their highly complex system work accurately. What started as a simple testing experiment resulted in our customers' gaining insight into our world, and caused them to change their attitude about IT itself.[10]

In *Project Retrospectives*, author and retrospective facilitator Norm Kerth describes witnessing a similarly enlightening epiphany experienced by a project's vice president when he visited the retrospective site. Eyeing a project-task chart that spanned one entire meeting-room wall, he asked whether he could have the chart when the retrospective ended. He explained that he wanted the chart because it so superbly communicated what goes into a complex project. He added that the chart would enable him to provide better support to software initiatives whose value he had previously underestimated and then commented, "This shows me that building professional software is much more complicated than what we were taught in my college courses." For nearly a year thereafter, the chart was on prominent display in the corporate boardroom.[11]

There's nothing quite like firsthand experience to enable a person to empathize with others in difficult circumstances. When a knee injury forced me to hobble around on crutches for a month, I came to see the world differently. Bending over to pick something up became impossible. The distance between two sides of a room seemed like miles, and molehills literally

---

[10] Naomi Karten, *Managing Expectations: Working with People Who Want More, Better, Faster, Sooner, NOW!* (New York: Dorset House Publishing, 1994), pp. 137–38.

[11] Norman L. Kerth, *Project Retrospectives: A Handbook for Team Reviews* (New York: Dorset House Publishing, 2001), p. 127. For more information, see www.retrospectives.com.

became mountains. My most stressful experience occurred when a hotel I was staying in sounded the fire alarm and a loudspeaker warned against using the elevator, forcing me to place a panicky call for help. Fortunately, help came quickly, and soon thereafter, it was found to be a false alarm, but I came to *truly* appreciate what people for whom such a condition is not temporary experience daily. I'd much rather have gained that insight by using a Perspectoscope.

CONSIDER *THEIR* CASE IN MAKING YOURS

There are numerous occasions in which you can use your imaginary Perspectoscope to better understand the perspectives of others, such as when you're striving

- to persuade
- to dissuade
- to make a sale
- to address a complaint
- to resolve a dispute

The following sections suggest approaches you can use in these situations to understand and accommodate another party's perspective. In the process, a win-win relationship can be created in which both parties achieve their goals.

Being Persuasive

Have you ever made what you believed to be an irrefutable case, only to discover that those in charge refuse to see it your way? Before labeling these people as difficult, resistant, or stubborn, consider whether your inability to persuade them could be because you presented your case without taking their perspective into account. Before you can get people to see things your way, you must first try to see things their way. Here are some tips on how to do just that:

> *Clarify in your own mind what you are seeking.* People often grouse about a lack of management support or executive sponsorship, but when I ask them what they mean, they sometimes have trouble being more specific. In advancing your case, think about what *you* want. Perhaps you want a 15 percent increase in funding to be used for certain specified benefits? Do you seek the authority to proceed with a high-payoff project? Would you like management intervention to help you deal with a relentless squeaky wheel? It's not enough to demand more of whatever you feel you need. You must be able to articulate precisely what you want and need. Don't expect others to see it your way if you don't see it your-self.

> *Focus on the other party's WIIFM.* Pronounced "wiffum," the acronym stands for What's In It For Me. WIIFM means that if you want to be persuasive, you need to articulate how other parties will benefit from your proposal. Take time to understand what's in their logic-bubbles: their priorities, fears, and concerns. If you can't

yet say how the other party will benefit, it might be better to pay another visit to your drawing board.

Remember the importance of timing. Certain times are less conducive to successful persuasion than others. For example, someone who has just returned from vacation to find an in-box over-flowing with demands requiring immediate action may not be disposed to appreciate the merits of your case. Similarly, knowing whether someone is a morning person or an afternoon person could help you time a visit appropriately. Finally, when you sense stress all around you, it might be best to refrain from submitting pro-posals for which you'd prefer an answer other than "Absolutely, positively NO!"

Consider what you're willing to give in return for what you get. In other words, what's it worth to you? What are you willing to do to get what you want? What concessions or compromises are you willing to make? Be prepared for a certain amount of give and take. Nice though it might be, you can't count on having everything your way. Furthermore, if you're not willing to do a little giving in order to do the getting, it may be a sign that the issue isn't all that important to you.

Don't expect immediate acceptance of your idea. If your proposal requires a commitment in time, effort, or resources from the other party, or a major change (or perhaps even a minor change) in someone else's thinking or functioning, it's unrealistic to expect an instantaneous go-for-it. Many people need time to accept new ideas. Recognizing this fact can keep your frustration meter from veering into the red zone. Give your ideas a chance to take root and grow. Be per-sistent in making your case, but above all, be patient.

Seek realistic outcomes. You may not be able to get exactly the outcome you want, no matter how convincing your case. So, your best bet may be to seek outcomes that will move you in the right direction, even if they don't take you all the way to your target. Remember, getting some of what you want now is better than getting everything you want a century from now. By then, you'll probably be looking forward to retirement.

Being Dissuasive

It's hard to persuade people to do what you want them to do, but it can be even harder to *dissuade* them from doing what *they* want to do. Say, for example, that you want to dissuade a higher-up—a chap named Mr. DoItMyWay (DoIt, for short)—from purchasing a product you firmly believe to be a poor choice. Suppose, as well, that DoIt is sufficiently high up to make the purchase without your approval, or anyone else's. You, however, are responsible for arranging the purchase and supporting DoIt's use of the product.

How do you dissuade DoIt from making a colossal mistake? Ideally, you need only present the facts—that the product is nonstandard, incompatible, overpriced, buggy, and miserably documented—and DoIt will respond favorably and gratefully to the exquisite logic of your argument. But if that doesn't work, the following suggestions may help:

No matter how compelling your case, remember that it's your *case.* Resist the urge to heap negatives on DoIt's decision, or you'll discourage him from communicating further with you. If that happens, not only will you not get another chance to sway him about *this* decision, you also won't get to have your say the *next* time DoIt makes a decision that concerns you. If you must present your view, do so in a low-key fashion. But first show that you have an open mind by expressing interest in DoIt's decision.

Try to learn why DoIt made that particular choice. His decision may strike you as ill-considered, but the reasoning behind the decision may have been sound when considered in terms of DoIt's logic-bubbles. For example, the decision may have been based on how things were done at DoIt's previous company, or perhaps a respected peer recommended the product. Possibly a vendor touted its strengths and somehow forgot to mention its 1,001 glaring weaknesses. It's even possible that DoIt is implementing a decision foisted on him by *his* superior. So, ask some questions such as those suggested below—and try to be genuinely curious, rather than suspicious:

- How did you arrive at this particular choice?
- What alternatives have you had a chance to consider?
- How do you anticipate using this product initially?
- Do you have any thoughts on how you'll be using it a year from now?
- What sorts of things have you heard from others who have used this product?

Analyze how DoIt sees things. To change someone's mind about a strongly held opinion, look through your imaginary Perspectoscope, and try to see things as that person does. You may know positively that the desired product will wreak havoc and require endless support, but forget that for a moment and consider what you know about DoIt. For example, what issues matter to him? What must he accomplish to be successful in his job? What makes him feel good or important or powerful? Now put yourself in his place and ask: What would make me abandon my current viewpoint for this vastly different one?

Consider DoIt's communication preferences. Focus not only on the issues, but also on how you'll present those issues. How does DoIt like to receive information? For example, if he likes information in written form, write up your key points. If he's enchanted by multicolored charts, prepare some in his favorite colors. If he likes snappy, ten-minute presentations, give him one. Remember, in dissuading someone of a favored approach, how you make your case may be as important as the case itself.

Allow DoIt to save face. Some people cling to their viewpoint because of pride, ego, upbringing, or the absolute certainty that they are right. If you want DoIt to change his mind, you have to make it palatable for him to do so. Try to identify people whom DoIt respects but who support your particular viewpoint. Their gentle prodding may help sway DoIt, while sparing him from feeling that he's caving in to you.

Practice infinite patience. You won't have the luxury of time if DoIt wants to complete the purchase by tea time. But if the purchase is to be made some time in the future, present your case a little at a time. Don't expect DoIt to change his mind overnight. Even if you're ultimately successful in influencing him, achieving that success could take weeks, months, or even a year or more, so be gently persistent. DoIt may not hear your points initially, but if you drop a hint here and a tip there, over time your ideas may seep in so that DoIt's thinking eventually comes around to your own. If this happens, be generous and let him think it was his idea.

If DoIt proceeds with the purchase and it creates a million headaches exactly as you predicted, resist the temptation to shout, "I told you so!" Instead, do a personal retrospective of your dissuasion strategy and plan how you might handle things differently next time.

Making the Sale

Often when we communicate, we are trying to sell something, such as a product or a service—or an idea, a standard, or an opportunity. I'm reminded of a frustrated vendor who wrote a letter to a trade publication to complain about managers who were "determined not to see the merits" of his product. In his view, his customers were wholly responsible for his failure to sell. Instead of complaining that the managers didn't see his perspective, he might have spent his time more productively by trying harder to see their point of view. Consider the following factors the next time you try to make a sale:

> *Understand past history.* Often, there's more to a situation than meets the eye. For example, some people are leery of buying because they've been burned in the past. Take the time to learn about their history and take their negative experiences into account when you present your proposal. Ask what would need to change in order to complete the sale (anticipating, of course, that the answer could be "You!").

> *Find relevance.* Be cautious about presenting benefits in terms that are irrelevant to the buyer. What's important to the buyer may be very different from what's important to you. It's your job to understand these differences, and to frame the benefits accordingly.

> *Appreciate how people react to new things.* Some people are threatened by anything new or different. Hitting such a person over the head with the benefits of what you're selling will get you nothing but a person with a sore head. Instead, focus on the similarities between what you're

selling and what is already familiar to the person.

Give credit to others. Some people are willing to buy provided that they are credited with having made the decision to buy. Therefore, avoid presenting the sale as if you alone initiated it. Instead, try to reorient the transaction so that it becomes the buyer's idea. Remember that you may be more successful in getting the outcome you want if you're willing to "allow" a sale to happen without getting credit for "making" it happen.

Sell by not selling. Some people prefer to buy rather than be sold to, and so the harder you try to sell, the more likely you are to fail. With such people, your job as salesperson is to plant the seeds, so as to trigger interest, curiosity, and the eagerness to know more. When the buyer makes the decision to proceed, you won't have to say another word.

Allow time for decision-making. Some people simply need time in which to make decisions. The bigger the decision, the longer the sale will take. For certain individuals, every decision is a big one and there's not a thing you can do to expedite the process. The key is patient persistence. Don't give up, but don't be pushy either.

Avoid miscommunication. Consider whom you are communicating with before making your pitch. For example, be careful not to get overly technical when speaking with a nontechnical person or highbrow when talking with someone who is very down-to-earth. Make sure you first build a relationship or at least seek some level of human connection before seeking the sale.

Identify pertinent parties. Sometimes, the obstacle isn't the buyer, but the people above and around the buyer who also need to approve the decision. In other words, your buyer may need to do some selling before you can make your sale. Find out how you can help the potential buyer prepare a persuasive case to present to other decision-makers.

Addressing Complaints

If you handle customer complaints, remember that you have the power to influence a positive outcome. Your response to the grievance and to the person voicing it can determine whether the interaction results in an amicable resolution or a prolonged battle. Here are tips to keep in mind:

> *Don't interrupt.* Sometimes, the most powerful communication technique is silence. When a customer is voicing a complaint, don't say a word; just listen, and take in what you're hearing as a legitimate expression of the person's perspective. While sounding off, people sometimes defuse their own anger or figure out their own solutions. Often, they reveal what they'd like the solution to be—and it may be simpler than any solution you might have offered. Listening to the entire grievance gives you information to work with as well as more time in which to consider your response.

> *Demonstrate that you've really listened.* People often protest that their views aren't being heard. Avoid this reaction by restating or summarizing what you heard, emphasizing the points that seemed most important. Ask for confirmation that you understood the intended message. If the person knows you were listening and that you care about the message, he or she is more likely to find your ideas acceptable.

Resist the temptation to disagree. Not disagreeing is even harder than not interrupting, especially if you feel you've been misunderstood or unfairly accused. It's natural to want to defend your position, but if you challenge the validity of the customer's perspective, you risk escalating the argument. People who express complaints are telling you how the view looks from within their logic-bubble. Accept that perception as real and valid for them, even if you see the situation differently.

If the complaint is valid, say so. Customers are so used to hearing others deny responsibility for problems that you can surprise them by saying, "Yes, you're absolutely right." When a repairman came to our house on a service call, he agreed that my husband or I could have fixed the problem days earlier had we only been given accurate information by his company's service department. The repairman apologized and said that his job often included "protecting the customer from the company." Hearing his apology made a crummy situation a little less so. Just as anger often feeds anger, reasonableness begets reasonableness, paving the way to working together to seek a resolution.

Personalize your attention. It's hard to ooze enthusiasm for resolving a problem when you've just heard your three-hundredth complaint of the week. But that's not the fault of the latest person with a complaint. Therefore, treat every customer as if he or she is your most important customer, and never minimize the seriousness of the problem. Use *you* phrases, such as, "Let me check on that for you," or "I'll see what I can find out for you."

Do something. The person who has a complaint needs to feel that you share his or her concern and that an effort is being made to solve the problem. Fortunately, many complaints don't call for a grand solution, so start by suggesting a simple solution. Offering to do a little—*and then doing it*—will earn you far more credibility in the long run than promising to do something large and falling short.

Resolving Disputes

Think about some of the disputes you've been involved in, especially the real doozies. It's a special skill to be able to gracefully terminate disputes without anyone getting a black eye or a bruised ego. Even better, of course, is to keep the matter from becoming a full-blown dispute in the first place. Processing the dispute using the Satir Interaction Model described in Chapter 4 is one way to do this. In addition, the next time you find yourself embroiled in a divisive difference of opinion, you might try some of the following strategies:

> *Listen carefully to the other person.* With disputes, as with complaints, listening is key. If your goal is to trigger the other person's anger, then inter-rupting after every five words will do the trick. Otherwise, clamp down on your vocal cords and let the person state his or her case—difficult though it may be when you hear outrageous claims being made about you, your work, or those you care about. Listen with the genuine intention of trying to understand the other person's perspective. You'll gain a much better sense of the person's concerns. And different though those views might be from your own, to the person who holds them, they're real, valid, and important.

> *Ask for clarification.* Don't assume that you understand everything the other person is saying. In a heated situation, with an overlay of emotion, it takes triple the effort to really hear

what the other person is saying. Ask questions to clarify your understanding of both terms and ideas, and to avoid serious misinterpretation. Asking questions shows your good intentions and gives you time to digest what you've heard before responding.

Present your case calmly. Don't become a master intimidator. Make your points calmly and concisely so that the facts are not overshadowed by your demeanor or by a negative attitude. Watch both your tone of voice and your body language—speaking in a blaming tone or with blaming gestures can make the other party not at all disposed to considering your ideas. In fact, the more successful you are at speaking in a calm, congruent tone that acknowledges the validity of both perspectives, the more receptive the other party will be to what you have to say.

Explain, don't argue. If you're puzzled or upset by something the other person has said or done, resist the temptation to hurl accusations. Instead, explain your reaction. Providing an explanation is important: Disputes often arise because of an innocent misunderstanding that can be easily rectified. If you can clear up the confusion, you may even discover that you're both on the same side of the issue.

Let the other person save face. Although the urge to humiliate can sometimes be strong, people are more likely to accept your viewpoint if you don't make it embarrassing for them to do so. Once you scream, "You're an idiot!" loud enough to be heard on Jupiter, it's a lot harder to reorient the discussion so that the other person can save face. You may not agree with the other person's ideas, but try to respect his or her right to have an opinion that differs from your own. See this as an opportunity to practice being empathetic.

Rare is the situation in which you can't find merit in the other person's views. If you can avoid being vehemently one-sided, you're more likely to resolve the dispute to your mutual satisfaction.

Swap places. Trading places with someone else provides a way for both of you to put on an Empathy Suit. For some agreed-upon duration, discuss the issues as if each of you were the other person. Using your imaginary Perspectoscope, try to peer into each other's mind, and then explain the other person's viewpoint as if it were your own. Another approach is to get together with colleagues and create a scenario in which you take on the role of that other person and ask someone else to stand in as you. Or simply imagine yourself as that person, and make a case for his or her perspective. Don't be surprised if you actually begin to see the other person's perspective in ways you hadn't been able to imagine previously. With awareness of that perspective, you may see a new way of presenting your ideas—one that takes that perspective into account.

Seek a win-win solution. You're more likely to find a win-win solution if you actively seek one. Even if you are adamant that your position is the only acceptable one, look for ways for the other person to benefit. If you're determined to fight till you win, you may succeed, but you may also pay a price. The grapevine has a way of turning today's victories into tomorrow's losses. What does it say about you if the only way you can succeed is by bludgeoning the other person into submission? If you are both willing to give a little, together you can gain a lot.

TRY SOMETHING DIFFERENT

If reacting automatically or at a lofty decibel level has been your style, or if you have habitually dismissed or discounted those whose behavior you've found troublesome, dare to try new behavior. Be alert the next time someone provokes you. If today is an average day, you may not have to wait long. When you feel provoked, take a deep breath and count to one hundred. Then, with your imaginary Perspectoscope in hand, use the ideas discussed in this chapter, and keep on using them until they become second nature. If you treat people with respect, and adopt a collaborative, mutually beneficial manner, even when you disagree with them or are puzzled by their behavior, you'll save yourself a lot of trouble. In the process, you may find that your differences aren't so major after all.

8

The Care and Feeding of Relationships

At the start of a project code-named FixNet, the ten members of the team were enthusiastic about working together. But as the project progressed, tensions started to surface. One gnawing grievance was that the geographically dispersed team members communicated primarily by e-mail and some team members were convinced that the others weren't reading their messages.

For example, the team leader sent out biweekly updates to everyone on the team. When team members questioned matters that had already been explained in the updates, he complained that if people weren't going to read the updates, then he wasn't going to send them. One team member, when asked about a written procedure she had e-mailed to team members a few weeks earlier, groused, "If nobody read my last message, will another one that repeats the same procedure be any more likely to be noticed?"

If one or two people voice a particular complaint, it may be an isolated occurrence. But if three or more people express similar grievances, the situation bears looking into—and sooner rather than later. Nevertheless, although several team members had expressed frustration about their messages going unread, none of them noticed any overall pattern. Fortunately, however, members of this team had selected one of their teammates to observe their communication processes and to provide feedback.

Before unrest about unread messages could escalate, the observer noticed the pattern of complaints and informed the team so that teammates could address it openly. Several positive results ensued: First, team members acknowledged that they'd been lax about reading messages and made a commitment to read and heed future project e-mail. Second, they designated one team member to devise an on-line catalog of procedures and to notify everyone by e-mail when new entries had been posted. Third, team members laughingly agreed that only those who read, digested, and retained every single message could demand perfection of the rest.

An appointed, and therefore "official," observer can help groups notice and combat potentially damaging communication patterns. The role of such an observer is described in this chapter, and is critical in the care and feeding of relationships.

Clearly, not even a rock-solid foundation can guarantee everlasting freedom from relationship problems. Although an appreciation of one another's communication style and perspective is important, it is not enough. Relationships take work; they require mindful attention on an ongoing basis. This chapter focuses on communication techniques designed to help groups maintain a strong foundation and create a caring culture.

GIVE THANKS

As children, we learn to say "please" and "thank you." As adults, we sometimes forget the importance of these common courtesies. Yet what could be simpler? Many things, as it turns out, because we can easily fall into the habit of giving thanks-free thank-you's. Consider the following situations:

> *The "to whom it may concern" thank-you.* A program chairperson invited several well-known speakers to fly to an out-of-the-way city to speak

at her conference, and she requested that they waive their standard speaking fee. Eight speakers agreed to her terms, with the result that the conference was a major success. Afterward, the program chair e-mailed a single three-line message to all eight. The message began: "Thank you for participating in our conference." No names, no individual greetings, no indication that what each speaker had contributed had any particular value.

A thank-you ought to be personalized. Given that only eight speakers were involved, the program chair could easily have sent each person a separate message, in which, at the very least, she addressed each by name. There is, after all, a difference between the generic "Thank you for participating in our conference," (whoever you are) and the minimally personalized "Scott, thank you for participating in our conference." And there is an even bigger difference between a generic message and one in which details specific to the individual's contribution are noted. How much more acknowledged Scott and the other speakers might have felt to be personally appreciated, rather than to be part of an impersonal list.

The sideways thank-you. A company event to which I was invited included a recognition ceremony for people who had been involved in a complex and highly successful implementation. I was pleased that the IT director, John, had planned this acknowledgment, because so often, management views the successful completion of a tough job by employees as nothing more than "what they are paid to do." In other words, their effort is not worthy of any special attention.

Unfortunately, though, instead of looking directly at each person and saying, for example, "Sarah, thank you for the role you played in designing the customer database," or "Sarah, your role involved designing the customer database, and I thank you for your efforts," John looked at the audience and said, "Sarah's role was to design the customer database."

The difference between these expressions of gratitude is monumental. Instead of speaking *to* each person, John spoke to the audience *about* each person. He understood the value of public recognition, but his tribute would have had greater impact if he had expressed it *directly and personally* to the individual who earned it.

The clueless thank-you. A colleague of mine forwarded to me this e-mail message sent by a senior vice president to his managers and directors:

"I want to congratulate you for your superb work in recent months. I hope you will pass along my deep appreciation and personally thank those who report to you. I'm excited about our people and the performance the company has experienced through their efforts. We have a great year ahead. Let's maintain our momentum."

As positive as this message sounds, very few people felt truly thanked by the senior vice president. The message might have been effective if it had been part of a culture of appreciation—but it wasn't. In this company, the culture had fostered a prolonged pattern of *non*-appreciation, made worse by a reorganization in which employee concerns were treated as irrelevant. In such a context, an isolated, long overdue, impersonal thank-you, combined with a remotely issued pep talk, worsened morale and hastened turnover.

If you want people to feel *thanked* by your thanks, create a caring culture in which individuals are acknowledged personally and directly.

Express Appreciations

One effective way to convey your sincerity when thanking someone is by expressing an "appreciation." During the frantic workday, people sometimes notice only what goes wrong. Offering an appreciation is a powerful way to focus on the positive, by acknowledging someone's efforts and commenting on them, especially when you do so in a group setting, such as at a team meeting. Some teams devote a segment of their team meetings to appreciations.

As with a thank-you, an appreciation should be direct and personal, such as: "I appreciate you, Jonathan, because . . ." or "I appreciate you, Sandra, for . . ." Find the wording that's most natural for you, such as, "I really liked the way you . . ." or "I was so impressed when you . . ." or "It was great the way you . . ." In other words, when you give an appreciation, speak directly to the person you wish to acknowledge rather than speaking to others *about* the person.

Appreciations don't need to be reserved for significant undertakings. You can give one for anything, whether large or small, and whether critical to the team's efforts or simply a kind gesture. Appreciations among team members might include, "I appreciate you, Sandra, for your great advice when the network went down," as well as, "I appreciate you, Jonathan, for bringing me a snack when I couldn't get to lunch."

If you aren't accustomed to giving appreciations, you might be surprised at how satisfying it is to do so. Seeing people light up in response to your acknowledgment can be a delightful experience. When I expressed my appreciation to one member of a team for outstanding work on behalf of her project, she responded, "I'm startled to receive such glowing praise. This is the first time anyone has commented on what I've done, and it feels very, very nice. Thank you." The impact an appreciation can have on its recipient usually far exceeds the effort of giving it.

Sadly, many people are unable to graciously accept simple appreciations. One reason is that they have been unaccustomed to receiving appreciations at any point in their professional lives, and so when one is expressed, they don't know how to handle it. Other factors that may make it difficult for people to accept appreciations include a person's upbringing, past experience, a conviction that he or she is unworthy of attention, or the misguided notion that it's immodest to accept compliments. For such people, accepting an appreciation is uncomfortable, and they tend to respond by downplaying the compliment, saying, "Oh, it was nothing." However, a self-deprecating response discounts a sincere expression of appreciation. Therefore, if you are the recipient of an appreciation, accept it as such, and use the proper form for receiving it. It goes like this: "Thank you."

The Power of Appreciations

Never underestimate the power of a sincerely expressed appreciation as a technique for improving relationships. Just how powerful this technique can be was especially apparent near the end of a session I lead with a group that was in chaos, the aftermath of the recent merger of two groups. I invited people to offer appreciations to each other. Given their troubled history, I would have understood if they had felt reluctant to "go public." Yet not only did numerous people do so; some offered deeply felt appreciations. One participant looked at his former manager and described, with a quiver in his voice, how much he appreciated the boss's strong support when they were working together. He said this appreciation was long overdue. I thought he meant he should have given it last week or last month—until he said he'd been thinking about it for three years!

There's no need to wait for a group gathering to give an appreciation. Do it as soon as the thought strikes you. It's a wonderful habit, one that helps a relationship withstand the inevitable trials and tribulations it faces. I firmly believe that stress in the workplace would diminish if people would make a habit of giving appreciations.

Even if appreciations aren't part of your team's or your organization's culture, you can set an example simply by saying, "Thanks. I really appreciate you for that!" whenever someone does something that pleases you. If we each do this once, and then again and again, others will soon start doing the same. Together, we will set the stage for a more caring and productive workplace.

Appreciations of Self

The one very deserving person most people don't think to appreciate is the one they see when they look in the mirror. As a facilitator, I sometimes invite people to offer an appreciation to themselves: "I appreciate myself for . . ."

Self-appreciation is easier for some people to acknowledge than for others. At one end of the spectrum are people who are comfortable with self-appreciation; they know their contributions, they feel good about themselves, and they need little prompting to acknowledge their contributions publicly. At the other end of the continuum are people who have great difficulty in appreciating themselves. The possible reasons are many, and some of the reasons run deep. Except in professionally facilitated contexts, coaxing someone into expressing a self-appreciation isn't wise. However, people who seem incapable of expressing self-appreciation might be encouraged to think about what they appreciate themselves for and to write one appreciation a day, a week, or a month in a private journal.

Think about yourself now: What have you done that deserves your appreciation? The list may be longer than you anticipate.

CONDUCT A TEMPERATURE READING

The offering of appreciations, as I've described here, originated as part of a highly effective communication technique. Called a Temperature Reading, this technique was created by the family therapist Virginia Satir to help team members reduce tensions, strengthen connections, and surface information, ideas, and feelings that enable them to interact more productively.[1] For teams that work under pressure, a Temperature Reading is a particularly useful technique.

Some groups devote a portion of every staff meeting to a Temperature Reading; others conduct one at monthly intervals, at key project milestones, or at the conclusion of a project. Any member of the group can serve in the role of facilitator, which requires no special training. In some organizations, team members take turns facilitating, so that each gains experience at this skill.

A Temperature Reading consists of five segments, described in the five numbered sections that follow, and can take anywhere from fifteen minutes to an hour or more, depending on the size of the team and its circumstances.

Segment #1: Appreciations

In this first segment, anyone who would like to give an appreciation does so, using the direct and personalized format: "I appreciate you for . . ." In some groups, the person giving the appreciation asks the person to be appreciated to come to the front of the room and then gives the appreciation; however, as long as the two are in eye contact, an across-the-room appreciation is fine.

If time doesn't permit a full Temperature Reading, focus on this first segment and skip the rest.

Segment #2: New Information

This second segment provides teammates with an opportunity to share information. Often, some members of a team may have information that other team members may need to know or may find interesting. Information-sharing reinforces group connections, especially when work responsibilities drive people in many different directions.

---

[1] Virginia Satir et al., *The Satir Model: Family Therapy and Beyond* (Palo Alto, Calif.: Science and Behavior Books, 1991), pp. 309–16.

Anyone with information to share can offer it during this segment. For example, a team leader may mention an upgrade that has been planned but has not yet been announced. A team member may describe a technique he or she learned in a recent class. Another team member may want to share information about a visit to a remotely located team member.

Segment #3: Puzzles

In some work settings, it's risky to admit that you don't understand something. The Puzzles segment provides a sanctioned opportunity to mention something that has confused or puzzled you, and to request an explanation. Questions about scheduling changes, team responsibilities, and rumors are often brought up during this segment, and the very act of raising these issues rather than letting them fester helps to avoid future problems. Often, people come to realize for the first time that others share their puzzle. Lengthy explanations are best deferred until later on, so as not to bog down the Temperature Reading.

When I facilitate a Temperature Reading, I deliberately place the New Information segment before the Puzzles segment because the sharing of information may resolve an issue that would otherwise be presented during Puzzles.

Segment #4: Complaints with Recommendations

Most workplaces suppress or discourage complaints. By contrast, this segment explicitly invites complaints. However, to keep the session from lapsing into a gripe session, the person voicing the complaint must offer a recommendation for addressing the complaint or request recommendations from the group. Pairing complaints with recommendations enables grievances to be raised in a constructive manner.

Although "Complaints with Recommendations" is Satir's name for this segment, some groups call the segment "Recommendations for Improvement," aptly shifting the emphasis from what's gone wrong to how to do better.

Segment #5: Hopes and Wishes

This final segment focuses on the future. Participants express hopes and wishes pertinent to the group or any of its members, including those not present. Sharing hopes and wishes, and discovering how many they have in common, ends the Temperature Reading on a high note.

Other Applications of the Temperature Reading

If people in your organization resist trying a Temperature Reading because they are uncomfortable with its name, then change the name to fit your organization's culture. For example, call the Temperature Reading a Team Check-In. Or change "appreciations" to "kudos" or "praise" and express them as "Thanks for . . ." instead of "I appreciate you for . . ." One team that disliked the names "Appreciations" and "Hopes and Wishes" replaced them with "Looking Back" and "Looking Forward." Whatever you call them, regularly conducted Temperature Readings help teams interact and collaborate more effectively.

One reason Temperature Readings are so valuable as a communication technique is that, with only slight adjustments, they can be adapted for use in many situations. For example, you can use a Temperature Reading to gather customer feedback by translating the five segments into questions, such as,

- What's working well?
- What's coming up that could be important?
- What kinds of problems or puzzles have you been experiencing?
- What recommendations do you have for improvement?
- What are your hopes for the future?

Similarly, you can orient the segments for use in a post-project review by asking

- What worked well?
- What important information seemed to be lacking?

- What was puzzling or confusing?
- What improvements would enable us to function better in future projects?
- What are our hopes for the future?

By changing just a few words, you can adapt these questions for use in assessing the quality of your personal or organizational communication.

GIVE PERSONALIZED ATTENTION

Almost everyone likes attention, probably because we get so little of it. This makes personalized attention a great way to maintain a relationship, especially if you're a manager or an executive. In some organizations, managers have direct, open relationships with their employees; in others, managers barely know who their employees are, and vice versa. The manager keeps a distance, making an appearance mainly when things go wrong.

Such companies remind me of the one in which an IT vice president wandered through the employee areas every year just before Christmas, wishing everyone happy holidays. Most people didn't even know who he was. This may have been personal attention of a once-a-year sort, but it was certainly not personalized; indeed, it revealed how little the executive knew about his employees, their efforts, and their accomplishments. Recall that the director discussed in Chapter 3 was equally clueless: His response to an employee survey that recommended more communication was to increase the number of memos he circulated. Communication would have been better served if he had spent time moseying through employee areas, interacting with employees, and showing evidence that he knew they were there.

A few words are all it takes to be a certified attention-giver. For example, I discovered how easy it is to acknowledge someone's contribution—and how good it feels to be acknowledged—during aerobics class.

In case you've never partaken, aerobics classes entail a series of vigorous, fast-paced exercise routines in which your arms and legs flail in all directions to the beat of music that's much too loud. Doing that is tough when you have difficulty following directions that require one foot to do one thing while the other foot does something else. On occasion, my feet get into an argument that threatens to flatten me.

But every now and then, from across a crowded room, the instructor would say, "Nice job, Naomi," or "Naomi, keep up the good work." Hearing her acknowledge my efforts gave me a nice feeling. I may have two left feet, but the instructor saw to it that they weren't two anonymous left feet. This instructor was astute enough to realize that personalized attention is a picker-upper. And anticipating that she might deliver this little zing of attention felt great every time, even when I knew it was coming. In the end, my two left feet rallied and completed the class in unison.

Clearly, giving personalized attention isn't about coddling people or catering to their every whim. It's a way to treat them and to show respect for them as individuals. Few methods for maintaining contact are so easy! This technique is particularly effective in companies in which people in virtual teams or provider/customer relationships are great distances apart.

Sometimes you can do no greater good in building and maintaining a relationship than to give it attention—whether the relationship involves subordinates, peers, customers, coworkers, or others. By listening attentively, offering a compliment, asking about work in progress, and commenting on activities of interest to the person, you show people that you care about them as individuals. People like to know that others know they're alive, and a little attention can have a huge positive impact.

In fact, giving personalized attention may at times be more important to people than addressing their complaints. Indeed, their complaints may be a reaction to a *lack* of attention. Sometimes, when people come to you with a problem, what they want is simply to hear you agree that it really is a problem, and that they are justified in being concerned.

To whom can you give some personalized attention today? Don't plan it. Don't schedule it. Just look around and do it.

Pay Attention to Each Other

As valuable as it is to give personalized attention, when people are immersed in solving problems and meeting deadlines, it's often a challenge for them to remember to focus on the needs and preferences of others. I witnessed this firsthand when, on the final morning of a week-long workshop, I assigned an in-class project. Immediately, discussion among group members was off and running, with topic after topic raised without people taking even a moment to reflect on how they actually would work together. Anxiety about not having enough time to complete the assignment fueled their get-to-it-ness and anything that didn't look like visible progress felt like a waste of time.

Members of the group forged ahead, so eager to complete the project that they were oblivious to the growing tension. They also didn't notice that two classmates who previously had been active idea-generators had turned silent. A third person muttered wisecracks, while a fourth slid his chair out-side the circle the group was seated in.

Each of these behaviors could have several different expla-nations: Perhaps the Silent Ones simply needed time to reflect. The Wisecracker might have used quips as a way to release tension. The Chair Slider might have wanted to gain the per-spective of an outsider looking in. Another possibility, though, was that these people had become dissatisfied and even disil-lusioned with the proceedings and had mentally checked out. Sure, they were still physically present, but their minds and spirits were miles away.

As tension escalated, I stopped the group's effort and asked each member to offer the group a few words to describe what he or she was experiencing. Among their responses were the following comments:

- I'm feeling stressed.
- No one's listening to me.
- I'm not having any fun.
- No one's paying attention to my ideas.
- I'm feeling frustrated.
- I'm really nervous we won't get the problem solved in time.
- I hate the whole thing.

I then asked them what, if anything, surprised them about these responses. Several members of the group said they didn't realize they weren't the only one feeling stressed. Others said they didn't realize the extent of the stress. One person was particularly upset, noting, "I didn't realize so many of you were unhappy. I feel bad that I didn't notice."

People who know each other well often neglect to pay per-sonalized attention to each other when they're working to meet a deadline. The members of this group had been together for almost a full week, tackling tough issues, laughing with each other, and talking about common interests. Many of them cared about each other. Yet when problems arose, they didn't notice or, if they noticed, their rules for commenting prevented them from expressing what they saw. Once they again became aware of each other, they decided to take periodic time-outs during the remainder of the project to check in with each other. They made a commitment to pay attention not only to the project, but also to the people engaged in it. Afterward, they commented that paying attention to each other's experience during the project seemed to reduce the stress of that experience.

Pay Attention to Yourself

Paying attention to yourself is even harder than paying attention to other people. Consider what happened on one team that I observed during a problem-solving session. Moments after the group convened, a personable, outgoing fellow volunteered to facilitate the session for the group. Prior to the start of the session, this chap had told me with pride that he was a team player; he emphasized that he wanted his teammates to succeed and was highly motivated to contribute to their shared effort.

As it turns out, though, he did as much to obstruct the team effort as to support it. For example, he dismissed several ideas that differed from his own, and discounted some suggestions without trying to understand the reasoning behind them. He seemed unfazed when people spoke simultaneously, although none of their comments could be heard clearly. As the effort proceeded, he failed to notice expressions of annoyance on the faces of some team members—or if he noticed, he did nothing to alleviate their distress.

This fellow's heart was in the right place. He *was* a team player. How could he not be, given how genuinely he wanted the team to succeed? Yet from the way he worked, it seemed as if he'd been directed to see how many different ways he could come up with to make the problem more difficult to solve than it actually was.

The group's problems were not caused solely by the facilitator, however; some were due to the activities of other participants—team players all. For example, one woman said she was good at listening to simultaneous speakers, yet she misstated a speaker's key point moments later. Another member of the group said he'd support any solution as long as the session ended quickly, but he then proceeded to bring up idea after idea, prolonging the discussion. None of these people seemed aware that their behavior counteracted the very success they wanted the team to achieve. Their actions, motivated by time pressures, ensured that their effort would need more time rather than less.

Did they solve the problem by their deadline? Yes, just barely. But in the process, they demonstrated that people who view themselves as team players can still impede a team's ability to function successfully.

Paying attention to yourself is a process that I call "catching yourself being yourself." It requires that you, in a sense, reserve a part of yourself to step back and look at the situation, to take note of how you act. It requires practice, but is an excellent way to notice your own personal contradictions between what you say and what you do.

STAY CONNECTED

Relationships can be difficult to sustain when the people involved rarely see each other, whether they're half a world apart or within roller-skating distance. When people seldom see each other, it's especially important for them to regularly offer thanks, express appreciations, and pay attention to each other. The less frequently people see each other, the stronger the impact of these gestures.

Interestingly, however, relationships can be just as difficult to sustain when people work side by side. Often, people don't know what their coworkers in neighboring cubicles are up to, let alone what people who work far away are doing. Why don't they know? Too busy! Urgent demands! Priorities! No time to get together! When the pressure is on, staff meetings are all but impossible. Or are they?

Some organizations have found a technique to help group members stay connected and informed about each other's doings. The meetings these organizations hold are quite unusual, however, and work like this: Every Monday, promptly at 9 A.M., the entire group assembles. Each person gets exactly one minute to describe his or her plans for the week. One minute. That's it. Oh, and one more thing is required—unless prevented from doing so by a physical condition, everyone remains standing for the duration of the meeting.

Sixty seconds per person may not sound like much, but it's longer than you may think. In fact, one minute is just enough time for each participant to bring everyone else up to speed. Knowing they each will have sixty seconds to speak makes people think a little harder about what they'll be doing during the coming week and how to communicate it.

Brief though it may be, this type of meeting is surprisingly effective in surfacing redundancies, overlapping efforts, or the need for greater coordination. For example, one group that tried this technique discovered that a particular customer had contacted several different members of the group with the same request. The contacted teammates *each* had planned to spend time responding to the customer's request, while the customer presumably waited to see which solution he liked best.

Knowledge of task redundancy is clearly advantageous to a team but why should everyone remain standing during this meeting? Because when people settle into comfortable chairs, sit back, and relax, they tend to take longer to get to the point. They go on at length. They meander. They think of just one more thing to say and then talk about 27 more things. Before you know it, the sun is setting on yet another unproductive day. By contrast, keeping people standing assures that everyone will remain alert and goal-oriented and that each speaker will get to the point quickly.

Two ground rules are important in making this type of meeting a success. First, the information presented must be specific to the projects or activities people will be working on during the coming week (or alternatively, worked on last week, if that's your preference). They can't cut their minute to four seconds by saying they're working on the same old stuff. Each person must take his or her minute seriously, making the most of the opportunity to speak; any member who will be unable to attend the meeting must provide a written statement of the week's plan for a coworker to read to the others.

The second ground rule is that discussion is prohibited. If someone's one-minute presentation triggers ideas for further discussion, that's natural—but stick to presentation of planned tasks, and pursue any discussion after the meeting has concluded.

If you want to maintain a relationship, it's crucial to find time to stay connected. But as this technique shows, sometimes all it takes is just a minute.

CREATE COMMUNICATION METRICS

Although techniques such as Virginia Satir's Temperature Reading can reduce the frequency and intensity of conflict, few relationships are conflict-free. Cognizant that the presence of conflict can be easy to miss or ignore, consultant Bob King (whose Visibility Ratio is described in Chapter 5) devised the Conflict Metric and the Anxiety Metric. These two metrics can help people know when the time has come to communicate openly about the presence of conflict.

The Anxiety Metric measures internal conflict by focusing on feelings of stress and that sick-to-your-stomach, tied-up-in-knots feeling that signals that all is not well. This metric helps a person working on a project recognize strong reactions to what he or she is experiencing. Identification of the anxiety prompts the taking of appropriate action to resolve the stress.

When King notices that his anxiety is on the rise, his first step is to identify its cause. Once he has determined its leading cause, he then seeks out the person or people who are in the best position to help him relieve it. Often, that person is the one who contributed to the anxiety. In other situations, it might be someone who can offer some perspective on the situation. Either way, he aims to present his case in a non-blaming manner. As King points out, "if I don't do it, my anxiety merely continues to grow."[2]

---

[2] Bob King, "Life as a Software Architect," *Amplifying Your Effectiveness: Collected Essays*, eds. Gerald M. Weinberg, James Bach, and Naomi Karten (New York: Dorset House Publishing, 2000), p. 51. See also www.rc-king.com.

The Conflict Metric is King's externally focused metric that concentrates on strong feelings that exist between individuals and groups as they work together. But contrary to what you might expect, the metric does not measure the presence of too much conflict, but rather is used to detect just the reverse: the absence of strong feeling. Based on his experience as a software architect, King states, "I enter this arena fully aware that there will be places where conflict lurks. . . . The sooner these conflicts surface, and are resolved, the better for the project, so if the Conflict Metric seems too low, I suspect that I don't yet understand all of the project's business ramifications."[3]

King's point is worth taking to heart: A certain amount of conflict is normal. If you don't see or experience any, it's probably not because there is none, but that it just hasn't surfaced or is being deliberately concealed. As uncomfortable as conflict can be, the kind that hasn't yet surfaced is probably a greater risk to the success of an undertaking than the kind that emerges and can be addressed.

Identify Other Metrics

King's Anxiety and Conflict Metrics focus attention on information that people either seem oblivious to, or seem tempted to ignore even if they do notice it. Can you think of additional metrics that might signal the presence of excessive, prolonged or unresolved conflict? One, for example, might be called the Preoccupation Metric: the amount of time people spend obsessing over a particular conflict, unable to concentrate on their work, yet doing nothing either to resolve the conflict or to reduce their preoccupation with it. Another, called the Blaming Metric, reveals the extent to which a person privately blames someone else for the current mess rather than considering how to help to resolve it.

Metrics such as these or others you develop yourself will signal you that the time has come to take action. As a work group, you and your teammates can establish metrics that signal that it's time to openly discuss issues that are interfering

---

[3] Ibid., p. 49.

with the ability of group members to work well together. Groups that devise and discuss relevant metrics are more likely to air grievances that might otherwise remain beneath the surface.

Select the Appropriate Communication Channel

Many factors, including differences between Introvert and Extravert communication styles, influence how parties prefer to interact to resolve conflict. Some people prefer to discuss the issues in person or over the telephone, whereas others prefer to send written correspondence, such as a letter, memo, or e-mail message. Although many people advocate against the use of e-mail for conflict resolution, this advice is at times misguided. E-mail communication between parties may be preferable in many cases, at least at the outset, as it allows people to choose their words carefully, to check and recheck their messages to prevent possible misinterpretation, to receive and then reflect on the other party's comments, to seek input from others, and to take time to cool off if they overheat.

For example, when two colleagues became mired in conflict, they turned to e-mail to try to resolve their issues. I suggested to one of them that despite the travel involved, they meet face-to-face. However, he convinced me otherwise when he explained his reason for preferring e-mail: "Joe clearly has some major grievances that I'm not sure he'll surface if we're face-to-face. At this stage, e-mail gives me a chance to study his comments and carefully compose my own. If I can get a little clearer about what's really bothering him, then I'll consider getting together with him." E-mail was clearly the communication channel of choice in this situation.

In some situations, e-mail may be the communication channel of choice even when relationships are strong and people live and work side by side. In *Ice Bound*, Dr. Jerri Nielsen describes her experience living at a South Pole research station. Remarking on the fact that her colleagues at the station corresponded with each other by e-mail, Dr. Nielsen comments, "You would think that forty-one people living together in a little hole would just talk, but I think the writing helped us express our feelings more precisely and more freely."[4]

To resolve conflict, choose the communication channel that best fits your comfort level. Use e-mail to resolve disputes when it serves both you and the other party well. Although e-mail cannot capture the nuances of verbal communication, it has one compelling benefit over the spoken word: Once you've written a message, you can always hit the Delete key if you feel the message is not right. Nothing comparable yet exists with spoken communication.

CREATE RELATIONSHIP-TENDING ROLES

Despite the best intentions of individuals to maintain strong relationships, an organizational strategy can improve the odds that the relationship will remain strong even when those in the relationship are too preoccupied to care for it. As the FixNet team discovered, when you're immersed in your work and deadlines hover overhead, you can easily lose sight of the big picture.

Most organizations put more effort into taking care of relationships with people who are external to the company than they devote to caring for their own employees. Externally oriented positions with titles like client-relations manager or vendor-relations manager focus on relationships with customers and suppliers. Rarely, however, do groups have internally focused positions designed to help them monitor and improve their own functioning. Such positions can be extremely valuable in maintaining or strengthening relationships, because the people in these relationship-tending roles serve as extra eyes and ears.

Several roles can help the members of a group function congruently as they face the stresses and pressures associated with achieving their goals. The roles of Observer, Compassionate Listener, Guide, Team Jiggler, and, yes, even Corporate Fool, are described in the remainder of this chapter.

---

[4] Dr. Jerri Nielsen, with Maryanne Vollers, *Ice Bound: A Doctor's Incredible Battle for Survival at the South Pole* (New York: Hyperion, 2001), p. 172.

Observers

Some people describe themselves as good observers; others claim they're not good at observing. In truth, both claims are correct because everyone is good at observing some things at some point in time, while completely missing others. I learned how true this is firsthand.

You see, every autumn, when leaves begin to fall, I somehow find myself in the role of Designated Leaf Raker. One October, though, I hoped my husband, Mr. I Don't Do Outdoor Work, would see how busy I was and rake the yard himself. He didn't. I waited for him to notice the growing carpet of leaves. He didn't.

I decided to try something dramatic to get his attention. I raked a section of lawn, but—and here is the genius behind my idea—I left a pile of leaves in the shape of a heart in the center of the cleared area. I was certain Howard would look out the window, see the valentine, think how romantic it would be to lend a hand, and rake the rest of the yard.

A day or two passed, but Howard didn't notice the heart of leaves. I didn't worry; these things take time. How much time was something I had badly miscalculated, however. After several weeks, I was concerned that the leaves would damage the lawn, and so I went out and raked my heart out. Sure enough, the leaves had burned the lawn, leaving a perfect yellowish-brown lawn-heart. Then I raked the rest of the yard. It was clear he wasn't going to do it.

Soon enough, snow covered the yard. I forgot about the lawn. Spring came. One day, Howard looked out the window and motioned me over. "Look at the lawn," he said, sounding puzzled. "That section over there is the strangest color. And it's in the shape of a heart." I decided not to confess that I'd had a role in creating the heart shape, but I did adopt a more direct approach to getting his help with the yard that Spring, designating him as official Yard Observer. Which is why, in organizations as in households, it's valuable to have designated Observers, people whose explicit responsibility it is to see specific things.

Observers are people invited to unobtrusively watch a group, identify noteworthy patterns of behavior, and provide feedback and recommendations. Observers help to answer a variety of questions, such as: How are people getting along? Do miscommunications occur? What kinds of interactions are taking place? Are people communicating at cross-purposes? Are they unintentionally taking action that negatively impacts others? What issues are contributing to conflict? What important issues are not being discussed?

An Observer can provide both ongoing observation, such as during a project, and event-specific observation, such as during team meetings. Observers don't participate in the group's interactions, but instead pay diligent attention to what is transpiring. They offer feedback at whatever points or intervals are mutually agreed to, such as at designated periods during a meeting, at the conclusion of a project, or upon noticing a matter likely to benefit from feedback.

Outside consultants often serve as Observers. But another option—one that costs far less and yields considerable learning—is for a group to have its own members serve as Observers in addition to carrying out their normal responsibilities. By virtue of being assigned as Observers, these individuals tend to notice instances of miscommunication, misinterpretation, and misunderstanding that others miss. They see how easily even the most well-intentioned efforts can go astray. In fact, two Observers are better than one because they will see different things and will see the same things from different angles. Group members can rotate Observer duties, so that everyone has the opportunity to experience both the challenges and the benefits that the role entails.

Observers must offer feedback in an objective, caring, and nonthreatening way. The emphasis must be on describing intake—that is, what they saw and heard—rather than interpretation. When they do offer interpretation, they must be careful to qualify it as such: "When I saw . . . my interpretation was . . ." In return, those being observed must try not to be defensive as they listen to the feedback offered. Being both the observer and the observed takes practice.

A good starting point is for group members to create a list of things to observe. This list could include

- how often the group deviates from one of the published norms, such as the "no interrupting" norm
- patterns of complaints by group members
- evidence that people may be unclear about their responsibilities
- messages that don't get through
- evidence that team members are, or are not, staying connected

Any one or two of these would be plenty for new Observers.

If you'd like to get some practice as an Observer before an actual opportunity arises, you can easily do so during the next boring meeting you attend. When you reach that point in the meeting when you'd rather be having a root canal, put on your invisible Observer hat. Don't try to observe everything; you can't. Instead, pick something specific to observe, such as,

- how often people interrupt each other
- the words used by people who discount others' ideas
- how often the meeting veers off course—and who steers it that way

- how the most persuasive people convince others
- how often people smile or laugh

As a self-appointed Observer in this setting, you may see far more than you expect. In the process, you'll be refining your observation skills. And you'll survive the meeting. You may even look forward to the next one.

Compassionate Listeners and Guides

In an ideal world, people who have grievances would simply approach those with whom they have difficulties and work through issues together.[5] But sometimes people fear this direct approach, are reluctant to try it alone, or don't believe that it will solve the problem.

For situations like these, it is valuable to have a small team whose responsibility it is to ask: "How are we doing as a group?" Although many people are concerned with how well the group is functioning, appointing specific people within a larger team to pay attention to the answer is an effective organizational strategy. Typically, members of this team perform their role in addition to their other responsibilities.

Two possible roles for this team are Compassionate Listener and Guide:

> *Compassionate Listeners* provide confidential support, on request, to coworkers to help them through stressful or confusing situations. The role entails listening attentively, asking questions, seeking clarifying information, and helping to identify options and alternatives. Compassionate Listeners don't fix problems; they help others find ways to resolve their own problems.

---

[5] The Compassionate Listener, Guide, and Team Jiggler roles described in this chapter are adapted from the work of Eileen Strider (www.striderandcline.com), Marie Benesh (www.mbenesh.com), Rick Brenner (www.ChacoCanyon.com), and Kevin Fjelsted (www.pcte.com), who created the roles for a project the five of us, and others, worked on together.

Guides assist group members, on request, in resolving conflicts they are experiencing with each other. As with the Compassionate Listener, the Guide's job is to listen attentively, ask questions, and seek clarifying information. The Guide also helps the parties hear each other and find a resolution that will enable them to communicate more effectively, understand each other's perspective, and improve how well they get along. Certain situations might call for multiple guides, one supporting and guiding each party to the conflict. The Satir Interaction Model is one of the most commonly used tools in this process.

At first glance, it may appear that these roles ought to be restricted to those with relevant training or experience. But, in fact, almost anyone can serve in these roles provided he or she maintains confidentiality, brings a genuine concern to the role, and strives to remain objective.

Clearly, individuals selected for these roles must have the trust and respect of those who might seek their assistance. It's advisable for groups to have more than one person serving in each of these roles so that they can offer support, guidance, and encouragement to each other as well as to the rest of the group.

During one project on which I served on a team with Compassionate Listener and Guide responsibilities (designated a Care and Feeding Team), we periodically conducted a confidential survey to gauge how team members viewed the project, their roles, and their interactions with others. We published summary reports, keeping individual feedback confidential. (In such situations, if team members feel safe enough to disclose their views and all are willing, confidentiality may be waived.) We came to see this role as valuable for any project, as a proactive way to help teams avoid or resolve problems.[6]

One caution, though. Serving as a Compassionate Listener or Guide can be emotionally draining if a lot of support is needed—and in some situations, a considerable amount is

---

[6] Thanks to my Care-and-Feeding-mates, Eileen Strider (www.striderandcline.com) and Esther Derby (www.estherderby.com).

needed. Listeners and Guides might benefit by creating a metric to help them judge when demand for their efforts becomes excessive either for themselves personally or for the effective functioning of the team. If requests for assistance exceed a certain level, the group may require a larger and more proactive form of intervention.

Team Jigglers

Some interdependencies and potential task overlaps in a project are obvious; others are subtle and easily missed. As a result, even the most cautious team can make what appears to be a reasonable decision without realizing that it may negatively impact the work of other individuals or teams.

Another type of relationship-tending role is that of a Team Jiggler, a specialized Observer whose function it is to help raise awareness of interdependencies and overlaps. Team Jigglers do not function as part of their own team but instead help by joining in on all forms of communication among another team's members—with that team's prior permission only. Teams may invite a Jiggler to their meetings and include them on their e-mail distribution lists to help them develop and maintain their awareness.

A Jiggler's ideas and insights are especially valuable when team members are making important decisions and would like assistance in determining how their work affects or is affected by others. Jigglers don't interfere with the team's activities or decision-making (tempting though it may be to do so). Rather, they raise awareness, ask questions, and provide feedback. Because they have permission to offer feedback, they can contribute at will without being viewed as intrusive.

The Corporate Fool

The role of Corporate Fool is a special one. Described by David Firth in his book *The Corporate Fool*,[7] the fool's role in the

---

[7] David Firth, with Alan Leigh, *The Corporate Fool* (Oxford, U.K.: Capstone Publishing, 1998).

King's court can be adapted to fit a modern, corporate setting. Firth defines a Corporate Fool as someone who looks at issues from all perspectives, and in particular, from both the head and the heart. Although the role of Corporate Fool has elements in common with Observers and Team Jigglers, it has its own special function.

According to Firth, the Corporate Fool operates by four principles:[8]

- The Fool is an outsider, because (Firth maintains) it is only from the outside that one has a clear perspective.
- The Fool sees things as they really are. He or she doesn't become trapped by the psychological phenomenon of perceptual adaptation, which Firth describes as "the ability to see distortion as normality and not know it."[9]
- The Fool is honest. If the Fool sees that the emperor has no clothes, he or she isn't afraid to say so.
- The Fool is a master of communication and, in particular, of the ability to listen, understand, and build rapport in order to present his or her perspective in a way that people will find palatable.

Now, the truth is, I don't know of any organizations that have formally designated positions for Corporate Fools. Consultants sometimes play a comparable role (although some may be viewed as fools rather than Fools). Many consultants, however, find it difficult to communicate with absolute honesty; indeed, not all managers and executives who hire consultants want to hear the truth. Still, the very notion of a Corporate Fool is a fascinating one, if for no other reason than to provoke thought about what it takes to see, acknowledge, and respond to what's really happening. Ideally, we can all participate as Corporate Fools in our various ventures.

---

[8] Firth, op. cit., pp. 7–9.

[9] Ibid., p. 7.

Section 3
Service Gaps

Communication is vital to achieving customer satisfaction. But it is a two-way process—you can't learn about your customers' needs if *you* do all the talking. Talk too much and you risk alienating the very customers you hope to please.

My doctor exhibited this syndrome when I asked whether Condition A was related to Condition B.

As if I'd just pressed the "Chatterbox On" button, she proceeded to describe all medical research conducted on both conditions since Hippocrates was a lad. I was impressed with her
knowledge, but not once did she ask the reason for my question. The upshot, when she finally reached modern times, was
that there was no known connection between the two conditions. And given that fact, I didn't really care about all the rest.

When my refrigerator broke, I found that the repairman I
called was afflicted with the same condition. This guy gushed
with enthusiasm, eager for me to know as much as *he* knew.
However, developing refrigerator expertise has never been one
of my life's goals. All I wanted to know was, Will this refrigerator keep my ice cream cold again? The answer turned out to
be no. Case closed.

When I had a fellow help me configure some new computer equipment, he talked nonstop. This fellow knew all
(judging from the word count, at least) and was eager for me to
know just as much. He didn't even seem to need to breathe; he
simply spewed forth. Squeezing in a question was no trivial
matter.

These people, like many others who are eager to share their
knowledge, fail to consider their customer's preferences, and
as a result, create unacceptable communication gaps. Asking
pertinent questions—and then listening carefully to the
responses—can help doctors, repair staff, you, *and me* determine the best way to communicate with a customer. In fact,
showing an interest by asking questions is an amazingly
simple way to win customers over.

In the situations described above, I was overwhelmed with
information I did not want or need. The following approaches
would have worked better for me and they may work well for
you:

- Before educating me in medical history, my doctor
  might have asked why I was curious about the connection between Conditions A and B. By understanding
  what I wanted to find out, she could have tailored her
  response accordingly. Or she might have simply said,

"There's no known relationship. Why do you ask?" Then, if I wanted more information I could have asked for it.

- As he dissected our ailing refrigerator, the repairman might have asked if I wanted to know what he was doing. That would have given me the option to encourage or suppress his chattiness. Determining a customer's communication preference can be crucial in generating repeat business. But this guy, well-meaning though he was, got on my nerves. Hopefully, our new refrigerator will provide twenty years of ice-cream-friendly performance.

- And the computer techie might have periodically asked any of several questions, such as, "Is there anything you want me to explain?" Or, "Am I giving you the amount of detail you want?" Or (my favorite), "Do you have any questions?"

Ideas and techniques to help you question, listen to, and interact more effectively with your own customers are provided in the three chapters that make up Section 3.

- Chapter 9 focuses on prevalent customer grievances and suggests steps that will help you achieve a higher level of customer satisfaction.
- Chapter 10 offers strategies and guidelines for gathering feedback from customers, so you know how well *they* think you are doing.
- Chapter 11 explains why and how to establish a service level agreement, a communication process that helps providers and customers build win-win relationships.

As this section emphasizes, success in working with customers requires more than competence at doing the job. It also requires an understanding of how your customers want to be treated. Sometimes, it's as simple as doing less talking and more listening.

9

The Communication of Caring

While waiting in a restaurant for a client with whom I had a dinner date, I noticed several signs touting the importance of customer service to the establishment. Clearly, this restaurant valued good service, and I looked forward to having dinner in a place that cared about its customers.

My client arrived promptly for our reservation but, although the restaurant was only half full, we waited a long time to be seated and even longer to be given menus. Then the waiter hovered over us, overly eager to take our orders. After he brought our dinners, he repeatedly interrupted us to find out if everything was okay, which it was—except for his interruptions. Lingering over coffee, we suffered only one more interruption: presentation of the bill, which—guess what?—had a sizable error in it. As we paid the corrected bill and got ready to leave the restaurant, the maître d' smiled pleasantly and said he hoped we'd return soon. Not likely.

Beware: Neither saying that you care about customer service nor posting signs in every nook and cranny will convince customers that you mean it if they experience something to the contrary. If your service is shabby, displaying such signs will only widen the gap between service as promised and service as delivered. It's what you do that customers notice, not what you claim to do.

It's often said that customers don't care how much you know until they know how much you care. This sounds clever, but it's not quite true. What matters is not how much you care, but how skillfully you exhibit evidence of caring. How deeply you care matters little to customers if you ignore their calls, discount their views, treat them rudely—or serve them Glitch du Jour, as my client and I experienced in the restaurant. If you deliver poor service, customers don't want to hear that you care, because it's clear to them you don't!

As the IT customers in one company I consulted with some years ago know well, visible declarations of caring sometimes signal just the opposite. To reverse an extended period of net-work outages, application failures, and flawed technical sup-port, the IT division established a new goal: Deliver world-class service. To emphasize this goal, management had it printed as a slogan on IT business cards and posted on plaques and posters throughout the division. What a laugh customers had. World-class service, indeed! Customers weren't even get-ting neighborhood-class service.

This disparity between expressions of caring and actions that suggest otherwise—that is, between service as promised and service as delivered—reflects a prevalent communication gap. The more the struggling IT division touted how excellent its service would be in the future, the more its customers' attention was riveted on the inferior service they were receiving then, at that minute.

If you want to successfully communicate that you care, con-sider the strategies and recommendations presented in this chapter.

CONTRIBUTORS TO CUSTOMER SATISFACTION

Reflect for a moment on your own experiences as a customer. What's important to *you* when you're at the bank, car dealer-ship, doctor's office, airport, or supermarket? What about when you're on the telephone ordering pizza or awaiting technical support? When you've had a negative experience as a customer, what made it negative? And what about your positive experiences?

I've collected feedback from many hundreds of technical and business professionals about what matters to them as customers. About 15 percent of their responses focus on what I refer to as *product expectations.* These are what customers expect about particular attributes of the product or solution, such as reliability, functionality, price, value, and quality.

The majority of their responses—approximately 85 percent—concern *process expectations:* the very human matter of how they want to be treated. And here's a key point: The majority of process expectations are communication-related. For example, customers want to be treated with respect, friendliness, and honesty. They want the basic courtesies. They want to be listened to—not ignored, interrupted, or spoken to as if they were dummies. They want to be informed of their options and consulted about matters that concern them. How providers respond to these process expectations significantly influences customer satisfaction.

Process expectations may vary from one situation or time to another, but everyone has some process expectations that, if not met, will result in a dissatisfying experience. Even when all else seems to be in order, ignoring your customers' process expectations can lead to their dissatisfaction. That was Pete's experience, as we saw in Chapter 3. Despite an on-time delivery of the required solution, Pete's client Carl was dissatisfied because he never knew the status of the project while it was in progress. This information was important to him, and not having it was sufficient, in his mind, to undermine his impression of an otherwise successful project.

An Investment in a Relationship

Focusing on how you treat customers—that is, how well you meet their process expectations—is an investment in a relationship. Customers who appreciate the way they've been treated are often much more tolerant of goofs and glitches in the service they receive. In other words, paying deliberate attention to these process expectations can buy you some leeway in delivering your product, service, or solution.

Granted, in certain circumstances, customers may willingly tolerate being treated in an obnoxious manner. A manager once commented to me that one software product his group had purchased was so superior that "we're willing to put up with a certain amount of crap from the vendor." But in such a relationship, it may take no more than a slight slip in product quality—or the customer just plain getting tired of being treated so poorly—for the customer to pull the plug and take business to a vendor that treats its customers better.

Conversely, most of us, as customers, have taken our business elsewhere precisely *because* of dissatisfaction with how we were treated. The product and the price may have been just right, but something about our service experience displeased us and so we took our business elsewhere. However, it's not just customers at the consumer level who take this type of action, but dissatisfied customers at all levels. An IT vice president who was making a mega-hundred-thousand-dollar purchasing decision told me: "Vendor A has a superb product at a good price, and I know I should go with it. But I just don't like the way the company is treating us, so we're going to go with Vendor B." Could Vendor A be you?

Rudeness, disrespect, a dismissive attitude, and a failure to return calls may seem like minor matters until they add up to equal angry, complaining customers. Richard Whiteley reports in *The Customer-Driven Company* that research conducted by The Forum Corporation revealed that nearly 70 percent of the identifiable reasons customers left typical companies had to do not with the product, but with poor service quality—in particular, a lack of personal attention and a manner of service that was rude, unhelpful, and otherwise unsatisfactory.[1]

---

[1] Richard C. Whiteley, *The Customer-Driven Company: Moving from Talk to Action* (Reading, Mass.: Addison-Wesley, 1991), pp. 9–10.

Customer Care Made Simple

As I discovered at my local print shop, even a smile—the simplest form of interpersonal communication—can make a huge difference to the customer. The woman who handled my printing needs for several years was friendly and forever smiling. When she left to take another job, she was replaced by a brusque woman whose manner was glum and gloomy. What a striking contradiction it now was to be asked, "Can I help you?" while looking at a face that said, "Go away, you're bothering me." Her words suggested she cared but her expression suggested the opposite—and the expression was far more persuasive.

Even when you're unaware of it, your demeanor communicates a message to customers that affects their overall satisfaction and influences how readily they'll forgive and forget any slipups. I recall being quick to dismiss Ms. Friendly Face's goofs as no big deal, but I felt annoyed when her replacement made even trivial mistakes.

This emotional component plays an important part in the psychology of customer service: Customers who are pleased with whatever aspect of their service experience is important to them will tend to respond favorably to other aspects that might otherwise have disturbed them. Conversely, once customers become displeased, they tend to find fault with other service components, not just with the aspects they initially viewed as important. As for me, I actually began to feel glum and gloomy whenever I went into the print shop.

In an editorial published in the monthly magazine *Customer Support Management,* editor Kathy Grayson described her positive experience in reaching a human being at one airline's customer-service area—this contrasted sharply with all the other airlines' automated telephone response systems, which seemed to condemn her to a life of "press this, press that." She commented that she'd call this airline first for her next trip, reasoning that if the airline "cares more about me on the phone, they may care more about me in the plane."[2]

As Grayson admits, "My reaction may not be logical. . . ." Yet, her reaction is not unique; the seemingly small things— your smile, your friendly tone of voice, and your caring attitude—often have an impact that's powerful enough to outweigh inadequacies, flubs, and blunders. Numerous people I interviewed in one particular company's customer division confirmed this point when they commented about an IT liaison who didn't always have the information they wanted but who was so friendly and upbeat that they didn't mind. Once customers have had some contact with you, your demeanor and attitude enter the room before you and influence the response you get.

These ideas hold true when you're on the customer side of the relationship as well. Starting out with a smile, a friendly voice, and an upbeat attitude will get you service that's faster, of higher quality, and more attentive than if you enter fighting. Providers' process expectations, it seems, are remarkably similar to those of customers.

Identifying Individual Differences

If you haven't identified your customers' process expectations, you may be falling short in meeting them. Questions such as the following will help identify these expectations:

- What will you be looking for when we've completed this project so that you feel it's been successful?

---

[2] Kathy Grayson, "Live! From the Call Center . . . " *Customer Support Management* (July/August, 1999), p. 10.

- How would you like us to keep in touch with you as we deliver this service?
- What's important to you in the way we work with you in solving this problem?
- What is the most important aspect of this work for you?
- What have you experienced in past projects that pleased you?
- What have you experienced in past projects that concerned or disappointed you?
- What aspects of this project are so new or unfamiliar that they worry you?

You may find that what customers describe as most important to them differs from what you perceived to be most important. Keep in mind that most customers are unaccustomed to answering questions such as these and may need time to reflect on them before responding. Once you have identified their process expectations, it's worth reevaluating them periodically since responses may vary over the course of a project or relationship.

As you investigate your customers' process expectations, you may encounter important differences between customers who, at first glance, seem to want the same thing. For example, in a meeting with two client groups, a software team learned that it was very important to both client managers to be updated on the progress of their respective projects. However, each manager had a different preference for this reporting. One client manager emphasized that she wanted a weekly report. The other responded rapidly, "I don't have time for weekly reports. I just want to be told of any deviations from what we've agreed to. I'll assume that the project is on track unless you tell me otherwise."

Giving both managers the same kind of report would have left one of them unhappy. Discovering customers' preferences at the start allows you to take such differences into account—or for a compromise arrangement to be made if addressing individual preferences would be impractical.

UNIVERSAL GRIEVANCES

In conducting customer interviews and reviewing customer satisfaction surveys, I find that certain complaints are regularly and predictably expressed. These complaints seem so widespread that I've come to think of them as Universal Grievances. The most frequently cited grievances revolve around customers knowing the status of work that affects them, being forced to endure excessive, unexplained waiting, and being treated in a dishonest manner. In essence, these grievances concern whether and how the customers' provider has communicated with them.

Not surprisingly, these grievances are interrelated: Customers who can't get status updates for information they want feel as if they're being made to wait needlessly and view their provider as treating them dishonestly. Taken together, these grievances reflect gaps between how customers want to be treated and how they feel they're being treated. Given the prevalence of these Universal Grievances, they're worth paying attention to even if your customers haven't specifically cited them as being important. Let's look at how these grievances play out, and how to avoid them.

The Importance of Explaining "When"

Customers always seem to want to know when something will happen. "When will Tech Support respond to my problem?" "When will I hear back about my request?" "When will the repairman show up?" For many customers, the uncertainty of not knowing—and not knowing *when* they will know—is exasperating.

Exasperated is how I felt the time we had a plumbing problem, and the plumber who came to the house told us that we needed a part that he didn't have in stock. He said he'd make some calls and let us know when he located the part. Then off he went. After several hours, I wondered whether I should call him to check on his progress. I didn't want to annoy him if he was searching for the part, but I worried that if

I waited and he wasn't even looking, I'd never get the problem fixed. Not hearing from him left me feeling uncertain, exasperated, and anxious. I concluded that if he needed to be nudged, I didn't want to wait too long to do the nudging.

Relieving customer uncertainty rarely requires a Herculean effort but it does take sensitivity to meeting the expectations of others. While writing this chapter, I got a phone call from a colleague who was due shortly for a meeting and who wanted to let me know she'd been delayed. Offering this kind of information—"just wanted to let you know"—relieves uncertainty and eliminates a communication gap before one can even occur. It's simple courtesy with a big impact.

Unfortunately, my plumber didn't seem to know that providing a progress report goes a long way toward keeping a customer satisfied. After another round of waiting and wondering whether I should call him, I did the only thing I could think of: I told my husband to call him! And yes, the plumber was indeed searching for the part. But he was doing something more. He was contributing mightily to a Universal Grievance: the frustration of not being kept informed about a matter of importance.

If you've made a commitment to customers to perform a task or fix a problem, but they can't see or hear that you're performing as promised, many will conclude that you're not. If you've already built a strong foundation with them, they're likely to give you the benefit of the doubt at times when you cannot meet their expectations. Communicating about status is especially needed during times of stress—and the very fact of not knowing the status will, for some, create that stress. A finance manager put it succinctly when he described the uncertainty he had regarding his company's IT organization, "It's not their ability to fix the problem that concerns us; it's their ability to communicate during the fix process."

Of course, customers have responsibilities, too. In retrospect, I could have asked the plumber when he'd be likely to call—and saved myself a few hours of futile fussing. I could also have asked him whether it would be all right to call him in a couple of hours to see how he was faring in locating the part. All of us, as customers, are likely to receive better service if we take some responsibility for receiving the kind of service we want.

Be Trustworthy to Be Trusted

The state of not knowing the status of something is far less stressful if the relationship has been built on a foundation of trust. As noted by Freiberg and Freiberg in *Nuts!*, the story of Southwest Airlines' success, "Trust grows when we keep our promises and follow through on our commitments. . . . When people know they can count on you, your words and actions have more power to influence them."[3] Similarly, when your dependability and your ability to deliver as promised lead people to trust you, they usually tolerate the state of not knowing for much, much longer.

To establish trust, however, you can't just declare, "I'm dependable. Trust me on this." In *The Darwin Awards: Evolution in Action,* author Wendy Northcutt is right on the mark in pointing out, "Most of us know instinctively that the phrase '*trust me, light this fuse'* is a recipe for disaster."[4]

Clearly, you have to develop a reputation for delivering on your commitments, and the best way to do that is to *deliver on your commitments.* But here is a critical point if you're serious about building trust: If you determine you won't be able to deliver as promised, you must let your customers know in a timely manner. Doing so can actually strengthen trust because you'll have been open and forthcoming. Conversely, in the absence of trust, the longer customers are forced to wait for an explanation, the more upset they become. This is a perfectly reasonable customer response.

The worst-case scenario for customers occurs when they feel powerless to find out the status. In this situation, they are

---

[3] Kevin Freiberg and Jackie Freiberg, *Nuts! Southwest Airlines' Crazy Recipe for Business and Personal Success* (New York: Broadway Books, 1998), p. 109.

[4] Wendy Northcutt, *The Darwin Awards: Evolution in Action* (New York: Dutton, 2000), p. 1.

likely to also become dissatisfied with other flaws in service delivery that otherwise might not bother them. Many stories from the world of customer service show that customers who become dissatisfied with one valued aspect of service will tend to find fault with others as well.

According to a *New York Times* article, "When shoppers receive bad service online, they are not only less likely to revisit the retailer's Web Site, they may also spend fewer dollars at its off-line stores. . . ."[5] Similarly, the more that airline passengers complain about delays and cancellations, the more they also complain about inconsequential matters such as peanut-versus-pretzel preferences.

As customers, we may be willing to let the little things slide, but disappoint us about the big things, and we'll grouse about all matters large and small.

Nonresponsiveness

Customers have dubbed the state of not knowing the Black Hole. To astronomers, a black hole is a dark, distant place in the cosmos where things get swallowed up, never again to emerge. To customers, it's that and something more: a place that's overflowing with problems and information.

Numerous customers have told me that when they submitted a problem or question to their technical staff, they received no response—that is, no follow-up, no clue as to the status of their query, and—most frustrating of all—no word as to when they might be advised of the status. Maybe in a hundred-thousand years, the Black Hole will eject its contents and customers will finally get the responses they've been waiting for. But most customers aren't that patient.

It's not just those with direct customer contact who make the Black Hole such a congested place. Others in the service chain add to the congestion. I remember asking members of

---

[5] Reported in *The New York Times*, March 25, 2001. The result cited is based on a poll conducted by Jupiter Media Metrix of New York, revealing that 70 percent of the 1,900 American shoppers polled said they would spend less at a retailer's store if they were dissatisfied with their on-line experience.

one help-desk group what kind of response they had received regarding problems they had transferred to a Level Two support group. "Those problems? Oh, they just disappeared into the black hole," one woman told me.

I heard a similar comment from a software group for which I was reviewing customer-survey results. Customers generally gave the group high marks for responsiveness, but buried within the high ratings was a solid block of low ratings. "What are these ratings?" I asked. "Oh, those," said the service manager, verbally signaling that bad news was about to follow.

"*Those*," he explained, "were associated with problems that were too complex to be resolved within the time frame set by the front-line staff, and so they were passed on to the R&D group for investigation." A group, he added, that they had privately named The Black Hole because problems submitted to them seemed never again to emerge.

Of course, providers suffer similarly when their customers aren't forthcoming. Software developers can relate sad sagas about information that has been withheld by the very customers who expect them to deliver on time. Customers, at times, can be just as unresponsive as some providers when it comes to returning calls, delivering information, and providing notification of status.

My client Maureen became a major contributor to the Black Hole when she invited me to give a keynote presentation at a conference for which two dates were being considered. I told her I'd temporarily reserve both dates. Some weeks later, I was invited to speak at another event scheduled for one of the two dates I had on hold. I called Maureen for an update, but couldn't reach her and so I left a message. I waited two days but Maureen didn't call me back. I called again. No response. I sent her a fax and an e-mail message, and then I left a few more phone messages. The Black Hole filleth.

Generous Interpretations

When you can't get the information you need, it's easy to start imagining possible explanations, such as, "They forgot about me." "They're ignoring me." "They're angry with me." The next thing you know, you're attributing to the person the most egregious motives, the worst intentions, the greatest possible ill will. Yet, in situations like this, it's important to start with a generous interpretation because often, the explanation for someone's behavior is very different from what you might imagine. Starting with a generous interpretation may not relieve your frustration, but it allows for the possibility that the other party isn't being spiteful, devious, or intentionally difficult.

In Maureen's case, my generous interpretation was that something had happened that kept her from being able to return my calls. Finally, one day, I called and she answered. I identified myself. She responded in a manner as friendly as if we'd just spoken the day before. I told her I'd been trying to reach her. "Oh yes," she said, "I received your messages, but I didn't have the information you wanted so I didn't call you back." I was flabbergasted.

Was Maureen being malicious in not responding to my messages? I don't think so. I think it just didn't occur to her that it would have been preferable to tell me she didn't know, and would keep me posted, than to simply not respond. She may have felt awkward about not having the answer, or perhaps she had a rule for commenting that kept her from admitting she didn't have the information I wanted. Still, none of these possibilities diminished the frustration I felt about getting no response whatsoever.

In most cases, people who don't contact you when you are waiting for information aren't being thoughtless; it may simply never have occurred to them to notify you. Don't make the same mistake with your customers, however. If customer satisfaction is important to you, periodically ask yourself:

- Who is expecting a follow-up call from me?
- Who is waiting for information that's important to them?
- Who has submitted a request and wants to know its status?

You could also ask,

- Who would appreciate receiving status information, even if they're not actively waiting for it?

Contact those people. Tell them what you know. If you don't know anything, tell them that. If possible, offer your best guess as to when you'll be able to tell them something more. And if you can't even tell them that, at least tell them that you can't tell them. All of these efforts will demonstrate that you care.

Don't contribute to the Black Hole. It's crowded enough without your help.

Sincere Status Reporting

Granted, it's not easy to call someone and say, "I don't have the information you want and I don't know when I *will* have it." But most people would rather know that than nothing at all.

Instead of letting customers feel ignored or forgotten, savvy professionals provide periodic updates. They keep customers informed on a regular basis even if only to tell them their problem is still in the queue. If you can be similarly responsive with your own customers—whether by phone, e-mail, database posting, or skywriting—you will probably find that they will give you extra leeway if ever you have difficulty meeting your commitments to them. Why will they exude such generosity? Because leaving customers in the dark is so pervasive and frustrating a service flaw that they will sit up and take notice when you do just the reverse. They'll appreciate your attentiveness and thoughtfulness. In the words of one IT customer: "They don't always have it done when I'd like, but at least they always keep me up-to-date."

Providing updates can build trust even when service is substandard, as was demonstrated to me by Kevin, a Data Center Operations staff member who worked in a company whose customers had widespread dissatisfaction with its IT organization. Many of the customers I interviewed enthusiastically mentioned Kevin by name as someone they could count on. Did he fix problems faster than his coworkers? No. Did he prevent problems from occurring? Hardly. What he did was make a practice of keeping customers informed about the status of problems that occurred during his shift.

Kevin helped his customers in another way that made them appreciate his work, but I didn't understand just how effective he was until he attended one of the customer-service classes I ran for his division. In one exercise in which I asked people to pair up so that one member of each pair could play the role of an Operations staff member and the other a customer, we saw why customers thought so highly of Kevin.

In the simulation, the staff member who was to contact the customer about an outage didn't have any information about what caused it or how long it would last. The people playing customers were directed to show how upset they felt about yet another outage and how eager they were for information about its duration.

Those in the role of "customer" were encouraged to be as demanding, angry, and frustrated as they felt their own customers were with them. Most needed little encouragement! Yet, in successive pairings with different classmates, Kevin's "customers" found themselves unable to behave in a hostile, impatient, or angry manner. They commented that when paired with Kevin, their frustration was defused by his gentle, soft-spoken manner, his obvious concern about the seriousness of the situation, and his promise to get back to them with information just as soon as he had any. With both his actual customers and his classroom "customers," Kevin exhibited genuine caring.

Informing customers can go a long way toward minimizing their potential distress. Kevin made the conscious decision to keep customers informed. Even though he usually was the bearer of bad news, his empathetic manner earned him praise from both customers and peers.

Managing the Wait State

Anyone can make a commitment to notify customers as Kevin did. However, instituting customer notification as an organizational practice provides a more consistent approach than relying on one individual's initiative. Service standards, statements a service provider creates and then communicates to customers to let them know how long they'll have to wait for some action or event to take place, provide a way to standardize customer notification.

Some sample service standards are shown below. The time frames indicated in these examples are strictly for illustrative purposes; your own standards must communicate commitments that are realistic for *you*.

- *For acknowledging messages to the support desk:* "Within one hour of receipt of an e-mail request for support, we will acknowledge your message. This acknowledgment will assure you that we have received your message and will provide an estimate of when we will respond to your inquiry."

  Notice that this service standard explains what is meant by "acknowledge," so as to prevent misinterpretations.

- *For responding to service requests:* "Within one week of receipt of a service request, we will provide written details of our planned response, on the condition that all the required information is given in the request."

  Notice the constraint that is specified: To receive a response within a week, customers must supply all required information.

- *For describing variations in service levels:* "Our goal is to resolve problems with A-level products within one business day of notification of the problem and B-level products within five business days of notification."

  This service standard not only informs customers of the time frame for problem resolution but also encourages use of A-level products. Customers are not prohibited from using B-level products, but they are made aware that a different time frame will apply. Possibly if Ken, whose dilemma was described in Chapter 2, had communicated a similar standard regarding service levels, his customers wouldn't have persisted in requesting help for products his division did not support.

- *For alerting customers about the waiting time:* "Customers placed on hold will be notified of the estimated wait for the next available agent."

     In this service standard, the duration of the wait is, of course, variable; yet knowing how long the wait is likely to be can be reassuring to customers. That was the experience of a woman who called her vendor and later described her reaction to the message she heard, "When I was put on hold and the message said I'd have a ten-minute wait, I was pleased. Not pleased at having to wait ten minutes, but at being told how long the wait would be. The message gave me information I could use to decide whether I wanted to wait or whether I would be better off hanging up and calling again later. Just being able to make that decision helped me feel I had some control over the situation."

Service standards are at the heart of service level agreements (SLAs). Addressed more fully in Chapter 11, service level agreement standards are the outcome of a negotiation process that considers both customer needs and provider capabilities. However, even if you don't undertake the lengthy process of negotiating an SLA, you can create service standards so that the parties with whom you interact will know what they can reasonably expect from you.

Communicating in Times of Uncertainty

What about when you don't know what the time frame will be? For example, think about how you handled the situation the last time a malfunction or outage occurred that significantly inconvenienced your customers and you didn't know the cause, yet customers demanded to know when service would be restored. Did you at least try to tell your customers what you did know even if you couldn't tell them what they wanted to know?

I remember a great example of this that occurred during a flight I took years ago—or rather, *waited* to take. Departure time had come and gone, but the fully boarded plane sat motionless at the gate.

Too often in situations like this, passengers are told nothing at all, but this occasion was different. The flight attendants on this plane knew that it would be better to give whatever information they could rather than let us sit there, agitating, fuming, and (not incidentally) driving them crazy. Since they couldn't tell us when the delay would end, they did the next best thing: They told us when they would provide updates. Speaking over the intercom, the Flight Attendant in Charge of Giving Passengers Bad News announced: "We're experiencing a mechanical problem, and we don't know how long it'll take to resolve. However, we will give you an update every fifteen minutes even if we have nothing new to tell you."

Note the form of this announcement. The flight attendant said, in effect,

- We will keep you informed of the status of the problem.
- We have a timetable for keeping you informed.
- We'll follow that timetable even if we have nothing new to tell you.

It was clear from the speed with which the flight attendant made the announcement that the policy for keeping customers informed already existed; airline personnel didn't have to hastily decide what to tell us and when. You might say that the existence of this policy meant that airline personnel expected delays, and you'd be right. Delays are a reality. So are outages and malfunctions. It's better to anticipate delays, outages, and malfunctions—and to prepare what you're going to communicate before these situations actually occur—rather than to be forced to deal simultaneously with the problem and with your customers' angry reactions to it.

The policy shown by this airline provides a model for a service standard that you can use when you experience network glitches, server snafus, power outages, hardware failures, or other malfunctions. Translated into service-standard format, the airline's service commitment might go like this:

> During delays, outages, or malfunctions, the duration of which is unknown, we will update customers on a specified schedule. We will advise them of this schedule, and we will adhere to it even if there is no change in status.

In certain situations, you might even ask customers how often they'd like to be updated and in what form. If you work with a specific set of customers, and have a manageable number of points of contact among them, you might establish a notification timetable based on their preferences. If you request and then accommodate these preferences, you'll be giving customers at least a little control over the situation when they'd otherwise have none at all. And you'll be enabling them to be responsive to their own customers, without feeling like they're being held hostage until the next announcement.

When your plane remains parked at the gate well after departure time, is an update every fifteen minutes better than an on-time departure? Not at all. And if, promptly every fifteen minutes for the next six hours, you were told, "We still don't have a clue," would that be acceptable? You *know* the answer to that! Clearly, this type of service standard has a practical limit. But when delays occur, most customers— including your own—would rather have a little information than none at all.

If possible, you might also give customers an alternative way to carry out their business while awaiting the restoration of service. I recently received the following e-mail message from a travel agency that I've worked with:

> Please be advised that we are not able to receive external e-mails at this time. We will alert you as soon as service is reinstated. Please call our office for assistance.

Savvy folks! In one brief message, agency personnel did three important things:

1. Instead of risking that e-mail from customers would bounce or go astray, they proactively notified customers of the problem, thereby giving people something to know instead of something to wonder about.
2. They promised to alert customers when service was restored, and did so a few hours later. Amazingly, many service providers neglect to notify customers of service restoration, leaving them unaware that the problem has been resolved.
3. They reminded customers that phone service remained available.

It's too bad, though, that they didn't think to include the agency's phone number in the e-mail message, so that customers could have called without the extra step of retrieving their phone number—a step some customers might not bother to take, especially when other options for making travel arrangements are readily available.

Honest Lies

These strategies for keeping customers informed and sparing them excessive unexplained delays relate to another Universal Grievance that most people find extremely disturbing: dishonesty. Customers claim they want to be dealt with in an honest manner, but are they saying that a service representative who thinks their shirt is hideous should tell them so? No, of course not! Most people who say they value honesty still appreciate tact, which may entail your deliberately withholding ideas or opinions that could cause offense.

When I ask people for examples of what they consider to be dishonest, they describe situations like the following:

- A car mechanic who said the broken car part was functioning properly when it wasn't.
- A service representative who guaranteed morning delivery of a critical part—but as of 4 P.M., nothing had been delivered.
- A systems development team that can't meet the deadline promised to customers.
- A doctor's receptionist who claimed the doctor was on schedule when . . . well, you know how that goes.

On occasion, situations such as these have explanations other than dishonesty, such as,

- undetected errors (The car part really was functioning properly; it was some other part that was malfunctioning.)
- innocent misunderstandings (The representative said delivery would be made *tomorrow* morning but the customer misheard *today*.)
- new information (Technical complexities caused delays in meeting the development deadline.)
- policy snafus (The receptionist was instructed to tell patients that the doctor would see them soon.)

To the extent that these kinds of explanations apply, none of these situations reflect actual lies. Yet to the customer, they feel like dishonesty is at play. What customers mean when they say that they value honesty is that they don't want information to be deliberately distorted or willfully withheld. They want "truthful disclosure," as one customer put it. What's more, they'd prefer a straightforward "I don't know" or "I can't" to a false promise or a fictitious explanation. They don't want to be led on. They don't want to be told A now and B later. And if A turns into B, they want to know immediately so they can plan accordingly.

The vehemence with which people describe their encounters with dishonesty highlights the emotional nature of this issue. When people discover they've been dealt with dishonestly, they react with anger, distrust, and unprintable language.

The type of dishonesty that seems to anger customers the most is when information about bad news is withheld—whether it concerns delays, problems, glitches, or unanticipated changes. Customers complain that when problems arise, they aren't informed early enough to be able to cope with the situation. Repeatedly, customers have told me of being notified shortly before a deliverable is due that the schedule had slipped. Whether a schedule slips a week, a month, or even several months, in nearly all cases, customers could have been notified well before the deadline.

Customers also complain of being assured that their needs can be addressed, or that they can be addressed in a particular way, when the truth is otherwise. Numerous customers have told me with frustration, "If the answer is no, I wish they'd just say so, instead of saying yes now, and then no later on."

Do you ever withhold bad news from your customers? When I ask technical professionals this question, their first response is to say no. But then they pause and reflect, and most eventually admit, some sheepishly and some with a head-slapping jolt of awareness, that the answer is yes. It seems that many of the people who abhor being treated dishonestly do withhold information from their own customers. Is it any wonder customers become angry, resentful, and distrustful?

Bad News Bearers

Needlessly withholding important information from customers can reflect a rule for commenting: "We must delay telling customers the unpleasant truth for as long as possible." This rule destroys trust and damages relationships.

Certainly it's tough to be the bearer of bad news. It's understandable to want to delay revealing that news in hopes that circumstances will change and you can recover with no one the wiser. But customers stress that they'd rather have bad news now than worse news later. For them, not having the news till later automatically *makes* it worse because they have less time to make appropriate adjustments, including—oh yes—notifying their own customers. Customers emphasize that they, too, have deadlines to meet and people to serve; the sooner they know of a change or a problem, the sooner they can take steps to manage the situation.

As one customer put it, reflecting the views of many others: "I know you can't always get the job done when you said you would. But if that turns out to be the case, just let me know *before* the time is up."

Most customers are reasonable people. They know that things don't always work out as planned, and would much prefer to know the situation as it is, not as you would wish them to think it is. They want to have some control over their responsibilities, and in order to have that, they need to know the true state of things.

When customers seem overly demanding or unyielding, their behavior may be the consequence of repeatedly being on the receiving end of what they experience as blatant dishonesty. Dare to tell your customers the truth. They may not like to hear bad news, but they'll appreciate you for giving it to them.

Dishonest Honesty

Sometimes, it's not clear what's honest and what's not. When the topic of honesty came up during one of my presentations, an IT director raised a fascinating question: "If five possible options respond to the customers' needs and we know that two of them are technically the best, is it dishonest to present the customer with only those two?" After all, he reasoned, isn't it more efficient to simply present those options already identified as the best?

In my view, this issue deals less with honesty than with customers' process expectations about knowing their options. Customers have varying preferences and process expectations. Some customers that I've talked to about this very matter have told me that they would want to know all their options, whether "all" means three or thirty-seven. Others prefer to know only the top few options, largely due to time constraints and limited subject-matter knowledge. Still others want to know just the top two, as judged by those on the selection team. But keep in mind, too, that a customer's preferences are likely to vary from one circumstance to another.

What's important in honoring the process expectation of honesty is to respect the customer's view of what is and isn't honest. One approach is to ask customers whether they'd prefer to know all the options, just the top ones, or some other possibility. Another approach, suggested by the IT director, is to say to the customer, "I came up with five options, two of which are strong candidates. How about if we consider those first? If you then decide you'd like to know about the others, we can consider them as well." This is an honest approach because it respects the customers' wishes.

CLAIMS OF CARING

Communicating so as to respond to your customers' process expectations provides evidence of caring. But guard against telling people that you care if your actions suggest otherwise. The IT division in this chapter's opening story was guilty of just this type of contradiction. The division's published *service goal* of world-class service said, in effect: "We aim to rate with the best." But the flagrantly flawed *service delivery* said just the reverse: "We've got nowhere to go but up."

When providers care about delivering good service, their actions reflect that service orientation. They don't need to announce how much they care; their actions speak more forcefully than words ever could. Conversely, providers that declare one thing and do another are guilty of creating a communication gap that provokes cynicism, disbelief, and distrust among customers.

One place I often see evidence of this type of gap is the superstore in which the checkout clerk asks, "Did you find everything all right?" Invariably, these are the stores in which I've had the toughest time finding what I'm looking for—including someone to help me find what I'm looking for. When I can find neither the item I want nor anyone to help me find it, I figure the store doesn't really care much about my business, so by the time someone at the checkout counter asks whether I've found everything, *I* no longer care.

Sometimes, the gap occurs because of a contradiction between what a person says and his or her manner or tone of voice. When I returned a rental car at the airport several weeks ago, and the rental-car agent asked, "How was the car?" her gaze was fixed on her terminal, and her somber demeanor and hushed voice suggested something less than wide-eyed interest in my response.

I noticed a similar contradiction while checking in at a hotel that proclaimed its service excellence by means of a sign posted at the Front Desk, plaques in the elevator, and a feed-back survey card in my room that stressed how much the hotel staff cared about its guests. Unfortunately, on my first morning there, the caring staff failed to deliver my wake-up call and I had to rush to make it to my morning meeting on time.

The feedback card next to my telephone informed me that if I wanted an immediate response to any concern, I could describe it on the card and drop the card in the slot in the Front Desk. That was a hopeful indicator: Evidence that a service provider wants to right the wrongs its customers have experienced is an important sign of caring. So I jotted a note about not getting my wake-up call and, when I rushed out for the day, I dropped the card in the slot, mindful that all eyes were upon me as I did so.

Upon returning to my room that evening, I expected to find . . . what? An offer of a free night's stay? Not likely. A bouquet of flowers? Not really. I expected a message with an apology. Instead . . . nothing. No evidence whatsoever, either during the remainder of my stay at the hotel or thereafter, that the hotel staff knew of my complaint, cared about it, or intended to do anything as a result of it. Claiming to care about customers' complaints and then ignoring them is a risky message to communicate when customers can take their business—and your reputation—elsewhere.

It doesn't take many such episodes before customers question whether claims of caring are merely a promotional bluff. Why should customers believe a service claim when experience tells them something different? Whenever there is a contradiction between an organization's service philosophy and its actions, it's the actions that customers notice, remember, and talk about. And it's the actions that affect their satisfaction ratings.

It might be beneficial for you to reexamine what you communicate—intentionally or unintentionally—about your service commitment and to analyze how well that goal translates into action. Examine your actions, and question whether they accurately reflect your service orientation. If they don't, it may be best not to spout that orientation too loudly or visibly. Otherwise, when you fall short, customers will conclude that you really don't care.

The Communication of Non-Caring

Because I travel so much, I've accumulated numerous hotel stories, including one last traveler's tale with which to end this chapter. It transpired at a hotel I was staying at for four nights while working with a new client. As I was checking in, I was pleased to see signs in the lobby and in my room promising, "Your satisfaction guaranteed, or you don't pay." The service clerk pointed out this guarantee as I registered, and emphasized that it represented the hotel's policy.

For half the stay, I was very happy with the hotel. I enjoyed the comfy furniture in my room, the exercise room, and the friendly staff. Then two minor problems arose. The first was that when I called the Front Desk my third evening there to get some information, no one answered. I tried several times, each time letting the phone ring at least a dozen times. I finally gave up. The second problem was that the next evening, I had difficulty retrieving my phone messages. When I called the Front Desk for help, a woman gave me instructions that didn't work. When I called again, she told me she was finishing something else, and would call me back in a few minutes. She didn't call back. When, after a half-hour, I tried again, the man who answered gave me correct instructions.

As a frequent traveler, I've become accustomed to service glitches, and would have put both of these complaints behind me, but for the major problem that occurred: When I returned home after the trip, my husband told me he had tried to call me on my final evening at this hotel. The person who answered told him there was no one at the hotel by my name. He spelled it for her. She checked the log for the entire week, and insisted there was no record of my being there. Since I'd gone out for the evening and my cell phone was turned off, he had no idea where I was or what might have happened to me.

When I learned about this situation, I wrote a friendly letter to the hotel management describing my initial satisfaction and both my major and minor complaints. I asked to be reimbursed for one night's stay. As I complete this chapter, it's been more than a year since I sent the letter. I have received no response from the hotel and have received no reimbursement.

I don't have to wonder if this is a hotel that really cares. I already know the answer.

10

Gathering Customer Feedback

Scott, an IT director whose division was a profit center to internal customers, learned a tough lesson: Failing to regularly gather feedback is a great way to lose good customers. Scott's staff members had been proud of their long-term relationship with the payroll department, for which they had provided extensive computer services. Unfortunately, they had begun to take this important and profitable customer for granted, competently delivering services but neglecting to maintain contact. There'd been no complaints, so why worry?

Imagine their surprise when the payroll manager abruptly announced plans to transfer the department's computer needs to an outside vendor. Not for better service—service quality had been fine—but for a better price. The payroll department needed to cut costs, and the vendor had offered a competitive price. Scott's group, having neglected to regularly visit the payroll department, was oblivious to the department's growing cost pressures. The upshot: Their "happy" customer had upped and gone elsewhere.

Pete, the project manager in Chapter 3, also thought he had a happy customer, but he learned otherwise from a post-project satisfaction survey. Pete might have learned much sooner about Carl's grievance—and might have prevented it altogether—if he had solicited Carl's feedback while the project was under way.

In failing to systematically gather customer feedback, Scott and Pete fell victim to the dangerous assumption that the absence of complaints signifies happy customers. The reality is that unless a customer's experience is exceptionally negative, he or she will rarely offer unsolicited feedback. Oh, the customer may think, "Gee, I wish they'd . . ." or "They really ought to . . ." but most minor grievances don't trigger enough oomph for people to lodge a complaint.

Even with major grievances, many customers simply grouse to each other rather than to the source of their problems. Most customers who do go to the source eventually give up if repeated complaints aren't addressed. In one company, a software director commented that customer complaints had decreased in recent months—a good sign, he noted. But when I asked customers about this decrease, they had a different explanation: They had just plain gotten tired of complaining. As one of them asked in an exasperated tone, "What was the point, when nothing ever changed?"

Of course, not all service providers *want* to hear complaints. In *A Complaint Is a Gift*, authors Barlow and Møller emphasize that "In order for us to treat complaints as gifts, we need to achieve a complete shift in perception and attitude about the role of complaints in modern business relationships."[1] Their book helps readers gain an understanding of the emotional and interpersonal dynamics of disappointed people, which makes it easier to separate the content of the complaint from the emotion of being blamed for it.

Gathering customer feedback is a communication process that's woefully inadequate in most organizations. This chapter helps you learn how to successfully gather feedback from your customers, to avoid a gap between their view of your services and your own.

---

[1] Janelle Barlow and Claus Møller, *A Complaint Is a Gift: Using Customer Feedback As a Strategic Tool* (San Francisco: Berrett-Koehler Publishers, 1996), p. 13.

THREE FEEDBACK-GATHERING FLAWS

If you want to understand your customers' perspective, you must explicitly request their feedback. As Richard Gerson notes in *Measuring Customer Satisfaction*, "A customer is satisfied whenever his or her needs, real or perceived, are met or exceeded. So, how do you know what the customer needs, wants and expects? You ask!"[2]

In other words, if you don't ask for feedback, you may not get any. But even if you do ask, how you ask strongly influences the quality and quantity of feedback you get. When I review the ways that organizations gather customer feedback, I regularly encounter several flaws, three of which are serious enough to undermine the entire effort:

1. inconveniencing customers to get feedback
2. making customers uncomfortable about providing feedback
3. ignoring the service attributes that are most important to customers

Flaw #1: Inconveniencing Customers to Get Feedback

Customers who are especially eager to give you feedback may be willing to tolerate some inconvenience, but most customers aren't so enthusiastic. If you really want feedback, you must make it as easy and effortless as possible for customers to provide it. In particular, three directives should be followed:

- *Keep it short.* One IT customer-satisfaction form asked customers to rate eighty items on a seven-point scale. Eighty items! Not surprisingly, feedback quality suffers when the respondents' brains have turned to mush from the tedium of responding. Another survey, distributed by a help desk, was ten pages long—a discour-

---

[2] Richard F. Gerson, *Measuring Customer Satisfaction* (Menlo Park, Calif.: Crisp Publications, 1993), p. 7.

aging oh-no-not-another-survey length. With people already suffocating under an overload of demands, you will be most successful in obtaining high-quality feedback if you ask for it in as concise a form as possible. Try to design surveys that can be completed in ten minutes, and make sure the instructions emphasize your estimate of the required time.

- *Allow customers time to respond.* A caller from my local office-supply emporium said he was conducting a survey and asked what I liked or didn't like about the store. I told him I needed time to recall my experiences and asked him to call back the next day. He said he would, but he never called back. Apparently he hadn't factored my need for time into his survey design. Similarly, as I checked out of a hotel, the checkout chap asked if I'd mind filling out a feedback form. I did mind. I was in a rush to get to the airport and he wouldn't let me take it and mail it back after I'd filled it out. If you want useful feedback, give people time to reflect and don't wait till they're on the run to request their feedback.

- *Omit unnecessary steps.* As part of a badly needed service-improvement effort, the management of a rail line posted large notices in several train stations, asking customers for feedback. The only way to respond was by writing a letter and mailing it to the address specified on the posted notices. Because few people are willing to go to that much extra effort to provide feedback, the rail line received very little. In a seafood restaurant at which feedback was solicited by means of postcards placed on tables, customers were reminded, "Please do not forget to affix a stamp before mailing." Asking customers to do extra work in order to provide feedback ensures that most simply won't bother. Both the rail line and the restaurant could have provided forms for customers to fill out and a collection point for dropping them off.

Flaw #2: Making Customers Uncomfortable About Providing Feedback

Some customers feel inarticulate in expressing their grievances. Some fear retribution. Some don't want to make a fuss. Some would rather tolerate poor service than complain about it. Reasons such as these keep dissatisfied customers from voicing their complaints. Furthermore, in cultures in which saving face is a deeply held value, many people are uncomfortable giving feedback to others for fear of causing them to lose face, and any negative feedback they give may be couched in words that mask the complaint.

Therefore, if you want to know about your customers' concerns, it's not enough simply to ask them. You must think carefully about how you ask them. Even in cultures and companies in which feedback-gathering is commonplace, it's wise to help customers avoid experiencing any fear, awkwardness, or discomfort in providing feedback. For example, consider the following approaches:

- *Explain that their feedback will help you help them.* Many people respond favorably to a genuine request for help. By emphasizing that you value their feedback, you are, in effect, giving them permission to say what they might otherwise keep to themselves. Point out that you realize that their perspective differs from your own, and that their insights will help you understand their perspective. Explain that the more detail they provide about their service experiences, the better positioned you'll be to make adjustments. Offer to accept their feedback in more than one form, such as by phone instead of in writing, if they'd prefer.

- *Frame requests for feedback appropriately.* Even people who don't like to complain may be willing to offer helpful suggestions. (My on-line thesaurus supports this idea: It lists "suggestion" as a synonym for "complaint.") To encourage this, you can frame your request along the following lines:

- "What are two things we're doing well and two things you'd like to see changed?"
- "Based on your recent experience, what would you most like us to do differently?"
- "Please describe an experience with our service that pleased you and an experience that disappointed you."

This approach invites respondents to offer constructive suggestions rather than complaints. As a result, otherwise reluctant respondents will be more likely to offer their ideas.

- *Set the stage for feedback-gathering.* Giving feedback is less awkward for customers if doing so is a routine part of the relationship. For example, in the opening stories of this chapter, Scott and Pete could have explicitly talked with their customers about incorporating a feedback-gathering process into their work together. They could have agreed, for example, to meet at designated intervals and discuss what pleased or concerned each of them. With this type of agreement, they'd be giving each other permission to voice grievances. Talking about feedback early in the project or relationship is an example of communicating about how you're going to communicate, and it helps you build the strong foundation described in Chapter 4.

- *Have customers interviewed by their coworkers.* Rarely do providers invite customers to take an active role in gathering customer feedback. Yet one of the best feedback-gathering efforts I've ever seen involved IT customers who participated on a feedback team with IT personnel and assisted in collecting feedback from their own coworkers. With each feedback session jointly led by a customer representative and an IT staff member, customers openly described their grievances and recommendations.

- *Have an objective third party conduct interviews for you.*
  Although customers may suppress or edit their comments when asked directly by their supplier or vendor,
  they rarely seem reluctant to voice their concerns when
  an objective party asks for feedback. These third parties
  can be outside consultants, internal facilitators, or
  employees who are from internal groups other than
  those being critiqued.

- *Ensure confidentiality.* The fear of retribution is legitimate.
  Who can fault customers for preferring anonymity if
  complaints could cause the supplier to withhold service
  or shift priority to other customers? Even people who
  give enthusiastically positive feedback sometimes withhold their names, perhaps because they consider the very
  process of giving feedback too great a form of self-disclosure. Therefore, make signatures optional on written
  feedback, and ensure that revealed names will remain
  confidential. Where feasible, use on-line methods that
  allow anonymous comments to be submitted to a central
  location.

Flaw #3: Ignoring the Service Attributes That Are Most Important to Customers

If you request feedback based solely on what *you* think is
important to customers, you may conclude they're satisfied
when they're not—and fail to learn what *is* important to them.

For example, a hotel I stayed at was excellent in terms of
the attributes hotels generally ask customers about: check-in,
room cleanliness, room service, and so on. Yet when I heard
the chilling sound of someone trying to unlock my door, I
made a startling discovery. The peephole in the door was way
above my head. I had nothing to stand on to reach it, and no
way to see who was there without opening the door and
revealing that inside the room was a woman traveling alone—
and a short one, at that. Fortunately, the person soon gave up
and left, but when I checked the feedback form, I saw that it

didn't ask me to rate the peephole placement or provide room for me to describe my dissatisfaction with it.

In assessing customer satisfaction, find out what's important to your customers and ask how well you're doing with those things. Granted, other hotel guests may have found the size of the coffee pot, the location of the ice machine, or the choice of overpriced movies to be their particular pet peeve—concerns that in the greater scheme of things may be as narrowly focused as my own. But without finding out what's important to customers, you have no way of knowing which concerns have become dominant and, therefore, worthy of attention.

Eliminating the Flaws

In evaluating your current process for gathering feedback or your plan for a new process, keep these three flaws in mind. They are reminders that in gathering feedback, you're more likely to succeed if you do the following:

1. Make it convenient for customers to give feedback.
2. Help customers feel comfortable about providing feedback.
3. Focus on the service attributes most important to customers.

ASKING THE RIGHT QUESTIONS AND ASKING THE QUESTIONS RIGHT

Surveys remain the mechanism of choice for assessing customer satisfaction. Most surveys revolve around rating scales: rating the competence of support staff on a seven-point scale, for example. Certainly, ratings help establish baselines for detecting changes in satisfaction levels over time. However, a great many surveys request ratings without also requesting supporting commentary. Without comments, you won't get an understanding of the experiences, preferences, or expectations that led customers to assign the ratings they did. What value, then, are the ratings?

In some organizations, the primary reason for conducting a survey is to serve management's belief in quantification. As one fellow put it, describing an expensive survey his company was conducting, "It's overkill for our purposes, but the president wants to do it. He likes numbers." Despite the preferences of the quantitatively inclined, ratings alone give an incomplete and easily misinterpreted picture of the state of customer satisfaction.

Face-to-Face Feedback-Gathering

I'm a strong proponent of face-to-face feedback-gathering. Ratings-based surveys, whether on-line or on paper, provide only a limited insight into customers' concerns. The best way to get a more-than-superficial idea of your customers' concerns is to talk to them—and to *listen* to what they say. In doing so, you can invite customers to describe their issues in their own words. You can also seek additional details about their experiences and clarify ambiguous terminology. In an article on needs assessment, Dean Leffingwell observes that "The customer may launch into a stream of consciousness dialogue describing, in gory detail, the horrors of the current situation."[3] As he notes, this is exactly the behavior you're seeking! When customers hold forth in this way, don't interrupt them—and don't rush to the next question.

Needless to say, the face-to-face interview approach doesn't lend itself to collecting feedback from large numbers of customers, except at considerable expense. I was once called by a friend to comment on the merit of a proposal submitted to his company by a survey vendor. My friend's management was interested in having a large-scale customer-satisfaction survey conducted, but, as the managers had not previously conducted any formal assessments of customer satisfaction, the details of the proposal were unfamiliar to them. According to the survey vendor's proposal, the customer population would be segmented into several categories. Twelve customers from each category would undergo a seven-minute phone interview. In total, a squad of interviewers would conduct more than one hundred seven-minute interviews. The cost of designing and conducting the survey, analyzing the findings, and generating reports would exceed $150,000. My friend wanted to know whether I thought this was a wise investment.

Although this type of survey would surely yield some useful information, I view it as an overly complex and expensive starting point for assessing customer satisfaction. In my experience, a small number of in-depth customer interviews can generate volumes of high-quality information, at a fraction of the cost of a large-scale survey. I suggested to my friend that his company initiate its feedback-gathering process with some in-depth customer interviews. If serious patterns of dissatisfaction emerged, they could be rapidly addressed without the delays incurred in planning and running a mega-survey. Furthermore, a small-scale undertaking could serve as a prototype

[3] Dean Leffingwell, "Understanding User Needs," *Software Development* (August 1997), pp. 54–55.

in the event the company still wanted to carry out the big-bucks survey.

Before ending our phone conversation, I asked my friend what his company would be likely to do with the findings if it proceeded with the large-scale survey. "Probably nothing," he responded. "That's our usual approach. We collect gobs of data. Then we ignore it." Enough said.

The Impact of the Setting

The seemingly small matter of the setting for an interview or meeting can have a major impact on the quality of the feedback that's gathered. Author Wayne Strider emphasizes the effect of the physical space on how people interact.[4] He once observed a meeting in a windowless, freshly painted, newly carpeted room. Because the person who had scheduled the room didn't know about its unfortunate condition, people began filing in as expected. Paint vapors mingled with carpet-glue fumes in the airless room, conspiring to make the meeting short—an imaginative strategy, perhaps, if you're burdened by meetings that last forever. However, as you might imagine, the meeting was not only brief, it was also totally unproductive, with most of the discussion centering on the condition of the room.

Other environmental factors can reduce the odds of productive interaction. Consider my experience when I was interviewed at the local mall by a woman conducting interviews with consumers to determine name preferences for a new suntan lotion. She assured me it would take only a few minutes and led me to a cramped cubicle in a back office on the lower level of the mall. Bidding me to sit on one of two straight-back wooden chairs, she then asked me a series of questions about my reactions to a list of proposed names for the new lotion. Stating that I thought all the names sounded like medicine you'd take after your suntan lotion failed to do its job, I was thanked for my time and sent out to find my own way back to daylight.

---

[4] Wayne Strider, *Powerful Project Leadership* (Vienna, Va.: Management Concepts, 2002), pp. 20–21. For more information, see www.striderandcline.com.

What made this experience memorable, however, was not the uncomfortable setting or the off-putting lotion names, but the unprofessional way the woman conducted the interview. Staff members kept poking their heads into the cubicle, shouting questions at her. Repeatedly, she interrupted the interview to help them. At several points, she even left the cubicle to resolve problems. Each time she returned, she told me how grateful she was for my participation. "It'll only take a few minutes longer," she repeated for the umpteenth time, attributing the chaos to the fact that, as supervisor for the department, she was on call to handle every problem, big or small, because several key staff members hadn't shown up for work.

My interviewer became so flustered by the commotion that she read aloud not only the marketing-survey instructions for me, but also those intended for her as the interviewer, such as, "Allow the respondent to give multiple responses to this question." Because her client was demanding results, she was trying to do many jobs at once. I could appreciate her problem—who hasn't faced staff shortages and pressure from a demanding project? Still, if you want to appear professional, do the opposite of what she did.

For example, conduct the interview in a place that's free of distractions and interruptions. Strive to appear relaxed and confident, even if your insides are trying out for the trampoline team. Be prepared. Reading from a script is fine, but practice beforehand, so you don't sound as if you're reading it for the first time. If things go wrong, don't call undue attention to them. Repeated apologies are just plain annoying. Before you begin the interview, state how long it will take—and then stick to that time commitment. (My interview took about four minutes; the interruptions extended it to thirty.)

Making Surveys Work

If surveys are the route you choose, then take steps to make them work effectively for you. Use ratings if you like, but also allow respondents to offer feedback in their own words. In one well-run survey, employees were asked to rate several service groups they interacted with and then to respond in writing to the following four questions:

1. What are the reasons for your satisfaction rating with the group?
2. What would you describe as the group's three most important services, and how well are they being delivered?
3. How would you describe the group's strengths?
4. What do you see as opportunities for improvement?

Busy though employees were, they responded in detail, commenting on what pleased them and leaving little doubt about the service inadequacies that had upset them. Knowing only that the ratings averaged 3.2 on a 7-point scale would have meant little, but the verbal commentary that accompanied the ratings clarified what respondents meant and what was important to them.

These questions can also be used in an interview format, provided that people are given the questions in advance of the interview and are allowed ample time to review them. That way, people have a chance to recall their experiences, making it more likely that they'll consider the whole of their experience rather than just the most recent (or most unpleasant) interaction.

Esther Derby, a software development consultant and facilitator, recommends that when feedback is likely to trigger strongly felt responses, it's wise to begin by deliberately asking objective questions. In an e-mail discussion we had on this topic, Derby noted, "I find that when I ask people to remember events, words, and phrases before I ask about their gut reaction . . . , they are more able to see the big picture over a period of time, remember the good and not-so-good, and see patterns and progress."[5]

Derby has observed that beginning at this objective level has a calming effect by slowing down the natural thought process and encouraging people to pause consciously at each step. Derby finds that using this approach to solicit feedback in a group setting, such as during a project retrospective, helps those involved to reach agreement on the data before going further. Reaching agreement at the onset is especially important because different people see different things and draw different conclusions from what they see.

If we were to design a survey to evaluate services delivered by, say, the XYZ group, a set of objective-then-subjective questions that draw on Derby's approach might include the following:

1. It's been six months since we last asked for your feedback about XYZ's service delivery. What events related to your interaction with XYZ stand out for you in that interval? What pictures, words, or phrases come to mind?
2. What is your reaction to what you've just noted?
3. Overall, what pleases you about the service you've received from XYZ? What concerns you?

---

[5] Esther Derby, private communication. See www.estherderby.com for several of Esther's articles and information on her services.

4. (a) In reflecting on the past six months, how would you rate XYZ's service delivery, using a 7-point scale, where 1 equals terrible and 7 equals superb? (b) Can you explain the reason for your rating?
5. Please describe any suggestions you have for improvement in XYZ's services.
6. Add anything else you'd like to comment on.

The first question focuses on what customers actually saw and heard, the second focuses on meaning, and the third focuses on feelings, as though stepping through the Satir Interaction Model described in Chapter 4. Note that the request for a rating doesn't appear until the fourth question. Positioning the rating question midway in the survey, rather than at the beginning, improves the odds that the rating will reflect in-depth thought about services and service delivery.

An Innovative Approach to Assessing Customer Satisfaction

The case study outlined below describes one software company's approach to gathering feedback regularly, responding to it, and taking action based on it. You may find this company's innovative, relationship-building approach to be a suitable model to draw from when creating or improving your own process.

Case Study: Two or three times per year, a representative from each client company participates in a formal customer-satisfaction survey. But this formal survey isn't the kind that ends up in the "Long, Boring Surveys" file. The survey takes the form of interviews conducted by phone by an employee charged with this responsibility. The objectives of the survey are as follows:

- Identify patterns of concern.
- Generate ideas for service improvement.
- Identify complaints that should be addressed immediately.
- Pinpoint problems that deserve attention and create a plan for taking action.

- Provide an outlet for grievances that may otherwise be withheld.
- Communicate to clients that their views are important.

Prior to each interview, the interviewer e-mails a list of questions to the customer. The questions remain the same for all interviews and include the following:

- How have you found our response time in answering your calls?
- How confident are you in the knowledge level of our technical staff?
- How would you rate the ability of our support staff to resolve problems?
- Can you suggest one improvement in the way we handle upgrades?

Unlike ratings-oriented surveys, these interviews ask for verbal feedback only. The interviewer records the feedback and then assigns numerical ratings to the customer's responses. *What?* you may be thinking, but read on. The interviewer then e-mails the write-up of the comments and the assigned ratings to the customer and asks him or her to correct any inaccuracies. Customers are also asked to review the interviewer's ratings and to lower any they feel are too high. Interestingly, most of the changes customers have requested have been to *raise* the ratings. It seems the interviewer rates his company more severely than his customers do!

Escalation procedures ensure that dissatisfied customers or serious problems receive immediate attention. If customers express complaints, the interviewer schedules a follow-up call to determine that improvements have been made to the customer's satisfaction.

Every few months, survey results are compiled and stored on the company's intranet for access by all employees. Both employees and customers receive a description of the improvements being undertaken in response to customer feedback.

Lessons from This Approach

This feedback process illustrates several keys to success with feedback-gathering:

1. *Assess customer satisfaction regularly.* The very process of soliciting feedback periodically tells customers that you genuinely care about their viewpoint. This is part of the psychology of feedback-gathering. People may not always feel comfortable about offering feedback, but they generally appreciate being asked. The very fact of being asked for their feedback can lead customers to boost the ratings they give.
2. *Give customers advance notice of the survey.* Doing so allows them time to gather their thoughts and to recall their service experiences. If possible, show them the questions that will be asked, so they can prepare. After all, the idea isn't to trick customers, but to help them express what's important to them.
3. *Request open-ended comments.* Whether or not you use ratings, solicit comments. Verbal commentary invariably generates more meaningful information about what pleases or distresses customers than ratings alone. By inviting comments, you can get specific examples of matters that concern them, and you can ask follow-up questions to be sure you understand.
4. *Let customers confirm your understanding.* Give them a chance to confirm that you really heard their comments. Doing so further communicates that their views count. In response, they will often make observations they hadn't thought of before.
5. *Develop response-escalation procedures.* Ensure that serious problems identified through the survey are quickly addressed, so that dissatisfied customers don't become even more unhappy. Establish criteria for selecting complaints that deserve quick attention, such as a rating below a certain level or a particularly negative comment. Problems that cry out for immediate

attention provide a moment of truth: an opportunity to take action that will transform a negative experience into a positive one.[6]

6. *Follow up with dissatisfied customers.* While you resolve problems, stay in touch with the customers who reported them. Let them know you really heard their complaints. Express your appreciation for their feedback. Inform them of the changes you plan to make, and notify them once you've implemented the changes. If the complaints concern matters that you can't change or choose not to change, or if they stem from misunderstandings on the part of the customer, provide an explanation or clarification. Bottom line: Don't ignore dissatisfied customers. If treated appropriately, they can become your most satisfied customers.

7. *Distribute survey results widely.* Enlightened organizations disseminate feedback findings to both employees and customers. Granted, it's not so easy to disclose the results when customer satisfaction is slithering off the bottom of the scale. But employees are likely to feel more ownership of problems if they have direct access to the feedback rather than secondhand accounts. When customers are informed that you're making adjustments based on their feedback, they may hang in there with you.

8. *Systematize the feedback-gathering process.* The organized, step-by-step approach this case-study company has adopted makes its process easy to understand, document, and carry out. Both employees and customers know what to expect. The relationship that the employee who conducts the survey cultivates with the

---

[6] The term "moment of truth," popularized by Jan Carlzon, refers to the moment when the customer comes in contact with any aspect of your business and, on the basis of that contact, forms an opinion—positive or negative—about the quality of your service. By acting quickly, a negative situation can be transformed into a positive opportunity. See Jan Carlzon, *Moments of Truth* (New York: Perennial, HarperCollins, 1989).

customers makes them more willing to describe their grievances. By surveying client companies on a staggered schedule, the work load in conducting the surveys is relatively small at any point in time.

WHEN AND HOW TO GATHER FEEDBACK

Although surveys are the most familiar way to gather customer feedback, they are hardly the only way. Indeed, each instance of customer contact offers opportunities to obtain feedback. Therefore, the most effective feedback-gathering process is one that is ongoing and uses a combination of methods, such as surveys, interviews, focus groups, periodic meetings, gripe sessions, and casual chats. Every method can yield useful information; no one method alone is sufficient.

The following points during a customer relationship may be appropriate for seeking feedback. Consider how soliciting feedback at each of the points can help you improve service.

At the Start of a New Customer Relationship: Feedback right at the outset? Absolutely. As noted in Chapter 5, the earlier you learn about what's important to your customers—their plans, attitudes, fears, hopes, concerns, and preferences—the better positioned you will be to address their needs effectively or to help them understand why you can't. You might think of feed*back* at this stage as feed*forward:* gathering information that will help you successfully address their needs.

The best way to gather this type of feedback is face-to-face, through one-on-one sessions or small group meetings. These sessions are a way to achieve the following:

- Begin to build a strong working relationship with customers.
- Develop rapport.
- Learn about their service history and noteworthy service experiences.
- Identify their criteria for success.
- Understand their needs and concerns.
- Identify their service expectations.
- Help them understand what *they* can realistically expect from *you.*

At Regular Points Throughout Your Working Relationship: Basically, every contact you have with your customers, whether planned or unplanned, is a potential opportunity to assess their satisfaction with your services. Ideally, everyone who interacts with customers is committed to listening carefully to their comments, so as to detect and respond to complaints and concerns.

Formal methods such as service reviews, group discussions, focus groups, and off-site meetings are fine, but you don't need to post a "Feedback-Gathering in Progress" sign in order to ask customers how things are going. Sometimes, casual hallway conversations or just dropping by can help you find out what's on people's minds. Using a combination of formal and informal methods will help you to accomplish the following:

- Detect changes in satisfaction levels over time.
- Trap problems before they turn into crises.
- Identify requirements for changes in service delivery.
- Learn about customer concerns that might not surface otherwise.

- Learn what's working well so that you can be sure to keep doing it.
- Keep reinforcing the "we care" message.

When Redesigning Customer Services: When providers plan improvements to better serve their customers, they often ignore the views of the very customers they're striving to serve better. "Why'd they do *that?*" customers are left to wonder, especially when the changes aren't what they would have liked. Making important decisions on behalf of customers without first considering their perspective is a mistake.

Methods for obtaining feedback to support service redesign include asking customers for examples of service problems, interviewing customers to test ideas for new approaches, and—perhaps best of all—inviting customers to participate on the redesign team. By seeking feedback from customers during your redesign effort, you'll be more successful in doing the following:

- Ensure that you understand their needs as you plan the redesign.
- Avoid modifications that customers will resist or resent.
- Gain insight into their perspective of the proposed changes.
- Identify possible changes you would not have learned about otherwise.
- Gain customer buy-in in helping you help them, increasing the odds of success.

At Times of Service-Related Changes: When people are affected by change, they feel a greater need to know what's happening. As you implement major service changes, it's wise to keep customers in the loop. While formal get-togethers may be helpful, you can also benefit from spending time in customer areas talking with them. As one IT client liaison told me, "They tell you things when you're there that they don't tell you when you're not there."

By providing ad hoc ways for customers to give you feedback, you'll improve your ability to accomplish the following:

- Reduce molehills of confusion before they become mountains.
- Resolve customers' misconceptions, mistakes, and false assumptions.
- Relieve the fear or uncertainty customers may experience due to the changes.
- Build goodwill, confidence, and trust.
- Keep reinforcing the "we care" message.

At Selected Checkpoints During a Project: During lengthy or complex undertakings, the temptation is to just forge ahead without pausing to resolve conflicts. However, it's far better to deal with concerns in a timely matter and to diffuse tensions before they escalate into shoot-outs.

The feedback-gathering methods you employ during a project can vary depending on the needs and preferences of those involved. For example, you may at different times put emphasis on face-to-face meetings, conferences calls, or e-mail check-ins with individual customers. Feedback-gathering at these checkpoints enables you to achieve the following:

- Identify customers' concerns that have not yet been voiced.
- Solicit and answer questions that customers otherwise would not have asked.
- Discuss project status in a more casual manner than formal reporting methods would allow.
- Review expectations and confirm that you and they are still in sync.
- Identify business changes that could affect your project.

After Receiving Negative Feedback: When you receive a complaint or encounter evidence of customer dissatisfaction, it's natural to want to defend against it, dismiss it, or find fault with the customer—or all three. But when one customer offers some feedback that's hard to take, that person is rarely the only one with that view. And when many hold a negative view, it's foolish to ignore it.

Stressful though it may be, dealing with negative feedback is best done face-to-face or, if that's not feasible, voice-to-voice. This direct contact will help you to succeed at the following:

- Ensure that you understand the feedback.
- Get specific examples of situations that led to the negative reaction.
- Demonstrate that you are interested in addressing and resolving the problem.
- Provide an explanation if the situation was actually a customer misunderstanding.
- Involve customers in helping you make improvements.
- Rebuild confidence in your service delivery.
- Turn a negative situation into a positive one.

ACT ON THE FEEDBACK GATHERED

Clearly, customer interaction offers plenty of opportunities to gather feedback, and the methods for gathering it are many. But then what? When you receive customer feedback, do you analyze it, identify service improvements, and take action? Or do you do what so many organizations do: nothing at all?

Examples of this "doing nothing" syndrome are easy to find. For example, one IT survey revealed that many customers felt the IT group didn't understand their priorities. When I asked the manager what this complaint meant, he said he didn't know. He confessed that no follow-up had been done to learn more about the customers' concerns, let alone to address them. When was this feedback gathered? More than a year earlier!

In another company, when I asked about the status of a company-wide survey that a technology group had conducted, the manager went digging in his bottom drawer. He had stuffed the surveys in this drawer, and they'd been sitting there, untouched, for the eight months since the survey was conducted.

In a third company, three months had passed since a Web-based survey revealed widespread customer dissatisfaction with software services and support. Not only had the director not taken any action, he had not yet reported the feedback— even to his own division. Meanwhile, the problems cited by customers continued, unabated. Is it any wonder that customer dissatisfaction was on the rise?

Please take note: Gathering feedback and not taking action based on the findings can be more damaging to your reputation than not gathering feedback at all. You might as well send out a letter saying,

> *Dear Sir or Madam:*
>
> *Here at XYZ Corp., we pride ourselves*
> *on not listening.*
>
> *Yours truly,*
>
> *The Management*

Failure to act erodes customer confidence and respect because, having been asked for feedback, customers watch for changes to emerge as a consequence. When they see none, they question whether those who requested the feedback were really listening or were just going through the motions.

Not only must you take action, you must do so quickly, even if only to estimate when you will have more to report. When I visited the vice president of a division one month after his employees had participated in a large-scale customer survey, he complained, "They said they'd issue a report, but I haven't seen anything yet." He was oblivious to the complexity of the work in progress to capture, evaluate, organize, and summarize the feedback, and to write the report for distribution. These were not his concerns, and from his perspective, the absence of the promised report was part of the pattern of poor service. If he had simply been kept informed about the status of the survey and the estimated delivery date of the report, he might not have been so impatient.

PERCEPTUAL LAGS

If you make improvements in response to customer grievances, then you might reasonably expect customer satisfaction to increase. Yet, all too frequently, customers remain dissatisfied. The reason is that perception of an improvement often lags behind the implementation of that improvement. Far behind.

If you've worked hard to upgrade service, this perceptual lag is unfair, if not infuriating. Therefore, take action to minimize it before, during, and after you make your service improvements. In particular, communicate. That is, keep a description of the improvements and your progress in implementing them visible to customers who've agitated for them or who will benefit from them.

Here's how the situation played out for a network vendor who was unaware of this perceptual lag. Customers were dissatisfied with the service snags and snafus they'd been experiencing. They would have gladly obtained the same services elsewhere, if they had that option. But they didn't. They felt trapped and very unhappy.

Vendor personnel agreed that something needed to be done. They started by taking the courageous step of administering a full-scale customer-satisfaction survey. They knew what the results would reveal, and they were right. Ratings teetered at the bottom of the scale, and customers' comments were scathing. Difficult though it was to take, this feedback provided a baseline.

Group members set forth to make things better. The service environment was complex, but over the course of a year, they implemented numerous improvements. They were justifiably proud and badly needed a pat on the back from their customers. Yet, when I learned the group had conducted another full-scale survey, I became concerned. Group members expected ratings in this second survey to reflect a dramatic leap. I feared they were in for a colossal disappointment.

Although the ratings were somewhat higher than a year earlier and the comments were less stinging, customers were still dissatisfied. In fact, judging from the feedback, many customers barely noticed a difference. Others felt service was on the upswing, but still far from optimal. Vendor personnel were devastated. They had accomplished a lot, but hardly anyone seemed to notice or care. They were victims of the perceptual lag.

A Lag-Avoidance Strategy

When service has been bad, it typically needs to be a lot better for a long time before customers notice the improvement. And let's face it: If customers don't trust their service provider, they adopt a "prove it" mentality. They don't see what's been fixed; only what's still broken—particularly if the provider has done a poor job of publicizing the improvements. Furthermore, people quickly forget how difficult things had been in the past as they focus on current problems.

Most organizations fall short in publicizing the improvements they've made. As a result, customers may not associate an improvement with the feedback they provided. To minimize the perceptual lag, put on your public relations hat: When you've identified the changes you'll make, inform your customers. Let them know how they can help you help them. Keep emphasizing the connection between their grievances and the action you're taking. When you've implemented a change, inform employees, remind them, and then tell them again. Distribute graphs and charts that show your progress in implementing the improvements. Involve key customers in planning and implementing the changes, so they'll have a stake in your success. Communicate, communicate, communicate. Don't let them not know. And while you're at it, acknowledge that there's much left to do.

Supplement these activities with as much direct customer contact as possible. As much as anything else, customers want to know that you take their needs seriously. Visiting them is time-consuming, but it pays great dividends. Solicit their feedback to ensure that your improvements really work. Ask for their help in spreading the word. This kind of attention alone often leads customers to give higher ratings in subsequent surveys.

The most uplifting outcome is when your fiercest adversary becomes your strongest supporter—and yes, this does happen. For example, a provider that was recovering from a sorry service history called a meeting with several of its most disgruntled customers. One of these customers, Bruce, was a tough dude, whose very name sent chills through those in charge of supporting his service needs. After the provider team presented its findings, Bruce stood up and pointed to a chart depicting the provider's improvement over the past year. With a level of enthusiasm that matched his level of outrage before the improvements, he told everyone that he would make sure his staff saw the chart and understood the improvement they'd been experiencing. While he acknowledged his staff's complaints that things were far from perfect, he was adamant that his people give credit for the improvements that had occurred.

Obviously, you want to have happy customers. But while you're working toward that goal, do what you can to limit the perceptual lag.

11

Service Level Agreements
A Powerful Communication Tool

A service level agreement (SLA) is a highly effective tool for improving communication between service providers and customers. SLAs help provider and customer groups more effectively manage expectations, clarify responsibilities, and minimize conflict. Yet, despite the proven effectiveness of SLAs, not everyone believes in their value, insisting that if people trust each other, they should not need a formal agreement.

Working recently with an IT group whose members thought SLAs would help them better communicate the scope of their services, I was startled by the intensity with which one member of the department voiced his objections. The vehemence with which he protested suggested that he was reacting to something other than the current discussion. Perhaps he'd had a negative experience with SLAs that had left him skeptical about their merits. Or maybe he believed that trust made the world go around—or ought to, at least. Or perhaps he'd been a big-hearted kid who, for some reason, no one trusted, and he remained motivated ever after to demonstrate he was trustworthy.

In any case, he was mistaken in thinking that trust alone would suffice. Trust is crucial in any relationship, but it is foolhardy to rely on trust alone in a complex service environment in which much is at stake. Even when people make service commitments with the intention of following through on them, they can easily forget the specifics they agreed to or discover that they have different interpretations of those commitments. In some situations, service commitments are broken when people change jobs and, in the absence of an agreement, their successors don't know what commitments were made.

Service level agreements are valuable because people are—well, only human. SLAs don't diminish trust; they strengthen it. Whether you're the provider or the customer, SLAs can help you close existing communication gaps and prevent others from occurring. SLAs clarify the terms and conditions of service delivery and help keep service targets in clear view. They guide the process of monitoring and discussing service effectiveness. They provide a way to make service changes when such changes are warranted.

Although SLAs are especially valuable tools, not all SLAs are successful. Some fail to function as hoped. Others never get completed because insurmountable problems arise between the parties while their SLA is being drawn up. Whatever their value, the process of creating and managing SLAs is not without pitfalls. This chapter describes how to best handle this process so as to enhance communication and create win-win relationships between providers and customers.

WHY AN SLA SUCCEEDS OR FAILS

An SLA stands the greatest chance of succeeding if the parties involved view it as all of the following:

- *A mechanism for managing expectations.* An SLA helps the provider and customer set, achieve, and maintain shared expectations about service delivery. An SLA undoubtedly would have helped Ken, the director in Chapter 2, get through to his customers about the products supported by his help desk.

- *A conflict-reduction tool.* The communication process involved in establishing an SLA helps the provider and customer minimize the frequency and intensity of conflicts and more readily and amicably resolve those that do occur.
- *A living document.* Once an SLA is in operation, the parties manage it by monitoring service delivery, holding periodic reviews, and negotiating changes as necessary. As the SLA is managed, so, too, is the relationship.
- *An objective process for gauging service effectiveness.* In creating an SLA, the provider and customer agree on what they'll look at to gauge service adequacy. These indicators become the basis for open and cooperative discussions about service effectiveness.

While providing SLA training and consulting internationally, I became curious why so many SLA efforts fail. As I investigated the various situations, I discovered some common patterns. These patterns are identified below as the six key reasons for SLA failure, and are paired with six corresponding contributors to SLA success.

SOURCES OF SLA FAILURE	CONTRIBUTORS TO SLA SUCCESS
1. Using the SLA as a weapon.	1. Using the SLA as a win-win tool.
2. Rushing to complete the SLA.	2. Not arbitrarily rushing SLA development.
3. Creating the agreement unilaterally.	3. Creating the SLA collaboratively.
4. Omitting key elements.	4. Including all key elements.
5. Misunderstanding how to create an SLA.	5. Learning how to create an SLA.
6. Ignoring the implemented SLA.	6. Managing the implemented SLA.

Fig. 11.1: Why SLAs Fail (and How to Make Yours Succeed).

Success Factor #1: Use the SLA as a Win-Win Tool

The most important benefit of an SLA is that it should help the provider and customer work together collaboratively, rather than clobber-atively!

It is clear that SLAs cannot succeed if the customer or provider enters into the process with punitive intent, yet examples of just such an approach are common. Consider these three examples:

- An information systems vice president felt that his clients complained too much. He directed his staff to create an SLA to stop the complaints. It didn't occur to him that forcing his unhappy clients to honor a so-called agreement would simply give them one more thing to complain about.
- A chief information officer directed a technology team to produce an SLA "to make our clients more coopera-tive." He believed that this would encourage clients to put more effort into working in cooperation with his organization.

- A business unit upset with snafu-ridden service delivery demanded that its provider organization enter into an SLA. This business unit's management viewed an SLA as a club with which to bludgeon the provider whenever service slipped, as though each such blow would inspire improved service delivery.

For an SLA to succeed, both parties must view it not as a "gotcha!" but as a mechanism for building mutually beneficial relationships. An SLA that is used as a communication tool rather than a battering ram can contribute to improved service because all parties understand what to expect of each other.

When All Is Not Well

So what are the options when a provider views its customers as ungracious grousers or when a customer sees its provider as Snafu Central? When either party is dissatisfied, it is best not to jump right into enacting an SLA. Try first to understand the other party's perspective, take steps to address some immediate problems, and develop a plan to improve the relationship. The very process of attempting to understand these sources of dissatisfaction often reduces their intensity because—*at last*—someone is listening.

That was the experience in a company in which watercooler gossip in both the provider and customer organizations centered on the latest misdeeds of the other. Creating an SLA was a transforming experience for both organizations. Through a process of dialogue and discussion, the SLA managers—the provider and customer representatives who headed the SLA effort—gained significant insight into each other's challenges.

Tensions between the organizations diminished as the SLA managers learned about each other's circumstances and used this knowledge to formulate recommendations regarding ways the two parties could work better together. As frequently happens in an SLA effort, this communication process helped to improve the relationship before the agreement was even implemented.

An SLA should be created to build a sound relationship, not to suppress evidence of dissatisfaction with the relationship. So if you're considering establishing an SLA, think carefully: Are you doing so to whip people into line? If so, stop now before you invest heavily in implementing a solution that's certain to backfire.

Success Factor #2: Don't Arbitrarily Rush SLA Development

Creation and management of SLAs aren't effortless tasks to be left until you've finished everything else on your to-do list. They are big jobs and need to be taken seriously. Yet one of the most common misconceptions among people who attend my SLA seminars is that creating an SLA is a process that can be hurried through. In fact, many seminar participants arrive under orders from management to complete one the following week (or the *previous* week, as one distressed participant bemoaned). By the end of the seminar, these people realize that creating a successful SLA will take longer, maybe a *lot* longer, than management expects. Creating an SLA is a project, not a tiny task.

Why is it such a big job? Because creating a successful agreement requires much more than simply plugging numbers into a template. The process of planning, establishing, and implementing an agreement can last for months and can involve numerous tasks, such as: assessing service history, creating service descriptions, defining service targets, gathering customer feedback, negotiating service standards, establishing tracking mechanisms, designing reports, documenting procedures, gaining approvals, educating pertinent parties, and training front-line staff.

Furthermore, departments that interact so as to support customers may discover that they can benefit from creating agreements among themselves before they enter into agreements with their customers. Sometimes called operational level agreements, these agreements are virtually identical to

SLAs except that they are between groups within the provider organization rather than between the provider and customer. Creating these inter-department agreements can add weeks and even months to the length of time needed for the total effort.

The benefit of doing all this work is that creating a well-structured SLA vastly improves communication between providers and customers both during its creation and after its completion; invariably, the parties come to better understand each other's needs, priorities, and concerns. The process of creating an SLA helps providers and customers build the foundation for a strong, successful, long-term relationship. To rush this process risks sabotaging the entire effort.

Because this communication process has such power to enhance mutual understanding, I prefer to see it take whatever time it legitimately needs. Sometimes, of course, the deadline for SLA completion is driven by external factors, such as the release date of a product, which may force the process to be rushed. However, the duration of the effort should not be determined by an arbitrary deadline.

Be forewarned: Completing the SLA is not the end of the job; in a sense, it's just the beginning of a long-term commitment to communication. Once an SLA is in operation, managing it entails a number of ongoing tasks, such as tracking service delivery, holding service reviews, modifying the agreement, discussing problems related to the agreement, and maintaining contact with the other party. Managing the agreement, however, takes significantly less energy than the parties previously expended in resolving disputes, conflicts, and differences of opinion prior to completion of the SLA.

Factors That Affect the Duration of the Effort

Given the scope of the effort, how long does it actually take to create an SLA? Well, it depends. Key contributors to the duration of the effort include the following:

1. *The service environment:* The more services covered by an SLA, and the more complex they are, the longer it takes to discuss, negotiate, and document the conditions of service delivery.

2. *The proximity of the parties:* Face-to-face negotiation is crucial in establishing an SLA, even if all other aspects of the SLA development work are done on-line or by phone. Travel time can add significantly to the length of the effort.

3. *The span of impact of the SLA:* Establishing an SLA between local groups generally takes less time than establishing an SLA that spans great distances. Global SLAs face complex issues due to differences in culture, time zones, pricing policies, legal and other regulations, and customer expectations.

4. *The relationship between the parties:* When the parties to an SLA trust and respect each other, the effort proceeds more expeditiously than when the relationship is adversarial and needs repair.

5. *The contractual nature of the SLA:* An SLA designed as part of a legal contract, and requiring the involvement of legal authorities, typically takes longer than a non-contractual SLA.

6. *The availability of a model:* The first SLA a group creates usually takes the longest. Once it is in operation, the document and the process can serve as a model for subsequent SLAs. If the first SLA is successful, later ones usually proceed much more rapidly.

7. *Prior SLA experience:* The most expeditious efforts are those led by SLA developers with prior successful SLA experience.

8. *Availability of SLA development staff:* Typically, personnel assigned SLA responsibilities have other concurrent duties. The extent of their availability to focus on SLA work affects the duration of the effort.

How Long Should It Take?

Given these factors, how long should it take to establish an SLA? I have found three-to-six months to be a good rule of thumb. When circumstances are optimal, three months may be a realistic estimate, or perhaps even less. However, if the situation is complex, even six months may not be enough time. Complex global SLAs sometimes take a year or more to reach completion.

One major reason why the process sometimes founders is that the people in charge of establishing the agreement are unfamiliar with how to go about it. I recall one manager who energetically predicted that she'd have an SLA in place in six months—but six months later, the effort had gone nowhere. She admitted that once they initiated the effort, no one was quite sure what to do first and what to do next.

A second major reason why the effort sometimes stalls is that one or both parties fail to bring a serious commitment to the effort. When management refuses to allocate staff to establish the SLA, or the effort is given a low priority, or one or both parties are unwilling to negotiate in good faith, progress becomes impossible. Although it may take longer than six months to create an agreement, if significant progress has not been made within that time, it's best to stop the effort and examine why before either party invests more time and expense.

Success Factor #3: Create the SLA Collaboratively

Imagine an IS organization developing a service level agreement to improve its partnership with its clients and not inviting a single client to participate in development of the SLA, or even to provide input. This unilateral approach happens more often than one would guess, and it is a surefire formula for failure.

Both provider and customer personnel *must* be involved in the formulation of an SLA. If one party attempts to control the process, members of the other party are likely to resist its terms even if they might otherwise have supported them. An SLA cannot be created unilaterally by one party in the hope that the other party will shape up, tone down, or go along. Yet many organizations believe this, seeming to think the meaning of "agreement" is "Let's you and I agree to do things my way."

For example, a vice president decided to use an SLA to improve his department's relationship with customers who were dissatisfied with shoddy service. He had a team create a draft agreement and send it out to customers for feedback. Seeing the agreement as one more attempt by provider personnel to have their way, customers either trashed it, belittled it, or ignored it. The relationship between the two organizations remained strained for almost another full year until they undertook a genuinely collaborative SLA effort.

One-Way "Agreements"

Although the SLA process must allow both parties to have some say, it may be neither feasible nor practical for providers and customers to collaborate on every aspect of the SLA effort. That's why the one-sided approach—a unilateral agreement—is so prevalent in our everyday lives. Open your software package, for example, or click on the "accept" icon on-line, and you've agreed to the vendor's terms. You've also agreed to terms unilaterally established by your bank or credit card company when you are an account holder—as I realized recently when my bank sent me a flyer that outlined its services and fees, stating, "We may change these fees and terms at any time, and if we do so, we will notify you in accordance with the terms of your Account Agreement." Did I make an agreement? I suppose so. Clearly, I can agree to keep the account, or I can transfer it to another bank where I'll be greeted with a similar "agreement."

Read the fine print on the back of most tickets, whether to a sports event, a rock concert, or a ride at the amusement park, and you'll discover that by using the ticket, you've agreed to specific terms—ones about which you've had no say. As an avid skier, I've read the list of hazards, dangers, and warnings printed on the lift ticket many times, but not thought much about it. However, I came to see the risk in a different light when I wrenched my knee skiing on steep terrain and two ski patrollers had to load me into a rescue toboggan. When they debated whether to take the long, slow, but safest trail down or the steep, icy, but quickest route, I was given no say in the matter. Of course, they selected the fast, icy route. I feared they'd lose control and catapult me on a solo journey down to sea level (Headline: "Skier Missing. Believed Drowned."). I lived to tell the tale, but would have much preferred a collaborative decision.

When Is an Agreement an Agreement?

Given the prevalence of one-sided "agreements," perhaps it's not surprising that many organizations begin their SLA effort with an "our way" mentality. But to talk about an SLA under such circumstances is a contradiction in terms. An SLA is, first and foremost, an *agreement*. Creating one entails discussion, collaboration, and compromise. A well-designed SLA enables the parties to amicably resolve their concerns about service delivery. Because they've agreed on how to handle disagreements, they will actually have fewer disagreements; those they do have can be resolved more rapidly and with less gnashing of teeth.

Success Factor #4: Include All Key Elements

An SLA requires both service elements and management elements.[1] The *service elements* clarify the services provided, the terms and conditions of service delivery, and the responsibilities of each party. The *management elements* focus on how the parties to the agreement will track, report, and review service effectiveness; how they'll address SLA-related disagreements; and how they'll negotiate adjustments to the agreement.

Both service and management elements are necessary if an SLA is to be effective, yet many SLAs I've evaluated for clients lack some or all of the management elements. In fact, omission of management elements, such as service reporting or periodic reviews, is a leading cause of SLA failure. These all-important service and management elements are described in the sections that follow.

Service Elements

The three main service elements are context-setting information, service description, and service standards. Each element is more fully discussed below.

Context-setting information introduces the agreement, setting out such information as the parties to the SLA, its purpose and scope, the set of services it addresses, important underlying assumptions, the service glossary, contact information, and perhaps an executive summary. This opening section sets the

---

[1] For detailed guidelines on establishing SLAs, contact me regarding my handbook, *How to Establish Service Level Agreements*. A detailed table of contents is on my Website (www.nkarten.com), along with a downloadable excerpt and several articles on establishing SLAs.

tone by communicating to readers that the SLA is a collaborative effort jointly undertaken by both parties.

The *service description* focuses on the services covered by the SLA. It also may include the services not covered if customers might reasonably assume the availability of such services. It can also include a description of the customer organization; the business needs to be addressed; and information such as the costs, pricing structure, and terms of payment. Some organizations prefer to place pricing information in an appendix to facilitate updating pricing changes. Of course, any information documented elsewhere that is easily accessible can be omitted from the SLA and referenced either in the context-setting section or in a section headed "Related Documents."[2]

Service standards ensure that both parties share a common understanding about the time frames, levels of responsiveness, and conditions under which the stated services will be provided. As a result of the common understanding, both parties know what they can reasonably expect. In an SLA, service standards typically focus on availability, up-time, responsiveness, throughput, timeliness, and quality. For example, a service standard might state

> The Inquiry Database will have 99 percent availability between 7 A.M. and midnight Monday through Friday; 95 percent availability between midnight and 7 A.M.; and 92 percent availability at all other times, as measured over a calendar month, and excluding periods of scheduled downtime for maintenance. All stated times are Central Time.

Notice that this service standard describes

- availability levels for different time periods
- the time frame over which the availability is tracked

---

[2] Thus far, very few organizations that have created SLAs with their internal customers have posted their SLAs on their internal Websites for viewing by both parties. Those that have done so have benefited from the ease of linking related documents and, as a result, have minimized the length of the core document.

- the pertinent time zone
- service exclusions: conditions excluded from the calculation of availability, such as downtime for maintenance

A service standard might also describe different pricing for different levels of service, as well as service dependencies: other parties on whom the provider or customer is dependent in order to meet the terms of the agreement.

Management Elements

The four key management elements—service tracking, service reporting, periodic review, and change process—minimize conflict and strengthen relationships by ensuring that service delivery is tracked, reported, and regularly and objectively assessed. These elements interact to make the SLA a living document and are discussed more fully below.

Service tracking focuses on the gathering of service data as the basis for assessing service effectiveness. When data are collected and reviewed, problems can be identified and addressed before they escalate into crises. Ideally, service tracking incorporates both objective, quantitative measures and subjective, qualitative measures.

Objective, quantitative measures reflect *what is*—that is, actual service delivery—by capturing pertinent service data, such as problem resolution time for help-desk support, up-time for a network server, and transaction response time for a customer database. The provider and customer should track the minimum number of indicators that will enable them to assess service adequacy. Objective, quantitative measures help to quickly isolate unacceptable variations in service delivery by tracking their patterns; such measures also help answer questions such as the following:

- How has response time varied during the last six months?
- Is this month's percentage of downtime consistent with past months', or is it an aberration? If an aberration, what accounts for it?

- Does on-time delivery show seasonal variations?
- What kinds of problems have taken the greatest amount of time to resolve in the last three months?
- How do the number of call disconnects per hour vary over the course of the day?

Subjective, qualitative measures reflect *what is perceived*—that is, the customer's experience in receiving the service—which may differ from *what is,* and is at least as important in generating customer satisfaction. In gathering subjective feedback, focus on the guidelines presented in Chapter 10. Try to use a combination of methods to gather feedback, such as the following:

- periodic customer surveys to gather data from a large number of customers
- service-specific assessment forms to have customers rate and comment on recent service experiences
- customer interviews for obtaining in-depth feedback
- evaluation of complaints for quickly identifying and resolving problems

Service reporting focuses on when and how service data will be reported and acted on. This public display of service information helps to highlight performance targets and actuals. Although service tracking and reporting are extremely important features of an SLA, don't forget the power of the naked eye. Don't wait for a monthly report to notice a troubling pattern that you'd easily see if only you had looked earlier.

It's important to distribute service reports to both provider and customer personnel. Without an SLA, service information tends to be communicated to too few people. For example, one help-desk team prepared stunning charts summarizing monthly problem-solving patterns, but the team used the reports strictly for its own internal purposes. In reviewing the charts, I noticed the large percentage of time the help desk spent resolving printer problems. When I commented about this to a customer manager, she expressed surprise at this large percentage, and vowed to work with her employees so that they'd have fewer printer problems and could fix more of the problems themselves. In making this commitment, she took some ownership for the problem. Not all customers will take ownership as she did, but those who know about a problem are more likely to help prevent it than those who don't.

Distributing service information—or at least providing access to it—also fulfills a valuable public relations function in reminding others of the services you deliver and your experience in delivering them.

Periodic reviews, led by the SLA managers of the two parties, ensure the regular and systematic review of service status by both customers and providers. The objectives of a periodic review are to

- review service delivery since the last review
- discuss major deviations from service standards
- resolve any conflicts or concerns about service delivery
- reevaluate services in light of current business needs and available resources
- discuss changes that are planned or in progress to improve service effectiveness
- negotiate changes to service levels, service tracking, or other relevant matters, and to modify the SLA accordingly

The importance of the review warrants face-to-face or at least voice-to-voice contact, so e-mail is not an acceptable channel for conducting periodic reviews. However, on-line access to service reports, such as by means of a corporate intranet, can facilitate discussions about service data during reviews by phone.

These reviews are critical to managing an SLA because they provide a formal, systematically scheduled way to assess service adequacy and to negotiate service changes. Regardless of what issues are on the agenda, other issues invariably arise that would normally not have received attention until much later, if at all. In the process, these meetings help strengthen relationships.

For example, the members of two divisions of an organization I once worked with were located in two distant cities and barely knew each other. Their distance from each other exacerbated the difficulties that plagued their relationship. After creating an SLA, they began holding monthly service reviews, alternating between the provider location and the customer location. Each SLA manager invited people from his own organization to come along when visiting the other's site. Gradually, people from the two organizations met and became familiar with each other's facilities and work environment. Over time, their pattern of blaming each other for problems was replaced with a pattern of cooperation in diagnosing problems and devising solutions.

A *change process* makes the SLA a living document by facilitating changes to the terms and conditions of service delivery. The change process enables the parties to make changes as circumstances warrant and when both parties are in agreement. This opportunity to make adjustments to the SLA often reassures those who fear being locked into service commitments that may subsequently prove unworkable.

Changes might be made for such things as adding new services or service standards, modifying service levels, setting new service targets, and adjusting the division of responsibilities. Of course, changes should not be made casually. Ideally, they should be confined to such matters as changing business or service needs, significant variations from agreed-upon service standards, or unanticipated events.

Success Factor #5: Learn How to Create an SLA

Typically, the primary work of creating an SLA rests with each organization's SLA manager, the person designated to direct the SLA effort on behalf of his or her organization. Alternatively, some organizations invite a third party, often from a quality-assurance or quality-improvement group, to oversee the SLA effort or to help the parties establish the SLA.

In establishing an SLA, pay particular attention to the following steps, each of which entails communication that is often lacking in the absence of an SLA.

- *Gather background information.* Both the customer and the service provider need to gather internal information so that each has a solid basis from which to negotiate. Therefore, before eliciting commitments from their service provider, customers should carefully review and clarify their own service needs and priorities. And before making any commitments to customers, the service provider should examine its service history and determine the level of service it can realistically provide. This process of communicating with others in one's own organization before communicating with those in the other organization is valuable in and of itself, aside from the SLA effort. Often, the information gathered highlights problem areas that need attention before the SLA effort can continue.

- *Gather customer feedback.* Before establishing an SLA, it's valuable for providers to gather feedback from customers so that they have firsthand information about customer perceptions. Such feedback improves the provider's understanding of customer concerns and creates a baseline against which to assess customer satisfaction after SLA implementation. As previously noted, customer feedback can be obtained in numerous ways, such as through surveys, focus groups, facilitated discussions, and interviews in person or by phone. The very act of meeting with customers and listening to them can help to improve communication before SLA negotiation even begins.

- *Ensure agreement about the agreement.* The two parties to an agreement sometimes have different ideas about the role of the SLA and what it will accomplish. For example, one party may view it as a quick fix, while the other may view it as a mechanism for building a long-term relationship. One party may want the SLA to reflect more stringent service levels than the other does, or expect it to deliver benefits that are outside its scope. Each party may expect the other to carry more of the work load in developing the agreement. Therefore, it's advisable for the two parties to hold a discussion to ensure that they have a basic level of agreement *about* the agreement. Until they do, any further SLA effort may prove futile.

- *Establish ground rules for the working relationship.* In this step, the SLA managers focus not on the agreement, but on the process by which they will work together to create the agreement. Issues to be discussed include the division of responsibility for development tasks, scheduling issues and constraints, and potential impediments to the SLA's creation. In addition, they may benefit from discussing their communication styles and preferences, as described in Chapter 6. By identifying similarities and differences at the onset, they will be in an excellent position to minimize conflict and to recognize and resolve any communication problems that arise.

- *Create a service glossary.* The service glossary enables the parties to work out differences in their interpretation of crucial service terminology. While creating such a glossary may not sound exhilarating, it generally leads to a wide-ranging discussion of how each party perceives service terms such as availability, up-time, problem resolution, and turnaround time. The result is a shared vocabulary that reduces the likelihood of future misunderstandings, making this one of the agreement's most important features. I've even seen SLAs with a definition of "service level agreement" in their own glossary!

- *Create a draft agreement.* This is just one step in the process of establishing an SLA; it's not the entire process. In this step, the parties create a structure for the SLA document and then research, discuss, debate, negotiate, and document the agreement until—over time—they reach accord about its contents. In doing so, they may each solicit assistance, input, or feedback from others in their own organization.

- *Generate buy-in.* Note that the result of the previous step is a *draft* agreement, not a completed agreement. Before implementing an SLA, all members of both parties who have a stake in, or are responsible for, the success of the agreement should have an opportunity to review the draft, raise concerns and questions, and offer suggestions. Using this feedback, the developers can conduct further negotiations, gain the necessary approvals, and finalize the document.

- *Complete pre-implementation tasks.* This step entails the identification and completion of such tasks as developing tracking mechanisms, establishing reporting processes, developing procedures for carrying out stated responsibilities, preparing pertinent documentation, communicating expectations to staff, and establishing and communicating an implementation date.

Then, and only then, are you ready to implement the agreement.

Success Factor #6: Manage the Implemented Agreement

A common misconception is that once the SLA document is complete, the job is done. However, an SLA that is not managed dies upon implementation. Managing the SLA must be the responsibility of a designated individual or group within each party, whose role may include such duties as

- serving as a point of contact for problems related to the agreement
- maintaining ongoing contact with the other party's SLA manager
- overseeing the tracking and reporting of key performance indicators
- planning and conducting service reviews
- coordinating and implementing modifications to the SLA and to service delivery
- conducting customer satisfaction surveys
- assessing and reporting on how the two parties can enhance their working relationship
- keeping management informed of any concerns regarding conformance to the provisions of the SLA
- planning classes designed to improve service attitude, foster awareness of the elements of high-quality customer service, and provide skills in service delivery
- overseeing ongoing relationship-building efforts designed to help the two parties work together in a supportive and cooperative manner

ADAPTING THE TOOL

One of my most satisfying moments in providing SLA assistance occurred as two formerly adversarial groups neared the implementation date of an agreement with which both parties were pleased. During a private conversation, the customer's SLA manager told me, "I believe we've reached a point in our relationship where we could switch places and come out with the exact same agreement." Such a comment would have seemed inconceivable at the outset.

Both the SLA process and the resulting document are adaptable to numerous contexts and adjustable to the unique needs of all the parties. If you can't get the approval or buy-in to create an SLA, then undertake as many of the individual activities as possible. This approach, which I call "How to succeed by not quite establishing an SLA," can enable you, ultimately, to create an SLA.

For example, try the following as single activities:

- Assess your service effectiveness.
- Gather customer feedback regularly.
- Create and disseminate your service description.
- Create a service glossary.
- Formulate service standards.
- Track and report service delivery.
- Meet periodically to assess service adequacy.
- Make adjustments as appropriate.

Although service level agreements have been used primarily between technology groups and their customers, I regularly hear from and work with other groups interested in adapting SLAs for their own use. On numerous occasions, employees and managers from a company's business divisions who attend my SLA seminars alongside members of their organization's IT division have expressed interest in creating SLAs with other business units. The fact is, an SLA can be created to improve a relationship with whomever one interacts. A few people have even commented that they could use an SLA in their marriage or other personal relationships. However, couples-based SLA counseling won't be making an appearance in my seminars listing any time soon!

Section 4
Change Gaps

If your organization has never experienced change, and you're sure it never will, feel free to skip this section. Otherwise, read on.

You may find it hard to believe, but one of the first things I thought of when I visited an elk refuge was the experience of change, and how some environments seem to undergo constant change—and others don't.

Several years ago, Howard and I went on a ski trip to Wyoming. During a break from skiing, we visited a refuge where elk congregate for the winter. The high point of the visit for me was a tour by horse-drawn sleigh that gave us a close-up view of what elk do in the winter, which seemed to be mostly nothing. They just lie around looking bored. But occasionally, two of them would paw the turf, charge at each other, butt heads, and then lock horns, just like some managers I know.

During the tour, people asked the guide lots of questions: "What do elk eat?" "How much do they weigh?" "What are the antlers for?" You know, typical elk questions. The guide answered each question enthusiastically, as if he were hearing it for the first time.

Afterward, when we were safely out of the path of beasts that looked like they could have decided at any moment that we were lunch, I asked the guide how many of these questions he had heard before. "All of them," he said. And how many had he heard frequently? "All of them." But then how did he manage to answer every question with enthusiasm and still retain his sanity? He said he just got used to doing it; it was part of his job.

What struck me, as we sat there in the middle of the elk refuge, was how odd it must be to have a job that doesn't contend with constant change. This fellow hears the same questions repeatedly, and he gives the same answers repeatedly. Communicating when there is little or no change is challenging, but communicating during times of immense upheaval is challenging in a very different way.

The two chapters of Section 4 will help you consider the challenge of communicating during times of change in your very non-elk-reserve-like organization.

- Chapter 12 describes the experience of change, and presents a model for considering what that experience is like for you and for the people with whom you interact.
- Chapter 13 builds on the change model by presenting guidelines for communicating effectively during times of change.

I can envision a sign posted on the sleigh at the elk refuge. It's labeled "Frequently Asked Questions About Elk." In bold letters, the sign says:

What do elk eat? They eat . . .

What do elk weigh? They average . . .

What are the antlers for? They are used for . . .

However, the tour guide probably wouldn't want this sign in his sleigh. Why? Because although he may get bored answering the same questions over and over, he probably prefers that to the alternative—dead silence. That's an alternative you are unlikely to encounter when you manage change.

12

The Experience of Change

In times of uncertainty, such as those triggered by technological or organizational change, most people have an intense need to know what is happening and how it will affect them. Yet, so often, communication in the form of information, empathy, reassurance, and feedback is in short supply.

Not that no one's communicating. Griping, for example, is common. So are venting, grousing, and gossiping. The rumor mill runs at full speed. But most of this communication is among those affected by the change. Those who initiated it, in contrast, are silent; or so it seems to those affected. The result is a gap between those who introduce change and those who are on the receiving end.

As always, Scott Adams tells it like it is. In *The Dilbert Principle,* he notes that people hate change. The reason, he contends, is that change makes us stupider because our relative knowledge decreases every time something changes. "And frankly, if we're talking about a percentage of the total knowledge in the universe, most of us aren't that many basis points superior to our furniture to begin with. I hate to wake up in the morning only to find that the intellectual gap between me and my credenza has narrowed."[1] Point well-taken.

FAILURE TO COMMUNICATE

During a recent conference at which I gave a presentation on managing change, a member of my audience asked why senior managers are so poor at communicating during times of change. Why, she wanted to know, do they tell us so little, when almost anything would help—even just an acknowledgment of what a stressful time it is for everyone?

Actually, it's not just senior managers but managers at all levels who communicate inadequately during times of change. These managers include the many who introduce or implement change as well as those who oversee the people affected by it. They may be project managers or team leaders or consultants. Two factors stand out as responsible for creating this Great State of Noncommunication. One is that, despite having experienced nearly nonstop change themselves, many managers simply do not appreciate the jolting impact that change can have on others and fail to recognize even the small steps they can take to help others adjust.

The second factor is that even when those in charge do understand the jarring impact of change, many prefer not to take any action. They avoid communicating because doing so means dealing with those messy "people issues" (such as feelings, for example). As William Bridges notes in *Managing Transitions*, "Managers are sometimes loathe to talk so openly, even arguing that it will 'stir up trouble' to acknowledge people's feelings."[2] Of course, as Bridges emphasizes, it's *not* talking about these reactions that creates the problem.

---

[1] Scott Adams, *The Dilbert Principle: A Cubicle's-Eye View of Bosses, Meetings, Management Fads & Other Workplace Afflictions* (New York: Harper-Business, 1996), p. 198.

[2] William Bridges, *Managing Transitions: Making the Most of Change* (Reading, Mass.: Perseus Books, 1991), p. 23.

Far too often, in place of communication, management uses a "get" strategy: trying to *get* people to change. As one vice president put it regarding the resistance of his company's sales force to use of a complex, new customer-relationship management system, "Our biggest challenge was to get them to change their habits and use it for planning."

Alas, no one can *get* anyone else to willingly do something that person doesn't want to do or doesn't know how to do. No one can *get* others to adopt enthusiastically what they fear, resent, or distrust. In a fantasy world, all those affected by a given change would welcome, endorse, and support it, openly and joyfully. Rah, rah, the change is here! But in the real world, change is unsettling. It always has been and it always will be.

The *Get* Strategy at Work

Inadequate communication was a key contributor to intense negative employee reaction in two companies, the first of which faced technological change and the second, organizational change. The first company embarked on a large-scale, company-wide desktop upgrade. The transition to the current platform a few years earlier had been easy for some employees, but a terrible trauma for others. Although the technology acted temperamentally at times, everyone was used to it by now.

Randy, the project manager of the upgrade implementation team, repeatedly asked his CIO to set the stage for change by issuing a company-wide announcement. Randy reasoned that employees would be more receptive to the upgrade if they knew the reason for it, how they'd benefit from it, when it would take place, and what they could expect as it proceeded. However, the CIO did not provide information to employees. As a result, some employees didn't become aware of the upgrade until Randy's team contacted their department to explain and schedule it. Most others learned about it through that most unreliable form of communication, the grapevine.

Employees reacted angrily when technical staff members arrived to "tamper" (their word) with their computers. Anger subsequently turned to outright hostility when employees experienced an unanticipated period of degraded system performance while implementation team members resolved bugs and fine-tuned the network. People fumed, "Why are you pushing this down our throats?"

Called in to meet with several of these employees, I discovered that there had been so little communication that some didn't even realize that the upgrade was company-wide. They believed it had been designed only for their particular department. The way they experienced it, the change was being done to them, not for them. They were victims of a *get* strategy.

In the company coping with organizational change, inadequate communication also contributed significantly to employee anger and distress. Describing this experience, Don, a director, bemoaned the dismal morale and escalating staff turnover that followed his company's merger with a corporate giant. Although a reorganization of his division was certain, and rumors were rampant, months had passed without the release of details by company executives.

Hoping to stop the exodus from his division, Don urged senior management either to talk directly to employees about the upcoming reorganization or, at least, to acknowledge their concerns and let them know when information would be forthcoming. Management ignored his recommendation.

Believing that employees would benefit from an understanding of the psychological nature of how people react to change, Don tried another approach. He offered to give a presentation to his division on the implications of change. Management rejected his offer.

Don was determined not to give up. Trying one last approach, he inserted a slide depicting the experience of change into another presentation he was preparing to give to his staff. When he previewed the presentation for senior managers, they directed him to remove the offending slide before giving the presentation to the troops.

Many months later, senior management rammed a comprehensive reorganization into place without informing, involving, or preparing employees. Morale worsened. The company, once a leader in its field with a sterling reputation as "the place to work," now became a liability. Turnover led to more turnover, and the company's severely damaged reputation made staff vacancies difficult to fill.

Why Change Packs a Wallop

In both Randy's and Don's companies, management's view seemed to be, in effect, "If we don't tell them this is a big change, maybe they won't notice that their guts are knotting up in response." Yet these are hardly isolated cases. Perhaps with each wrenching change that they implement, management's hope is that this time will be different. Maybe, this time, employees will go along meekly and passively, and won't make a fuss. Maybe, for once, management can just drop the changes into place and tiptoe away. Maybe, people won't notice that no respect has been shown—either for them or for the fact that big changes always create turmoil.

However, people always notice.

The reason people notice is that significant change is a felt experience. People's responses to change are much more emotional and visceral than logical and rational. Change efforts trigger a wide variety of reactions—eagerness, enthusiasm, and excitement, as well as fear, trepidation, anxiety, uncertainty, anger, and stress—feelings, in other words, that are both positive and negative.

Change, after all, signifies an end to something. As Bridges notes in *Managing Transitions*, "When endings take place, people get angry, sad, frightened, depressed, confused. These emotional states can be mistaken for bad morale, but they aren't. They are the *signs of grieving*. . . ."[3]

The importance of the grieving process is acknowledged rarely enough in personal circumstances, but it is given recognition even less frequently in the workplace. Yet, grieving is a

---

[3] Bridges, op. cit., p. 24.

response not just to death, but also to other kinds of loss: the loss of a job, a role, a team, a location, a specialty, a valued skill, a way of doing work—the loss, in other words, of a familiar way of life and its attendant safety, certainty, and predictability. People grieve when they lose something that matters to them. Failure to acknowledge people's need to come to terms with change doesn't eliminate that need; in fact, it places a greater burden on those who are trying to cope.

What this means is that if you are in a position to introduce change or manage its impact, then what, when, and how you communicate during the course of that change can dramatically influence the success of the effort. Your challenge—and this may signify a change for *you*—is to communicate with the affected people in a way that acknowledges and respects their reactions, while helping them to accept the change and adjust to it as expeditiously as possible.

THE STAGES OF RESPONSE TO CHANGE

Jake offered a splendid example of the stages people go through in responding to change. No, Jake isn't a colleague or an employee; he's a first-grader, and the son of a friend of mine. Back when he was three years old, his sister Erica was born.

Jake's parents did their best to prepare him for Erica's arrival, but when she arrived, Jake totally ignored her. For several days, he kept his distance and avoided any contact with her. He refused to look at her and acted as though she simply wasn't there.

Gradually, over the next several days, Jake started to acknowledge Erica. First, he gazed at her from a distance; then, he circled around her, moving closer and closer, checking her out. Finally, he dared to approach her, gently poking her hand and softly patting her head. By a week later, the two were great friends. Jake became very fond of Erica, and very protective of her.

What a wonderful illustration of how three-year-olds—and adults—often respond when confronted with change. First,

Jake tried to ignore Erica—the intrusion in his life. Then, he slowly acknowledged her existence and took tentative steps toward her. At length, he warmed up to her and accepted her. In the process, he came to realize that she was apparently here to stay, that he wasn't going to lose his parents' love and attention, and that maybe she wasn't so bad, after all.

Of course, I don't *really* know what was going through Jake's head as he attempted to cope with Erica's arrival. But his reaction to his new sister is analogous to the way adults cope with major change. They may take a different amount of time to reach acceptance, and they may encounter a different amount of distress in the process, but the experience of change is strikingly similar.

Jake was new to the change game, but most of us have had copious experience with it. Businesses change continuously as the world shrinks and becomes increasingly connected. Companies merge, split, realign, and morph in unimaginable ways; organization charts created in the morning are obsolete by lunchtime. Methodologies change, compressing multiyear development cycles into cycles measured in months. Technological change is nonstop and at times teeth-grittingly maddening. And people often fend it off, hoping it'll go away or at least not affect them. Yet, as pervasive and familiar as change is, the people responsible for introducing it are no more eager to accept it than anyone else—when it affects them. At times, it's easy to agree with that great philosopher of change, the poet Ogden Nash, who said, "Progress is fine, but it's gone on long enough."

CHANGE MODELS

Numerous models depict the stages of change and the importance of communication in helping people prepare for and adjust to it. The models vary in emphasis and terminology, but each offers insight into how people respond to, experience, and integrate change.

In *Managing Transitions,* Bridges describes the typical response to change in terms of three phases: ending, the neutral zone, and beginning. *Ending* is the time during which familiar ways must be given up. The *neutral zone* is that disconcerting, and sometimes immobilizing, phase between giving up the old way and accepting the new. Bridges warns that the trip through the neutral zone may be quick in some situations and in others, long and slow: "when the change is deep and far-reaching, this time between the old identity and the new can stretch out for months, even years."[4] The third phase, *beginning,* is what people seek and want, but also find scary once they're face-to-face with it.

Bridges makes a distinction between change and transition. Change, he states, is situational: the new person or thing, such as the new project, new team, or new manager. Transition, by contrast, is the psychological process people must go through to come to terms with the change. Thus, change is external, but transition is internal.[5]

Other change specialists also use stages, or phases, to describe the journey through change. In *The 7 Levels of Change,* Rolf Smith divides change into distinct levels as a way to develop a strategy for innovation and self-improvement. Smith calls the levels Effectiveness (doing the right things), Efficiency (doing things right), Improving (doing the right things better), Cutting (doing away with things), Copying (doing things other people are doing), Different (doing things no one else is doing), and Impossible (doing things that can't be done).[6]

---

[4] Bridges, op. cit., p. 34.

[5] Ibid., p. 3.

[6] Rolf Smith, *The 7 Levels of Change: The Guide to Innovation in the World's Largest Corporations* (Arlington, Tex.: The Summit Publishing Group, 1997).

Elisabeth Kübler-Ross describes the stages many people experience in coping with a terminal illness as Denial, Anger, Bargaining, Depression, and Acceptance. In her book *On Death and Dying*, Kübler-Ross describes the power of communication to help patients come to terms with the prospect of dying.[7] Although most organizational change is not of a life-or-death nature (though it may feel like it at the time!), people may experience similar stages as they adjust to it, making Kübler-Ross's advice highly applicable.

THE SATIR CHANGE MODEL

In my work with organizations, I've found Virginia Satir's Change Model extremely valuable in the way it provides a context for understanding the role of communication during change. The Satir model, which depicts the impact of change on performance or productivity, can help you better understand how you respond to change as well as how you can help your organization cope with it.[8]

Satir herself used initial capital letters in naming the various elements and stages of the Change Model, and these have been retained in the figure below and in the sections that follow. As you read on, consider the impact of the presence or absence of communication during the various stages of change.

---

[7] Elisabeth Kübler-Ross, *On Death and Dying* (New York: Collier Books, 1969).

[8] For an overview, see Virginia Satir et al., *The Satir Model: Family Therapy and Beyond* (Palo Alto, Calif.: Science and Behavior Books, 1991). For an in-depth treatment of change, see Gerald M. Weinberg, *Quality Software Management, Vol. 4: Anticipating Change* (New York: Dorset House Publishing, 1997).

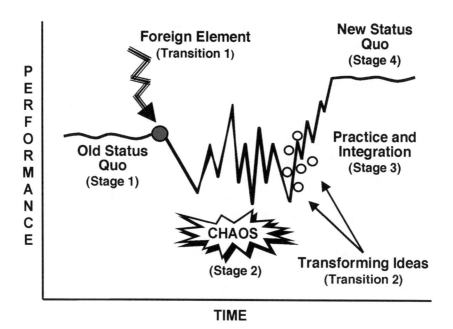

Fig. 12.1: The Satir Change Model.

Stage 1: Old Status Quo

Old Status Quo is the pre-change stage characterized by the known, the familiar, and the predictable. People in the Old Status Quo stage experience a sense of relative stability. Even when they're unhappy with the Old Status Quo, many people prefer it to the turmoil and disruption of change. It's like that old saying, "The enemy we know is better than the enemy we don't know." Recall that the employees coping with an upgrade in Randy's company were comfortable with their current hardware and software, and wanted to keep the familiar system despite its many bugs. Given the choice, most wouldn't have opted to leave the Old Status Quo. In Don's company, although many people were disenchanted with the existing organizational structure, they preferred it to the uncertainty of what might come next.

In *Teamwork: We Have Met the Enemy and They Are Us*, authors Starcevich and Stowell capture the experience of Old Status Quo in noting that most of us have two competing forces motivating our behavior: "Number one is the drive or desire to achieve, succeed, live, experiment, and take appropriate risks and to experience change and variety in our lives. Number two is the drive or desire to be cautious and avoid losses, play it safe, go with the status quo, avoid exposure to risks, and protect our own importance."[9]

People particularly favor the status quo when they feel stressed; at such times, the known seems more reassuring and trustworthy than the new and different. Thus, when urged to change, many people pull back, tug-of-war-like. Although people who prefer the status quo may be viewed skeptically by those who impose change, this behavior is perfectly normal. To believe otherwise is fruitless. According to the psychiatrist Dr. Pierre Mornell, most people are "allergic" to change and thus you can count on resistance occurring. The reason, he notes, is simply that most people like things the way they are. "And when you start changing direction, people start talking about the good old days, even if they weren't very good at all."[10]

By beginning to communicate about a change before it is implemented, you might be able to help people feel more comfortable with the idea of it so that they can begin to adjust to it.

Stage 2: Chaos

Satir used the term Foreign Element to describe something that upsets the Old Status Quo and throws the system—individuals or groups—into an unsettled state of decreased or impaired performance known as Chaos. Imagine the reaction, for example, when management in one company announced that the entire organization would be moving out-of-state and that employees had a month to decide whether to move with the company or terminate their employment.

---

[9] Matt M. Starcevich, and Steven J. Stowell, *Teamwork: We Have Met the Enemy and They Are Us* (Bartlesville, Okla.: The Center for Management and Organization Effectiveness, 1990), p. 76.

[10] Pierre Mornell, "Nothing Endures But Change," *Inc* (July 2000), pp. 131–32. Mornell is author of *Games Companies Play* (Berkeley, Calif.: Ten Speed Press, 2000).

This abrupt and unexpected news was a Foreign Element that propelled the entire company into a sudden and intense state of Chaos. Work came to a halt. Gossip and discussion took over. Some people were elated at the opportunity to move; others felt as if they'd been punched in the stomach, severely shocked by the idea of having to either move or find a new job. Reactions were many and varied. Most people became unable to focus on anything other than the implications of the move.

As this situation illustrates, people experience Foreign Elements in different ways. For that reason, I sometimes refer to Foreign Elements as Foreign *Elephants,* as a lighthearted reminder of the wisdom offered by the poem of the blind men and the elephant. As the poem reveals, each blind man, exploring a different part of the elephant—the ear, trunk, tail, knee, hide—had a different idea of what he was touching.[11] The men's stories were seemingly incompatible, yet each one aptly captured that man's experience.

---

[11] From the poem "The Blind Men and the Elephant" by John Godfrey Saxe (1816–1887), as quoted in David A. Schmaltz, *Coping with Fuzzy Projects: Stories of Utter Ignorance, Theologic Wars, and Unseen Possibilities* (Portland, Oreg.: True North pgs, 2000), pp. 5–6.

There are many different types of situations that someone somewhere will experience as a Foreign Element. How many of the situations listed below have you experienced? Have any been Foreign Elements, driving you into Chaos?

- the announcement of an impending layoff (or even just a rumor)
- the arrival of a new CEO or manager
- the arrival or departure of a team member
- yet another reorganization
- the realization that you caused the bug that crashed the system
- the decision to get married or divorced (or remarried or redivorced)
- a call from the Squeaky Wheel
- an unanticipated promotion
- an abrupt change in priorities
- the announcement of a new methodology, technology, or standard
- the news that you've won the lottery
- a visit to an unfamiliar country or culture
- an outsourcing decision
- the arrival of consultants
- an unexpected business trip to Hawaii
- a natural disaster
- remodeling your kitchen
- the realization that you overslept and will miss an important meeting
- your most feared error message
- an interruption while you were deep in thought
- the discovery that you've lost your keys
- your phone ringing during the night
- the sound of a siren behind your car

As you can see from this list, a Foreign Element can be short-lived or long lasting, expected or unexpected, good news or bad news. It can be seen as positive for some people, negative for others, and neither for still others. It can even be positive for a given person at one point in time and negative at another.

The Chaos stage is a time of uncertainty. While in Chaos, people may have difficulty concentrating, and may become more error-prone, preoccupied, or forgetful. For example, a colleague with whom I had scheduled a phone meeting didn't call at the agreed-upon time. When I tracked him down, he explained that he had received news that threw him into such turmoil that he simply forgot about our appointment. I could certainly relate to the impact a distraction of that magnitude can have. When I try to write while in Chaos, I make so many typing errors that my spell-checker overheats.

During Chaos, you may feel anger, frustration, fear, confusion, excitement, or a range of other emotions. You may also experience physical symptoms such as a headache, backache, or stomachache. While you can't always directly observe these emotions or symptoms in others, you can certainly notice them in yourself. Of course, having a stomachache doesn't necessarily mean you're in Chaos; the all-you-can-eat pizza shop could somehow be implicated. But if you experience physical distress shortly after being told that you're now in charge of your least favorite customer, these physical sensations might signal that you're in Chaos.

You as a Foreign Element

When I ask people to identify examples of Foreign Elements in their work, they generally cite the loss of a job, a major reorganization, new technology, and other such items. However, not all Foreign Elements are "out there." *You* can be a Foreign Element for others. Almost certainly, you *are* at times, by virtue of your role and responsibilities.

The very way that you communicate—how you introduce a new idea, argue your point of view, offer unexpected information, lobby for a new approach, or present bad news—can serve as a Foreign Element that propels recipients of your message into Chaos or causes them to latch onto the Old Status Quo and hold on tight. So if you propose something and people are quick to reject it, refute it, or discount it, they may simply be responding to the introduction of a Foreign Element. However, if you present your information thoughtfully and allow people time to adjust, they may find their way through their Chaos and become receptive to your idea.

It would be absurd to worry excessively about how everyone you interact with will respond to what you say and do; however, an awareness of Foreign Elements and of the Chaos stage may encourage you to find alternative ways of presenting information and ideas so that people are more likely to accept them.

Chaos Is Normal

Chaos is a normal response to change. You can't prevent people from experiencing it, and you shouldn't even try. However, what, when and how you communicate with those experiencing Chaos can affect how long and how intensely they experience it. Acknowledging the Foreign Element and the resulting Chaos is an important first step. Talking with employees about their fears and uncertainties can ease their way. Being empathetic if they attempt to revert to the Old Status Quo—that exceedingly common reaction often described as resistance or denial—may provide reassurance.

In the medical context, Kübler-Ross describes denial as "a buffer after unexpected shocking news. . . ."[12] In organizations, the news is not always unexpected, but it can still cause employees to respond with denial. As management consultant Steve Smith points out, resistance to a Foreign Element entails "denying its validity, avoiding the issue, or blaming someone for causing the problem."[13] Helping employees understand that these reactions are normal can ease their adjustment to the Foreign Element. At the same time, it may be helpful to make

---

[12] Kübler-Ross, op. cit., p. 35.

[13] Steven M. Smith, "The Satir Change Model," *Amplifying Your Effectiveness: Collected Essays,* eds. Gerald M. Weinberg, James Bach, and Naomi Karten (New York: Dorset House Publishing, 2000), p. 97.

it clear that the change is here to stay and to emphasize the importance of getting past it.

You can't always tell when people are in Chaos, but one sign you can watch for is a change in their communication patterns. When an even-tempered person becomes a Master Griper or when the department comedian turns serious, these may be signs of an individual in Chaos. Whispering and gossiping are common among people in Chaos. Puzzling interactions, such as those described in Chapter 4, may occur more frequently. Of course, not all mumbling and grumbling signifies a state of Chaos. This behavior, after all, is perfectly normal for some people, or simply a sign of preoccupation or garden-variety stress.

The tricky thing about being in Chaos is that when you're experiencing it yourself, you don't always realize it; you can be so tightly in its grip that you lack the presence of mind to stop and say, "I'm in Chaos." Learning to recognize when you're experiencing Chaos is a worthy goal because by doing so, you're more likely to prevent yourself from misspeaking, saying what you don't mean, making claims you'll later regret, heaping blame where it doesn't belong, or taking abrupt action that you'll later wish you didn't. Most importantly, you'll avoid making irreversible decisions that you'd never have made otherwise. By becoming more conscious of what propels you into Chaos, and of how you experience it, you can have more control over your own behavior.

Stage 3: Practice and Integration

In most situations, Chaos doesn't last forever. It's a temporary state of tremendous learning that occurs when the old ways no longer apply and the stage is set for a person to try new approaches. With the help of some Transforming Ideas—new ways of looking at the situation—people start to adjust to the changes brought (or wrought) by the Foreign Element. This adjustment stage is called Practice and Integration and it leads to a New Status Quo.

Transforming Ideas can come from many sources, such as quiet reflection, brainstorming, training, research, or talking with others. A woman in one of my workshops described how the Chaos she experienced during a reorganization dissolved when her new manager offered her the opportunity to participate in a new, exciting project. For her, this was a Transforming Idea that enabled her to see new possibilities for herself and therefore to emerge from Chaos and start moving toward a New Status Quo.

Unfortunately, even the very best ideas will not become Transforming Ideas if you're unaware of them or unwilling to accept them. When in Chaos, many people are quick to dismiss possible Transforming Ideas as ridiculous, unworkable, irrelevant, or deficient in any number of other ways. Therefore, this is an important time to notice people's communication patterns, especially your own.

To avoid this tendency to dismiss ideas, observe your reaction to the ideas other people offer while you're in Chaos. If you hear yourself summarily rejecting ideas or finding fault with them, think twice. One of them might prove to be the germ of a Transforming Idea. And if other people are quick to reject your potentially Transforming Ideas because they're in Chaos, be gently persistent. Sometimes people need time for an idea to settle in before they can accept it.

Practice and Integration is a stage in which communication plays a key role. It's a time of trying things out, making mistakes, moving forward and slipping back, and gradually becoming more comfortable with the new way. Thus, people who are adjusting to new software, for example, may initially make more mistakes than usual until they become familiar with its features, navigation paths, and menu options. A group emerging from a reorganization may have reduced productivity until group members become accustomed to the new responsibilities, reporting relationships, rules, and procedures.

Just as people sometimes respond to a Foreign Element by reverting to the Old Status Quo, people in Practice and Integration sometimes slip back into the turbulence of Chaos. Some managers don't appreciate that Practice and Integration is a necessary component of the adjustment to change, and may expect employees to accept the Foreign Element instantly and effortlessly. They may communicate frustration and dissatisfaction as employees take time to adjust to the new way of working.

Enlightened managers, by contrast, understand that this adjustment takes time—and, to the extent feasible, they allow that time. During this period, they interact with employees, listen, and empathize. But they do something more: They help employees understand the ups and downs of Practice and Integration, and they allow employees some leeway to practice new skills and integrate new ways of functioning. Not only do these managers not expect perfection; they help employees understand that unfamiliarity with the new way may temporarily result in an increase in errors and inefficiencies.

Stage 4: New Status Quo

After emerging from Chaos and experiencing the roller-coaster ride of Practice and Integration, an individual or group achieves a New Status Quo. This is a return to relative stability with respect to that particular Foreign Element. Communication at this stage ideally takes the form of reflection, discussion, and evaluation of what's been learned, because those who learn from their experiences are better equipped to cope with change.

META-CHANGE

Over time, and with experience and reflection, individuals and groups can develop expertise in managing the kinds of change that at one time would have provoked intense Chaos. Changing the way you manage and cope with change as a result of this growing expertise is called Meta-Change. By becoming conversant with the change cycle, you can become more sophisticated both in experiencing it yourself and in influencing its impact on others, taking on the role of Change Artist.

The Satir Change Model can help you become a skilled Change Artist in your organization, but you can also use it to manage personal change more effectively. To improve your ability to cope with change personally, consider your own behavior:

1. What behavior do you exhibit when you are in Old Status Quo—especially when you really want to stay there?
2. What kinds of things are Foreign Elements for you? When confronted with a Foreign Element, how do you respond?
3. What is Chaos like for you? What happens to your mental state? your emotional stability? your ability to concentrate?
4. How do your communication patterns change when you're in Chaos? What might others notice about you?
5. When you're in Chaos, what do you want from others? How do you let them know?
6. When you're in Chaos, what might be some sources of Transforming Ideas for you? How can you become more open to those sources?

7. When you've reached a New Status Quo, what can you do to learn from the experience so you can minimize the duration and intensity of future Chaos?

8. What can you do differently to improve the way you respond to change?

The questions listed above will help you reflect on how you handle matters of a personal nature but you also can use them to improve your skill as an organizational Change Artist. Review the questions as they pertain to your team, department, division, functional group, or business unit. The following questions can be extremely instructive for a group to contemplate and discuss:

1. What kinds of things are Foreign Elements for your organization? How do you respond, individually and as a group, to these Foreign Elements?

2. What kinds of differences have you observed in how people respond to a given Foreign Element?

3. How does Chaos exhibit itself in your organization? How do people behave? How can you help them when they are in Chaos? How can you let each other know what would be most helpful to you?

4. What changes occur in the ways people communicate with each other while they are in Chaos?

5. While your organization is in Chaos, what are some sources of Transforming Ideas? How can you help others become receptive to these ideas?

6. How can you provide support during Practice and Integration?

7. When your organization has achieved a New Status Quo, how can you help people reflect on what they've learned?

8. What can the people in your organization do differently to improve the way they respond to change?

People who possess self-awareness learn what propels them into Chaos and become better at responding to it in the future.

By becoming attuned to the experience of Chaos, they become increasingly able to minimize its duration and intensity, and increasingly skilled at managing change.

CHAOS AS STATUS QUO

People experience different things as Foreign Elements. They experience Chaos for different lengths of time and at different levels of intensity. They respond to different Transforming Ideas. They have different experiences in Practice and Integration as they achieve a New Status Quo. At any point in time, people are at different points in numerous different change cycles. While the Satir model shows the Foreign Element as creating Chaos, a Transforming Idea can also act as a Foreign Element to create additional Chaos. Sometimes, people in Old Status Quo go through smaller-scale versions of the entire change cycle as they attempt to avoid change in the first place.

All of this is perfectly normal, and quite simply, the way things are. The miracle is that companies are able to achieve so much, given this constant state of flux. (Or could it be that this constant state of flux is precisely what enables them to achieve so much?)

In many companies, nonstop change *is* the status quo. This state of constant change may be the culture of the organization. Often, what's seen as constant change is actually a lot of smaller changes that overlap in time and impact. As Bridges points out, "Every new level of change will be termed 'nonstop' by people who are having trouble with transition. At the same time, every previous level of change will be called 'stability.'"[14] The tendency people have to view the current "nonstop change" as unique to them or their time in history is a delusion. Constant change has always been the status quo.

---

[14] Bridges, op. cit., pp. 75–76.

13

Changing How You Communicate During Change

Drawing from the Satir Change Model, this chapter provides guidelines for communicating during change. As general communication caveats, these guidelines apply to all interactions in the workplace, even ones occurring during those rare times of stability. But they are particularly applicable if you are responsible for introducing, influencing, or managing change. The following actions will help you become a skilled Change Artist.

1. Respect the matter of timing.
2. Expect individual differences in response to change.
3. Allow time for adjustment.
4. Treat the Old Status Quo with respect.
5. Allow people to vent.
6. Listen proactively.
7. Provide information and more information.
8. Say something, even when you have nothing to say.
9. Empathize, empathize, empathize.
10. Choose your words carefully.
11. Dare to show people you care.
12. Involve people in implementing the change.
13. Educate people about the experience of change.
14. Deal with it!

RESPECT THE MATTER OF TIMING

The sooner people know about an upcoming Foreign Element, the sooner they can start to adjust to it and the sooner you can harness their energy and ideas to help the change effort succeed. Timing is a delicate matter, best decided on a case-by-case basis. In some situations, notification of the change too far in advance can itself be a Foreign Element, causing unrest and a drop in productivity. Some organizational changes do require discretion, if not absolute secrecy, preventing any advance notice at all. For example, company officials sometimes tread a fine line between alerting employees of an impending layoff and withholding information which, if publicly released, could damage the company for those employees who remain. In general, withholding information about an upcoming change in the name of kindness—in this case, shielding people from bad news—is a form of self-delusion.

Offering advance notice is a simple strategy that can have a strikingly positive impact. That was the discovery of a manager in one of my classes who complained that his wife usually reacted angrily whenever he told her that he needed to be away on business the following week. "Why can't she be more supportive of the travel demands of my job?" he asked.

After hearing my presentation describing the components of the Satir Change Model, he told me he now interpreted his wife's reaction differently: His travel announcements were Foreign Elements to his wife, creating Chaos for her because she had so little time to make arrangements to handle family matters during his absence. He decided to try a simple modification: He started informing her an extra week in advance of his out-of-town trips.

"Amazing!" he reported when we talked some months later. "She's suddenly become supportive." Yet, nothing but his timing had changed. In adjusting that timing, he displayed respect for her need to know and enabled her to plan accordingly.

At times, it may be prudent to delay the introduction of a Foreign Element, especially when those it will affect are already in considerable Chaos from a previous Foreign Element. The cumulative effect may intensify and prolong their Chaos. You don't always have control over the timing, nor can you ever know all the overlapping states of Chaos others are in. But by being sensitive to the timing, you may be able to minimize the Chaos that they (and you) experience.

EXPECT INDIVIDUAL DIFFERENCES IN RESPONSE TO CHANGE

Imagine a continuum. At one end are people who cling to the safety and security of the status quo. These people are risk-averse. They need certainty and predictability; for them, a sure thing is a good thing. If it ain't broke, don't fix it, they'll say. In fact, stay away from it so it doesn't break. Any iota of change is disruptive, if not downright mortifying, for these people. They survive by following a fixed routine and a time-tested, trustworthy approach to doing things.

At the other end of the continuum are those who thrive on change and get bored if five seconds pass without something new or different happening. These people detest sameness. They enjoy change for the sake of change. If it ain't broke, they yearn to break it, and then break it again, and again, because there are so many fascinating ways to fix it. These people start from Point A to go to Point B, but become distracted by the charms of Point C, . . . and oh, look, Point Q . . . and what about Point H? Indeed, they'll enjoy the entire alphabet whether or not they ever reach Point B.

Hardly anyone is superglued to one end of the continuum or the other. Most people reside somewhere in between, the specific location depending on numerous factors. For example, receptivity to change is associated with personality type. People with a preference for perceiving, as described in the Myers-Briggs Type Indicator (see Chapter 6), tend to be more open to change than people with a preference for judging. What may seem to those with a preference for judging like an abrupt or unanticipated change might, for the perceiving type, be another interesting possibility or even just a ho-hum adjustment.

Furthermore, people with a preference for intuition tend to be more comfortable with change than people with a preference for sensing. Sensing types take in information from that which is concrete, real, present, and immediate, and they therefore tend to be more trusting of the present. Intuitive types, in contrast, are less bound by current reality and tend to function well in a world of imagination, speculation, and hypothesis.

In addition to personality type, one's response to a given change may vary, depending on factors such as past experience, upbringing, life experiences, the availability of pertinent information, the context, the nature of the change, the effect change has on the person and on others, and the person's belief in how well he or she can cope with it.

For example, I consulted with the members of a technical-support group that was frantically trying to keep up with its customers' relentless demands. When I met with the group, one fellow's relaxed and easygoing manner was in stark contrast to the others. Afterward, I asked him privately how he could be so calm in the midst of such Chaos. He said, "This is nothing—it was much worse where I was before." He then described the extraordinary customer demands in his previous company. Clearly, past experience influenced his reaction to his current situation. "These people don't know how easy they have it," he told me.

In any group, even a seemingly inconsequential change can trigger a range of responses. To reinforce this point, I sometimes introduce a Foreign Element into groups I'm speaking to about change. One way I do this is by asking everyone to move to a different seat, to see things from a different perspective. After a few moments of musical chairs, people get settled, and I continue with the presentation. A while later, I ask what their reaction was to this minor reorganization. Following are some typical responses:

- I didn't want to move—I liked where I was.
- It seemed like a fun thing to do.
- My seat had a bad leg—I was glad to move.
- I had the perfect seat and I wanted to stay there.
- I was annoyed—I specifically sat where I was before, so I could see.
- What was the point?
- It seemed silly.
- I was curious where this was going.
- I didn't understand why you wanted us to move, but it was no big deal.
- I resented having to change where I was.
- I got here early to get the best seat and you made me move.
- I ask people to move around in my own classes, so I didn't mind.
- I was thinking of refusing to move, but finally I went along.

This range of reactions—from resentment and mild anger to eagerness and curiosity—is typical, even in an artificial, short-lived, nonthreatening change such as this one. The presence of so many different reactions is an eye-opener for many attendees and a shaker-upper for those who assume everyone else must have had the same reaction they did.

As is often the case in adjusting to change, the woman who said she had the perfect seat and wanted to stay there later admitted that her new seat wasn't so bad—in fact, it was just fine. Her reaction provided a delightful illustration of the transition from Chaos to New Status Quo.

Another participant, in describing his reaction, said, "I arrived late. When I saw that everyone was just sitting down, I was relieved to discover I hadn't missed anything." He didn't realize until later that people weren't seating themselves, but *reseating* themselves. His comment illustrates that people entering into a changing environment at different points may have very different views of what is transpiring; as a result, they may misinterpret the reactions of others.

ALLOW TIME FOR ADJUSTMENT

> I informed you of this change yesterday, so what's your problem?

I've never actually heard anyone make this statement, but the attitude sometimes conveyed by those who impose change on others suggests that these words aren't far from the tip of their tongue. The implied expectation—that people will instantaneously embrace the Foreign Element—shows how persistently optimistic we humans are. But the sooner we accept that people need time to react to a Foreign Element, to experience Chaos, and to journey to a New Status Quo, the sooner we can focus on steps that will help speed that process. In other words, *accepting the fact that implementing change takes time will save time in implementing change.*

If you want to know how long the process takes, consider Hofstadter's Law, created by Doug Hofstadter, an eminent physicist and computer scientist:

> It always takes longer than you expect, even when you take into account Hofstadter's Law.[1]

---

[1] Cited in Donald A. Norman, *Turn Signals Are the Facial Expressions of Automobiles* (Reading, Mass.: Addison-Wesley, 1992), p. 144.

Thus, experienced Change Artists anticipate and allow for negative reactions to a Foreign Element. Those who are inexperienced in managing change are less likely to be patient. For example, a consultant named Jay had for a long time silently tolerated being treated in a condescending and overbearing manner by Vic, a colleague Jay depended on for referrals. When Jay finally decided to break the cycle, he announced to Vic that, henceforth, their relationship would change and that he would expect to be treated with respect.

Daring to disrupt their dance took courage on Jay's part. He felt empowered by his move, and expected Vic to immediately begin to treat him respectfully. However, when he was encouraged to think about what he'd done within the context of the Satir Change Model, he realized that his declaration might have been a Foreign Element for Vic and that Vic might respond by clinging to his previous pattern. After all, this abusive behavior was Vic's Old Status Quo. Therefore, Jay concluded that he'd need to stand his ground and reinforce his expectation of their new relationship while Vic absorbed the Foreign Element and dealt with his Chaos.

Even a positive Foreign Element upsets the Old Status Quo and triggers a temporary dip in performance. This performance dip is familiar to those who achieve a level of mastery in a sport or hobby and then undergo a period of awkwardness as they strive for the next level. Some people can't tolerate the discomfort of this temporary ineptitude and revert to the comfort of Old Status Quo. Learning new skills is much more satisfying for those who can cope with—or enjoy—this very normal part of the learning process.

To help people move through Chaos as expeditiously as possible, consider stating explicitly that you know they need time to adjust to the Foreign Element. Emphasize that adapting to something that's new and unexpected isn't always easy. Show respect for the reality of Chaos.

For an example of what not to do, consider the mistake made by a particular service provider engaged in establishing a service level agreement with its customers. After extensive negotiation resulted in an agreement that represented a compromise between the customers' fondest dreams and the provider's worst nightmare, the SLA manager simply said to the service staff, "It's done, so live with it." Big mistake!

For the many service staffers who were inexperienced with SLAs, the agreement itself was a Foreign Element. SLA-driven changes to service strategies were also Foreign Elements to them. So were the changes they had to make in the way they functioned. Everyone who would have responsibility for the success of the agreement needed time to grasp what was in it and to understand how it would affect his or her work load, responsibilities, and ability to succeed.

The organizations that are most effective at easing people through SLA-triggered Chaos do two key things before making the agreement operational. First, they communicate the terms of the agreement to affected personnel, explaining how these terms came to be, and allowing employees a chance to voice their concerns and questions. Second, before making the agreement operational, they seek feedback from those who will have a role in the success of the agreement.

This process of two-way communication—presenting information *to* affected personnel and soliciting information *from* them—gives people time to adjust to Foreign Elements. It's an especially valuable process when the Foreign Element is a new technology, methodology, tool, or process.

TREAT THE OLD STATUS QUO WITH RESPECT

People become emotionally invested in the way they do their work. Even when that way is cumbersome, tedious, or circuitous, it has a special status as the way that's most familiar. Therefore, you have nothing to gain but resentment by demeaning that way of working. Resentment is certainly what erupted within a certain IT organization that embarked on a major technology infrastructure change. The problem: IT personnel were mighty attached and fiercely loyal to their current technology.

To initiate the change process, management summoned successive groups of IT employees to a series of presentations that introduced the wonders of the new technology. Sprinkled throughout the presentations was the message that life would be ever so much better than with the current technology. They'd be able to do what was now difficult or impossible; the problems they experienced with their current platform would vanish. Say goodbye to the old way, everyone: Good times were ahead.

Many of the IT professionals responded to the presentation with derision and sarcasm. This response was particularly fascinating given that these people often put their customers in the position of accepting whatever changes *they* imposed. Not for the first time, and certainly not for the last, IT people were shown to be no more eager for change than anyone else—at least, *when it affects them.*

Although a new way of carrying out work—a New Status Quo—may bring substantial improvements, many people's attention is riveted not on what they'll gain, but on what they're being asked to give up. ("What?" they ask. "You want me to give up the clumsy, tedious, awkward, slow, inefficient way of doing things that I profusely and relentlessly complain about? Nothing doing! I *like* this way!")

Even when the current way is full of potholes, people know what to expect of it. It's part of how they operate and think and behave. It's part of how they see themselves. It's part of who they are.

People who introduce change often believe that the more benefits they attribute to it, the more readily others will accept it. Although this may be true at times, it's still unwise to discount or discredit what people hold dear.

To accommodate this reality, it's far better to express respect for the Old Status Quo and for the role it has played in people's lives. Instead of describing how different the new way is, describe how it's similar to the current way. Helping people understand these similarities will ease their acceptance of the differences. This is a particularly useful strategy when they are averse to the change.

As William Bridges points out, "People have to understand that the point of change is to preserve that which does not change."[2] Experienced Change Artists keep in mind that although much will change, a great deal will stay the same. As Jerry Weinberg notes in *Quality Software Management, Vol. 4: Anticipating Change,* "When you concentrate on the process of change, it's easy to forget that most of the time, you don't want to change *most* things in your organization."[3]

ALLOW PEOPLE TO VENT

While immersed in Chaos, people need a safe way to express themselves, especially to someone they believe will listen and empathize. I've frequently witnessed the psychological benefit of this venting when I've conducted confidential, one-on-one conversations with people who are grappling with change. With little prompting, they vent about their uncertainties, fears, and disappointments. Some of them have had little previous opportunity to sound off to someone other than their cubicle-mates. They're fully aware that venting won't vaporize their frustration, yet many appreciate being able to have their say.

In addition to holding one-on-one sessions, you might also facilitate a group venting session. This can be risky; there's a fine line between healthy venting and out-of-control griping. However, a major plus of group grousing is that it reminds people they're not alone in their Chaos. Also, if the venting session is carefully managed, the negative energy can be transformed into a search for ways to change the experience into a positive one. Presenting the Satir Change Model, for example, or some other such model of your choice, can help people put their experience in perspective and recognize choices that they may have overlooked.

A potential pitfall of group venting is that the context may not feel safe for everyone. If that's the case, some people will

[2] William Bridges, *Managing Transitions: Making the Most of Change* (Reading, Mass.: Perseus Books, 1991), p. 76.

[3] Gerald M. Weinberg, *Quality Software Management, Vol. 4: Anticipating Change* (New York: Dorset House Publishing, 1997), p. 70.

withhold their views for fear of being judged, belittled, or rejected by the others. For that reason, it's wise to precede a group session with one-on-ones, to learn privately about each person's concerns. In *Winning the Change Game*, authors Kathy Farrell and Craig Broude strongly support this approach.[4] They favor starting a change effort by meeting with key clients individually, before bringing them together as a group. Their reasoning is that you're more likely to hear clients' genuine concerns this way than in a public forum where some may clam up to avoid a backlash from the others.

In addition to one-on-one meetings, an anonymous poll provides a safe way for individuals to express their views about a planned or potential change. I used this approach when I asked the people in a particular group to imagine how they'd react if told that their recently created teams would be disbanded and new ones formed. I asked them to privately and anonymously write their reaction on an index card. Then I collected the cards and displayed them along a continuum of receptivity to the idea.

One-quarter of the group was enthusiastic about the idea of creating new teams. About half of the members of the group were somewhat opposed, and the remaining quarter was vehemently opposed. Clearly, the idea of a change in team makeup was appealing to some and loathsome to others. The feedback that I gathered helped people see how their reactions compared with those of the rest of the group, and it gave me insight into their feelings about team reorganization.

Allowing participants to describe their reactions anonymously may be critical to their sense of safety; requiring them to reveal their identities could distort the results. People who introduce a new idea sometimes make the mistake of posing it to an assembled group and asking people for reactions. In that setting, many may withhold their views or appear to go along, rather than risk being seen as resistant or unsupportive. As

---

[4] Kathy Farrell and Craig Broude, *Winning the Change Game: How to Implement Information Systems with Fewer Headaches and Bigger Paybacks* (Los Angeles: Breakthroughs Enterprises, 1987), pp. 27–28.

noted in Chapter 10, if you want useful feedback from people, you have to make it comfortable for them to provide it.

LISTEN PROACTIVELY

Budget permitting, you can easily bring in a consultant to serve as a hired listener. But instead, what a powerful message you would send by personally listening to the concerns of those who are affected by a major change. Listening proactively means creating opportunities to listen: inviting people affected by a change to describe their feelings, ideas, and opinions about what they are experiencing. It's not enough to tell people that you're interested in their perspective, or to announce that you have an open door policy. Despite your professed willingness to listen, do not assume that people will seek you out. The fact is, some won't.

This was the case with a group of internal consultants in transition to a more proactive, business-focused consulting model. Bill, the director of the group, was new to the organization and eager to implement the model. Unfortunately, he failed to appreciate the Chaos his group was experiencing—a state that was largely due to his own vague and ambiguous management style.

In fact, the difference between Bill's view of his efforts and the consultants' view was striking. Bill saw himself as forthcoming, decisive, goal-oriented, and open to the consultants' ideas. The consultants, however, felt that his strengths as a director were far outweighed by his weaknesses in leading this organizational change. They saw him as confused and confusing, unable to make decisions, uninterested in their views, unsure of how to implement the new model, and out of sync with the culture of the organization.

One of the group members' dominant complaints was that although Bill repeatedly claimed to be interested in their thoughts, he never explicitly asked for their input. A few days after my visit, I received a lengthy e-mail from a woman in the group, describing her analysis of the new consulting model. I found her ideas thorough and sophisticated, but I was especially struck by one of her comments: "I have been here for a year, but I have never presented Bill with these opinions simply because he has never asked me."

Like many people who oversee change, Bill never knew the views of those in his group, even highly capable members such as the woman who wrote to me, because he never explicitly asked. Perhaps these people should have been more forthcoming with their ideas, but that's exactly the point: Many people aren't. It's often a mistake to conclude that people who don't present their ideas have none to offer. Go to them and ask.

Make listening part of your change-management strategy. Set aside time to listen to whatever may be of concern to those affected by the change. Hold one-on-one sessions or gatherings of small groups to talk about issues of concern. Saying that you're interested in people's views is just communication blather; if you mean it, prove it.

PROVIDE INFORMATION AND MORE INFORMATION

During times of change, one of the strongest needs people have is the need for information. They want to know what is happening and how it will affect them. They want an understanding of the big picture and of how they will fit into that picture. They want answers to some very important questions: What will be expected of them? How will they be judged? How quickly will they be expected to adapt? What assistance will be available during the transition?

Some people enjoy the temporary incompetence that's part of learning a new skill. For many, however, the loss of control—when that familiar Old Status Quo is yanked away—is unsettling. During times of change, many people have an intense fear of being humiliated or being seen as incompetent. As noted by author Jerry Weinberg, the fear of looking foolish is worse than the fear of failure.[5]

---

[5] Gerald M. Weinberg, "Tools, Fools, Rules, and Schools—What Hinders Improvement in Development Methods?" Software Quality Engineering Software Management Conference, San Diego, Feb. 13, 2001.

The rumor mill starts churning as soon as a change is announced. When information about the change isn't forthcoming, the people affected by it are quick to assume the worst. By providing information early and often, you'll go a long way toward minimizing the spread of rumors and their messy effects. Furthermore, when given some information rather than being kept in the dark, people are more likely to tolerate a certain amount of turmoil. Often, demonstrating that you are *willing* to communicate is as important as the precise information communicated, because it tells those involved that they are an integral part of the process. Most important, it lets them know they haven't been forgotten.

Of course, honesty is critical during times of change, especially when the news is bad. People quickly see through an attempt to conceal bad news. Whether that news is hidden or shared, people take action to protect themselves. As one CIO explained as his company took a financial nosedive, the minute employees sense that management is trying to put one over on them, they walk.

Another executive held weekly meetings with entire divisions to answer questions and eliminate rumors. Divisional meetings may be overwhelming for some people, but a mix of gatherings of different sizes, along with other forums in which people can ask questions, can help people put their fears behind them. In addition to providing information proactively, ensure that people have a point of contact for reliably getting a response to questions—whether by phone, in person, or by e-mail.

Making information readily available can help reduce people's resistance to change and their very human fears about it. Therefore, it's a good idea to increase the dissemination of information not just about the change itself, but also about its impact on processes, responsibilities, expectations, and opportunities. For example, video presentations, Q&A sessions, demos, periodic e-mail updates, and information posted on intranets can be helpful in reaching different groups of employees. And of course, face-to-face communication is also critical in getting the word out during these stressful times.

This personal contact presents an opportunity to help people gain the Transforming Ideas that will help them emerge from Chaos.

Authors Farrell and Broude offer a Why-How-What approach to providing information.[6] At the outset, when people are still attached to the current way of doing their work, provide Why information: Why should they change? But don't present this information in boring logicalese. Instead, personalize it by explaining why the new way will help people avoid current aggravations and accomplish tasks they couldn't until now. Identify people's hot buttons. Find strong reasons for them to want to change—not just practical reasons, but emotional ones, too.

Next, provide the How information to help people understand how to actually go about making the transition to the new way. This information is very specific, focusing on steps, procedures, schedules, plans, forms, and so on. Its purpose is to respond to people's concerns as they begin to wonder: How in the world will we get there from here, anyway?

Finally, provide the What information. Farrell and Broude advocate drawing people in by giving them a sense of what the new way will look and feel like, and how they'll feel using it. This information focuses on benefits and tries to make the new way as real and tangible as possible. As Farrell and Broude suggest, it's a good idea to offer different Why-How-What information to the different functional areas and levels of personnel that are affected by the change; after all, they have different needs and perspectives.

SAY SOMETHING EVEN WHEN YOU HAVE NOTHING TO SAY

When people are in Chaos and helpful information is not forthcoming, they tend to believe it's being deliberately withheld. That belief makes people angry. And the longer the information seems to be withheld, the more likely people are to imagine dire possibilities and to fear the worst.

---

[6] Farrell and Broude, op. cit., pp. 50ff.

Sometimes, however, the information is not being withheld; it just isn't available yet. In that situation—when you don't have the answers people want—say so. As was discussed in Chapter 9, people become upset when they are not kept informed or are made to endure unexplained, excessive waiting. And that's in normal times. During times of change, such reactions are significantly intensified. At such times, no news is definitely *not* good news.

If you assure employees that you know they're eager for information but explain that you simply don't have the information they want, you give them something to know rather than something to obsess about. Knowing that you aren't deliberately withholding information may not relieve their stress, but at least they won't accuse you of ulterior motives. And if you do have information but for various reasons are unable to disclose it, be open about that, as well. Explain that circumstances prevent you from telling them what they'd like to know, but that you will tell them as soon as you can. Whether you don't yet know something or can't yet disclose what you do know, periodically remind them of this fact so they won't begin to suspect otherwise.

Trust, of course, plays an important role in your employees' acceptance of your explanation. If trust is lacking, they will see your response as part of a pattern of obfuscation. On the other hand, if you have a reputation for playing it straight, they will accept that you are not needlessly withholding information. I once worked for a director who kept me informed about far more than I expected him to tell me. However, when I inquired about a particularly sensitive issue, he started to hem and haw, which was not characteristic of his up-front manner. I told him that I'd be satisfied if he simply told me he couldn't tell me. So, he told me . . . that he couldn't tell me. And that was sufficient.

EMPATHIZE, EMPATHIZE, EMPATHIZE

Empathy can help to reduce the duration and intensity of the Chaos associated with change. This was the realization of a group whose primary responsibility was to help its clients implement change—literally. As a facilities group, its role was to relocate individuals, groups, and entire divisions from one company location to another. This responsibility entailed everything from moving an individual to another floor to moving a building's worth of people to a newly built campus, several states away.

Think about the last time you moved, whether to another state, another home, another job—or even to another cubicle. Think of all the taking down and putting up, all the packing and unpacking, all the things that turned out better than you had imagined and all the things that turned out worse. For many people, stress is the dominant theme of such an experience.

So it's not surprising that although some people look forward to a change in location, to gain better digs or a shorter commute, they may still find the move itself unpleasant at best. The facilities group not only had to manage people's attachment to their current space—people form strong emotional attachments to their home and work spaces—but relocations without incident were rare because of the complexity of accommodating employees' work-space needs.

I presented the Satir Change Model to this group as a basis for discussing what people might do to minimize their clients' stress—and, not incidentally, their own. One of their decisions was to exhibit more empathy for their clients' situation. They felt they could do this by connecting more frequently and more effectively with their clients.

In particular, they agreed to make initial contact with people further in advance of a planned move and to follow up periodically as the moving date approached. They also decided to send out reminders about pertinent particulars that people often forget in the hubbub, and to give their clients an opportunity to express concerns about the move. They realized that some people simply needed to vent about an upcoming move and that empathetic listening was one of the most important services they could provide.

Furthermore, the group members resolved not to react defensively when people complained about being relocated; instead, they agreed to acknowledge people's anxieties and to seek additional input to ensure they hadn't missed important details.

Expressing empathy during times of change is not about uttering sympathetic oohs and aahs. It's about communicating proactively and with sincere concern. One considerate way to exhibit empathy, particularly with subordinates and customers, is to assure them that you don't expect perfection as they start to emerge from Chaos. Remember, Practice and Integration is a time of trial and error, a time of trying and slipping and trying again, a time of inching toward the New Status Quo, occasionally interrupted by return trips through Chaos.

When people are learning a new way of working and start to feel like they've "got it," they may find it depressing to suddenly slide back. Yet that's the nature of Practice and Integration. Practice is needed before integration of the new way is complete.[7] Allowing for mistakes during Practice and Integration is a valuable form of empathy. Even small signs of empathy are helpful, because they say, "We're listening and we care."

---

[7] Some Satir practitioners view this stage as Integration and Practice rather than Practice and Integration. They see it as a process of first integrating the many aspects of the change and then practicing them. My own perspective, and that of other Satir practitioners, is that it is through the process of practice that integration occurs. The truth is probably somewhere between the two views: Practice and Integration are inextricably bound, and together, they help achieve the New Status Quo.

CHOOSE YOUR WORDS CAREFULLY

The very words you use to introduce a change can make a huge difference in how—or whether—people accept it. They will be more likely to support a New Status Quo if they feel they have a say in the matter than if they feel forced into it. On the other hand, if they are given the impression that henceforth they *must* begin to do something a certain way, they may resist it, even if they otherwise would have supported the idea.

For example, the members of a business unit felt that their needs as customers were being ignored, and they wanted to create a service level agreement with their technology provider. Their desire for improved responsiveness was valid; their provider's service had been subpar. However, their attitude of "We want it—*so do it!*" was poised to backfire, more likely to elicit resistance than acceptance and agreement.

As we discussed how they might best present their needs, they agreed to undemandingly explain the level of responsiveness they needed and to ask how their needs might fit what the provider could deliver. They would say, in effect: "Here's what I need and why. How is that for you?" This approach would create a basis for discussion and negotiation that would prevent the provider from summarily rejecting their requests without consideration.

Their strategy worked. Afterward, the customer manager delighted in reporting how forthcoming the provider proved to be. Provider personnel weren't so hardheaded after all; like most of us, they preferred to be asked rather than bullied. When they discovered that this customer wasn't demanding the impossible and was willing to negotiate, they became even more willing to provide what the customer needed.

In addition to being cautious about the words you use to introduce a change, be sensitive to the words you use to describe a person's response to change. That description will influence how you interact with the person. Once you label people as resistant to change, you will probably continue to consider them resistant. Doing so fails to acknowledge them as people—individuals who are uncomfortable with a given change and who may have valid concerns that have not yet had a fair hearing. At a fundamental level, labels disregard the reality that people vary in the way they respond to change.

In *The Tipping Point*, Malcolm Gladwell emphasizes our tendency to think in terms of absolutes: "that a person is a certain way or is not a certain way."[8] He describes the psychological tendency known as the Fundamental Attribution Error: "when it comes to interpreting other people's behavior, human beings invariably make the mistake of overestimating the importance of fundamental character traits and underestimating the importance of the situation and context."[9]

As noted by Dale Emery, an expert on transforming resistance during change, "Resistance is a word that stops conversation."[10] He suggests that when you are tempted to describe people as resistant, you should consider some alternative interpretations:

- I don't understand their point of view . . . yet.
- They did something I didn't expect.
- They did something I didn't want them to do.
- What they did doesn't fit into my model of how change happens.
- Either I know something they don't, or they know something I don't.
- Maybe I've made a mistake.
- I've created a problem for them.
- I'm asking them to do something that feels unsafe.

These are generous interpretations of your own reaction to someone else's apparent resistance. Rather than sitting in

---

[8] Malcolm Gladwell, *The Tipping Point: How Little Things Can Make a Big Difference* (Boston: Little, Brown and Company, 2000), p. 158.

[9] Ibid., p. 160.

[10] Dale Emery, "A Force for Change—Using Resistance Positively," Software Quality Engineering Software Management Conference, San Diego, Feb. 14, 2001. Dale is an expert on the subject of resistance. For readings on resistance, see www.dhemery.com.

judgment, seek additional information that would help you understand the person's reactions.

DARE TO SHOW PEOPLE YOU CARE

When change is taking place, many people would like nothing more than to have someone in a position of authority ask them how they are doing and what concerns they have. Evidence of caring is a powerful tool for building trust, reducing stress, and easing the uncertainty of those in a state of change-induced turmoil.

In *On Death and Dying*, Kübler-Ross describes a seriously ill hospital patient who was never asked straightforward questions about how he was doing. The hospital nurses and staff never offered him a chance to talk about his condition, instead mistaking his grim look as a sign that they should keep their distance. However, this perception was drastically incorrect: ". . . in fact, their own anxiety prevented them from finding out what he wanted to share so badly with another human being."[11] And indeed, when it comes to organizational change, few measures are as effective at demonstrating that you care as asking employees how they are doing and giving them a chance to talk about what they are experiencing. Sometimes, simply asking, "How are you doing?" is all it takes.

In fact, not talking with people about changes that are taking place is tantamount to donning a cheerful mask, so as to conceal from them what is destined to become evident eventually. But the mask doesn't work because employees don't work in a vacuum. They see what's going on around them. As Kübler-Ross notes, the more people who know the truth of the situation, the sooner the patient (or in the organizational context, the employee) "will realize the true state of affairs anyway, since few people are actors enough to maintain a believable mask of cheerfulness over a long period of time."[12]

---

[11] Elisabeth Kübler-Ross, *On Death and Dying* (New York: Collier Books, 1969), p. 31.

[12] Ibid., p. 32.

INVOLVE PEOPLE IN IMPLEMENTING THE CHANGE

During a period of major change, people feel a loss of choice about how they run their lives. You can minimize this feeling by involving them in the change. For example, invite personnel to discuss the types of information that will help them gain familiarity with the change. Ask selected employee groups for help in devising ways to ensure that their peers become comfortable with the new procedures. Conduct interviews to identify the biggest concerns in each group and take steps to address them.

If it's feasible, present a specific problem regarding the change and invite people to comment. The problem might revolve around identifying aspects of the change effort that might inadvertently be overlooked. For example, you can challenge people to analyze the change effort from their own perspective and to come up with three ways it may fall short if certain considerations are overlooked. Or ask the type of question that's at the heart of Dietrich Dörner's *The Logic of Failure:* How can we prevent the solution from creating a new problem?[13] Challenges such as this can help you to harness the energy of people who oppose the change.

Another way to involve people is to give them some control over the situation. For example, when a Foreign Element takes the form of a major outage, most people are eager to know when it will be resolved. Providing periodic updates during the interim can help to assure them that the situation is being rectified and that they haven't been forgotten. One way to offer a modicum of control is to ask how often they'd like you to provide these updates—assuming you'll be in a position to act on their wishes. Your inquiry, itself, gives them some say in the matter when, otherwise, they'd have none at all.

---

[13] Dietrich Dörner, *The Logic of Failure: Recognizing and Avoiding Error in Complex Situations* (Cambridge, Mass.: Perseus Books, 1996).

EDUCATE PEOPLE ABOUT THE EXPERIENCE OF CHANGE

If your role entails managing, implementing, or influencing change, you'll find it helpful to study a variety of change models, such as those cited in Chapter 12. Most such models map to each other, to some degree, and each of them can be valuable in helping you better understand the experience of change. With this background, present the Satir model or any other change model to the people who will be affected by a change.

Acknowledge that people are likely to have different reactions to change, and show respect, in both word and deed, for those reactions. Help employees understand the normal stages that people go through when confronted with unexpected or unwanted change—or even expected and wanted change. Teach them the terminology and concepts of change, including terms such as Foreign Element, Chaos, and Transforming Ideas (from the Satir Change Model); Transition and Neutral Zones (from Bridges' model); or pertinent terms from other models. This terminology provides a vocabulary for communicating about a shared experience and for helping each other drive toward the New Status Quo. It also helps people describe the state they're in at any given time.

I find the terminology of the Satir Change Model extremely valuable in communicating with colleagues and friends who are familiar with this model. When confronted with a situation that unsettles or disorients me, I can simply say, "Wow, that's a Foreign Element!" and they can relate to what I'm experiencing—regardless of whether they've been in the same situation. If any of us mentions that we're in Chaos, the others may not understand the specific nature of the person's Chaos, but we can appreciate that the person is feeling jostled and try to be sensitive and supportive.

DEAL WITH IT!

By now, you may be thinking how much easier it would be if you could just focus on the task at hand and not get bogged down in all this people stuff. It may even be that some of these guidelines are Foreign Elements for you. Unfortunately, focusing on the technical aspects of a change—to the exclusion of its impact on people—guarantees that your change effort will be an interminable jackhammer of a headache. You can't effectively manage change without paying attention to the human factors.

How do you deal with the human factors? Build trust. Prepare people. Talk to them. Listen to them. Empathize with their reactions. Involve them in the effort. Explain the experience of change. Reassure them. Tell them what you can—and when you have information that you can't divulge, say so. Explain the reasoning behind your thinking. Don't expect immediate acceptance of your ideas. Treat people's concerns with empathy and respect. Be persistent without being pushy. Communicate early, often, and in multiple ways. In other words, follow the guidelines in this chapter, and throughout this book. Above all, use your common sense. It will help you through the rough spots.

14

On Becoming a Gapologist

Although I've described some effective ways to close communication gaps, truth in book-writing compels me to reveal that you can't ever be gap-free. Opportunities for communication gaps are everywhere, and despite your best efforts, you will at times create them, contribute to them, or fall victim to them. By becoming alert to the possibility of these gaps, though, you'll minimize the ones that could have an adverse impact on your projects, activities, and relationships. With vigilance and practice, you'll become a certified Gapologist.

I challenge you to become mindful of the potential for gaps and to channel that awareness into improving your personal and organizational effectiveness. Lucky person that I am, I seem to have awareness-raising experiences quite often—even in elevators.

Take, for example, the time I was staying at one of those big-city hotels, the kind with glass-fronted elevators that climb up and down the sides of a center atrium thirty stories high. I was alone in one of the elevators, ascending to my room on the twenty-second floor.

For the first twenty-one floors, the ride was uneventful. I peered through the glass wall down to guests the size of ants, milling about in the lobby below. Suddenly, just as number 22 lit up on the elevator's display panel, I heard the grinding of gears and the metallic ping of a part popping off. The elevator slammed to a stop. I waited for the doors to open. They didn't.

Trying to remain calm, I pressed the Door Open button. Nothing. Nervously, I pressed the button for the twenty-second floor again, and then, in rapid succession, the buttons for *all* the floors. Still no response. Feeling slightly more desperate, I pressed the Alarm button.

A second or two passed and then, over the elevator intercom, I heard a deep, soothing voice. "What seems to be the problem?" asked the voice.

I quickly explained, "I'm on the twenty-second floor and the doors won't open."

"Have you tried the Door Open button?" the voice asked. I answered that I had.

"Don't worry about a thing," the voice reassured me. "We'll be right up to get you out."

That response disturbed me. To me, the words "Don't worry about a thing" are a sure sign of an incipient gap. All I could think of was that I was in a glass prison, suspended by a thread, twenty-two stories above terra firma—quite a gap!—and a disembodied voice was blithely telling me not to worry.

In times of stress, minutes feel like months. Believing I had waited long enough, I pressed the Alarm button again, and again I heard the voice, asking, "What seems to be the problem?" Impatiently, I explained that I was *still* stuck on the twenty-second floor and the doors *still* wouldn't open.

"Have you tried the Door Open button?" the voice asked. I was shocked. Was this an automatic voice response unit? ("Press 1 if the doors are stuck. Press 2 if you're falling through space. . . .") Tactfully, I brought the conversation back to the fact that we had previously spoken. "Don't worry about a thing," the voice chirped. "We'll be right up to get you out."

I don't know about you, but when I'm told someone will be right up to get me out, I take that to mean *today*. Still nobody came to rescue me and so, a third time, I pressed the Alarm button. And *again*, I heard the voice: "What seems to be the problem?" I couldn't believe it. In exasperation, I shouted, "I don't know if you remember me, but I'm stuck on the twenty-second floor *and the doors won't open!*"

The voice replied, "Don't worry about a thing. . . ."

What seemed an eternity later, I heard two men outside the elevator. One sounded like the voice. The other I assumed to be a voice-in-training. Together, they pried open the elevator door. That's when I discovered I wasn't actually at the twenty-second floor, but several feet above the twenty-first floor, with just a few feet between the floor of the elevator and the top of the elevator doorway (yet another gap!).

"Okay," said the apprentice, "You can jump down now."

"I will *not*," I said, emphatically. "You will lift me out." Which he did.

The experience was not one I would want to repeat—ever!—but it did provide me with a useful case study for the customer service class I presented the next day in that very hotel.

This experience reminded me that when it comes to closing communication gaps, little things do matter. Things like listening (*really* listening) and recognizing the impact of stressful situations on people. And *not making people wait forever!* I truly came to appreciate these things while watching the lobby ants from Floor 21.5.

AFTERWORD

If you have stories about your own communication gaps and those you've observed, as well as what you've learned about preventing or minimizing gaps, I'd love to hear them. You can e-mail me at naomi@nkarten.com. Please visit my Website, www.nkarten.com, for more on this subject, including additional experiences of my own and stories readers have sent me. Perhaps you'll want to submit your own. In matters of Gapology, we can learn lots from each other. Good luck, and let's stay in touch.

Bibliography

Adams, Scott. *The Dilbert Principle: A Cubicle's-Eye View of Bosses, Meetings, Management Fads & Other Workplace Afflictions.* New York: HarperBusiness, 1996.

Barlow, Janelle, and Claus Møller. *A Complaint Is a Gift: Using Customer Feedback As a Strategic Tool.* San Francisco: Berrett-Koehler Publishers, 1996.

Bohjalian, Chris. *The Law of Similars.* New York: Vintage Books, 1999.

———. *Water Witches.* New York: Simon & Schuster, 1995.

Brandreth, Gyles. *The Joy of Lex: How to Have Fun with 860,341,500 Words.* New York: Quill, William Morrow and Company, 1980.

Bridges, William. *Managing Transitions: Making the Most of Change.* Reading, Mass.: Perseus Books, 1991.

Bullock, James, Gerald M. Weinberg, and Marie Benesh, eds. *Roundtable on Project Management: A SHAPE Forum Dialogue.* New York: Dorset House Publishing, 2001.

Carlzon, Jan. *Moments of Truth.* New York: Perennial, HarperCollins, 1989.

Crum, Thomas F. *The Magic of Conflict: Turning a Life of Work into a Work of Art.* New York: Touchstone, Simon & Schuster, 1987.

de Bono, Edward. *de Bono's Thinking Course*. New York: Facts On File, 1982.

———. *I Am Right—You Are Wrong: From This to the New Renaissance: From Rock Logic to Water Logic*. London: Penguin Books, 1991.

———. *Lateral Thinking: Creativity Step by Step*. New York: Perennial, Harper & Row, 1990.

DeFleur, Melvin L., Patricia Kearney, and Timothy G. Plax. *Fundamentals of Human Communication*, 2nd ed. Mountain View, Calif.: Mayfield Publishing, 1993.

DeMarco, Tom, and Timothy Lister. *Peopleware: Productive Projects and Teams*, 2nd ed. New York: Dorset House Publishing, 1999.

Dörner, Dietrich. *The Logic of Failure: Recognizing and Avoiding Error in Complex Situations*. Cambridge, Mass.: Perseus Books, 1996.

du Maurier, Daphne. *The Breaking Point*. New York: Avon Books, 1959.

Ekman, Paul. *Telling Lies: Clues to Deceit in the Marketplace, Politics, and Marriage*. New York: Berkley Books, 1986.

Elgin, Suzette Haden. *BusinessSpeak: Using the Gentle Art of Verbal Persuasion to Get What You Want at Work*. New York: McGraw-Hill, 1995.

Espy, Willard R. *An Almanac of Words at Play*. New York: Clarkson N. Potter, 1975.

Farrell, Kathy, and Craig Broude. *Winning the Change Game: How to Implement Information Systems with Fewer Headaches and Bigger Paybacks*. Los Angeles: Breakthroughs Enterprises, 1987.

Farson, Richard. *Management of the Absurd: Paradoxes in Leadership*. New York: Touchstone, Simon & Schuster, 1996.

Firth, David, with Alan Leigh. *The Corporate Fool: Doing the Undoable, Thinking the Unthinkable, Saying the Unsayable and Driving Your Sensible Organization Mad with Creative Folly*. Oxford, U.K.: Capstone Publishing, 1998.

Fisher, Roger, and Alan Sharp, with John Richardson. *Getting It Done: How to Lead When You're Not in Charge*. New York: HarperBusiness, 1998.

Freiberg, Kevin, and Jackie Freiberg. *Nuts! Southwest Airlines' Crazy Recipe for Business and Personal Success*. New York: Broadway Books, 1998.

Gerson, Richard F. *Measuring Customer Satisfaction.* Menlo Park, Calif.: Crisp Publications, 1993.

Gesell, Izzy. *Playing Along: 37 Group Learning Activities Borrowed from Improvisational Theater.* Duluth: Whole Person Associates, 1997.

Gilovich, Thomas. *How We Know What Isn't So: The Fallibility of Human Reason in Everyday Life.* New York: The Free Press, 1991.

Gladwell, Malcolm. *The Tipping Point: How Little Things Can Make a Big Difference.* Boston: Little, Brown and Company, 2000.

Gottesdiener, Ellen. *Requirements by Collaboration: Workshops for Defining Needs.* Boston: Addison-Wesley, 2002.

Hay, David C. *Data Model Patterns: Conventions of Thought.* New York: Dorset House Publishing, 1996.

Hirsh, Sandra Krebs, and Jean Kummerow. *LIFETypes.* New York: Warner Books, 1989.

Jung, C.G. *Psychological Types.* New York: Harcourt Brace, 1923.

Karten, Naomi. *How to Establish Service Level Agreements.* Randolph, Mass.: Karten Associates, 1998.

————. *Managing Expectations: Working with People Who Want More, Better, Faster, Sooner, NOW!* New York: Dorset House Publishing, 1994.

Kerth, Norman L. *Project Retrospectives: A Handbook for Team Reviews.* New York: Dorset House Publishing, 2001.

King, Bob. "Life as a Software Architect," *Amplifying Your Effectiveness: Collected Essays,* eds. Gerald M. Weinberg, James Bach, and Naomi Karten. New York: Dorset House Publishing, 2000.

Kroeger, Otto, with Janet M. Thuesen. *Type Talk at Work: How the 16 Personality Types Determine Your Success on the Job.* New York: Dell Publishing, 1992.

Kübler-Ross, Elisabeth. *On Death and Dying.* New York: Collier Books, 1969.

Larkin, T.J., and Sandar Larkin. *Communicating Change: Winning Employee Support for New Business Goals.* New York: McGraw-Hill, 1994.

Lawrence, Gordon. *People Types & Tiger Stripes,* 3rd ed. Gainesville, Fla.: Center for Applications of Psychological Type, 1993.

Lurie, Alison. *Foreign Affairs.* New York: Avon Books, 1984.

Lutz, William. *The New Doublespeak: Why No One Knows What Anyone's Saying Anymore.* New York: HarperCollins, 1996.

Mornell, Pierre. *Games Companies Play*. Berkeley, Calif.: Ten Speed Press, 2000.

Murray, William D.G. *Give Yourself the Unfair Advantage: A Serious Practical Guide to Understanding Human Personality That Will Have You Rolling in the Aisles*. Gladwyne, Penn.: Type & Temperament, 1995.

Nielsen, Jerri, with Maryanne Vollers. *Ice Bound: A Doctor's Incredible Battle for Survival at the South Pole*. New York: Hyperion, 2001.

Norman, Donald A. *Turn Signals Are the Facial Expressions of Automobiles*. Reading, Mass.: Addison-Wesley, 1992.

Northcutt, Wendy. *The Darwin Awards: Evolution in Action*. New York: Dutton, 2000.

Oshry, Barry. *Seeing Systems: Unlocking the Mysteries of Organizational Life*. San Francisco: Berrett-Koehler Publishers, 1995.

Ruiz, Miguel. *The Four Agreements: A Practical Guide to Personal Freedom*. San Rafael, Calif.: Amber-Allen Publishing, 1997.

Satir, Virginia. *Conjoint Family Therapy*, 3rd ed. Palo Alto, Calif.: Science and Behavior Books, 1983.

———. *Making Contact*. Millbrae, Calif.: Celestial Arts, 1976.

———, J. Banmen, J. Gerber, and M. Gomori. *The Satir Model: Family Therapy and Beyond*. Palo Alto, Calif.: Science and Behavior Books, 1991.

Schmaltz, David A. *Coping with Fuzzy Projects: Stories of Utter Ignorance, Theologic Wars, and Unseen Possibilities*. Portland, Oreg.: True North pgs, 2000.

Shapiro, Ronald M., and Mark A. Jankowski, with James Dale. *The Power of Nice: How to Negotiate So Everyone Wins—Especially You!* New York: John Wiley & Sons, 1998.

Smith, Rolf. *The 7 Levels of Change: The Guide to Innovation in the World's Largest Corporations*. Arlington, Tex.: The Summit Publishing Group, 1997.

Smith, Steven M. "The Satir Change Model," *Amplifying Your Effectiveness: Collected Essays*, eds. Gerald M. Weinberg, James Bach, and Naomi Karten. New York: Dorset House Publishing, 2000.

Starcevich, Matt M., and Steven J. Stowell. *Teamwork: We Have Met the Enemy and They Are Us*. Bartlesville, Okla.: The Center for Management and Organization Effectiveness, 1990.

Stirr, Thomas. *Miller's Bolt: A Modern Business Parable.* Reading, Mass: Addison-Wesley, 1997.

Stokes, Stewart L., Jr. *Controlling the Future: Managing Technology-Driven Change.* Wellesley, Mass.: QED Information Sciences, 1991.

Strider, Wayne. *Powerful Project Leadership.* Vienna, Va.: Management Concepts, 2002.

Underhill, Paco. *Why We Buy: The Science of Shopping.* New York: Simon & Schuster, 1999.

Weinberg, Gerald M. *An Introduction to General Systems Thinking: Silver Anniversary Edition.* New York: Dorset House Publishing, 2001.

————. *Quality Software Management, Vol. 2: First-Order Measurement.* New York: Dorset House Publishing, 1993.

————. *Quality Software Management, Vol. 4: Anticipating Change.* New York: Dorset House Publishing, 1997.

————, James Bach, and Naomi Karten, eds. *Amplifying Your Effectiveness: Collected Essays.* New York: Dorset House Publishing, 2000.

Weinberg, Gerald M., Marie Benesh, and James Bullock, eds. *Roundtable on Technical Leadership: A SHAPE Forum Dialogue.* New York: Dorset House Publishing, 2002.

Whiteley, Richard C. *The Customer-Driven Company: Moving from Talk to Action.* Reading, Mass.: Addison-Wesley, 1991.

Index